Decisions of the International Court of Justice are almost as replete with references to precedent as are decisions of a common law court. Even though previous decisions are not binding, the Court relies upon them as authoritative expressions of its views on decided points of law. In his lectures, Judge Shahabuddeen examines various aspects of this phenomenon. While the treatment of precedent in common law courts of last resort has become more flexible, the case law of the International Court of Justice has shown a remarkable jurisprudential consistency. In addition, Judge Shahabuddeen discusses the way in which parties to cases are themselves guided by previous decisions of the Court in framing and presenting their cases.

Precedent in the World Court

Titles published in the Hersch Lauterpacht Memorial Lecture Series

UNIVERSITY OF CAMBRIDGE
RESEARCH CENTRE FOR INTERNATIONAL LAW

HERSCH LAUTERPACHT MEMORIAL LECTURES

PRECEDENT
IN THE WORLD COURT

MOHAMED SHAHABUDDEEN

Honorary Bencher of the Middle Temple
Associate Member of the Institute of International Law
Judge of the International Court of Justice

GROTIUS PUBLICATIONS

CAMBRIDGE
UNIVERSITY PRESS

Published by the Press Syndicate of the University of Cambridge
The Pitt Building, Trumpington Street, Cambridge, CB2 1RP
40 West 20th Street, New York, NY 10011-4211, USA
10 Stamford Road, Oakleigh, Melbourne 3166, Australia

First published 1996

Printed in Great Britain at the University Press, Cambridge

A catalogue record for this book is available from the British Library

Library of Congress cataloguing in publication data

Shahabuddeen, M., 1931–
Precedent in the world court / by Mohamed Shahabuddeen.
p.   cm.–(Hersch Lauterpacht memorial lectures)
ISBN 0 521 56310 0 (hardback)
1. International Court of Justice. 2. Stare decisis. I. Title. II. Series.
JX1971.6.S49 1996
341.5'52 – dc20   95 – 49149 CIP

ISBN 0 521 56310 0 hardback

FOR RIYAH AND JAVED

Contents

Contents

Contents

Contents

Foreword

SIR ROBERT JENNINGS

The historical endeavour, extending from the First Hague Conference of 1899 until eventual success in 1920, to establish a permanent international court as distinct from *ad hoc* tribunals, was inspired by the belief that only a court established on a permanent basis could, besides deciding disputes, make an adequate contribution to the progressive development of international law as a working system of law. This belief implied a commitment to the acceptance of a case-law system as the way forward. This acceptance was confirmed by the decision to publish law reports for the Permanent Court of International Justice; for, given law reports, a system based upon case law invariably follows.

The principal features of this case law were economically and inimitably described and analysed by Hersch Lauterpacht in his *Development*;[1] it is therefore a happy circumstance that this new and considerable study by Judge Shahabuddeen was one of the series of Hersch Lauterpacht Memorial Lectures given in Cambridge University.

The formal basis of this case law is still that now laid down in the present Article 38 of the Statute of the International Court of Justice (for earlier drafts see p. 52 below) which lists amongst what the Court is to apply, 'subject to the provisions of Article 59, judicial decisions and the teachings of the most highly qualified publicists

---

[1] The first edition of Lauterpacht's *Development of International Law by the Permanent Court of International Justice* was in 1934; the revised edition under the title of *The Development of International Law by the International Court* was in 1958; see Chapter 1 of the later version and especially pp. 9–25, which deal with the question of judicial precedent in international law.

of the various nations, as subsidiary means for the determination of rules of law'.

This treatment of the writings of publicists and judicial decisions as sources that are on a par has been much modified by the practice of both World Courts, at any rate as regards the treatment of the Court's own decisions. The difference is very clearly stated by Fitzmaurice (see pp. 42 and 88 below): a publicist is cited because he has expressed a point in a way that is felicitous, or apposite, but a judicial decision is cited because it is 'something which the tribunal cannot ignore'. But there is a problem. A passage from a previous judgment may also be cited almost in isolation from the case as a whole, and because it happens to be a felicitous expression of a point the Court is desirous of making. How does one distinguish between using earlier judgments almost as if they were writings, and their use as authoritative and highly persuasive precedent decisions? What is the proper technique for determining the authoritative precedent which establishes principles and rules of law; and distinguishing it from that particular decision to which Article 59 refers?

This is the question, or rather set of questions, that Judge Shahabuddeen sets out to tackle in this monograph: the principle of *stare decisis;* the meaning of Article 59; the art of distinguishing the *ratio decidendi* and *obiter dicta*; the position of chambers; advisory opinions of the Court; separate and dissenting opinions of the Judges; and all the other important but delicate matters that arise. Being common law trained and now a very respected and experienced Judge of the World Court, he is particularly well qualified to do so; for the common law has a unique experience of the techniques of handling cases. This, as he makes clear, is not to suggest of course that the World Court could adopt anything like the common law doctrine of binding precedent. Indeed the necessary hierarchical court system which is the essence of binding precedent is in any case lacking in international law. Moreover, as a great common lawyer and international lawyer, A. L. Goodhart, pointed out, the Continental system of following a settled *jurisprudence* may be thought superior in practicality. For a 'system of law to be truly practical [it] must be one based on a series of experiments, tested by trial and error; this, however, is not the method of English law, for, owing to the doctrine of precedent, the first experiment must also be the last'.[2] Fortunately, as Judge Shahabuddeen points out, even the common law now shows a certain degree of flexibility at the top of the system.

It is an honour and a pleasure to provide a foreword for so accomplished a study of a topically apposite but hitherto relatively neglected subject. It is a happy coincidence that this study of the place of the World Court in the development of international law appears as the present Court is about to celebrate its fiftieth anniversary.

[2] See A. L. Goodhart 'Precedent in English and Continental Law', *LQR* 50 (1934), at p. 26.

Preface

In important ways the World Court was established on the Continental model, which knows no doctrine of precedent. Indeed, if curiously so, in 1920 it was the representatives of the legal systems where judge-made law prevailed who were foremost in insisting that decisions of the Court should not have precedential force as understood in Anglo-American judicial practice. That in principle remains the case. And yet decisions of the Court are almost as replete with references to precedents as are decisions of a common law court. This monograph is devoted to some aspects of this phenomenon.

The subject, by reason of its nature, attracts reference to the common law experience. I accept that a more rounded approach could benefit from perceptions made from the standpoint of other legal traditions. Even so, imperfections will appear to me as soon as the text leaves my hands; others will surface in due course. I own the shortcomings in advance.

Judge Sir Robert Jennings, a former President of the Court, Judge Gilbert Guillaume and Professor Elihu Lauterpacht have been good enough to read the work in draft. I thank them for their comments.

The study, which is limited to decisions of the Court itself, is based on the Hersch Lauterpacht Memorial Lectures of November 1994. I thank Professor Lauterpacht for inviting me to speak. Sir Robert Jennings took the chair at the lectures and has now provided a foreword. I appreciate this.

I would like also to thank my secretary, Miss Charlotte Kamers, for her willingness, patience and efficiency.

Abbreviations

AC Appeal Cases
AFDI *Annuaire français de droit international*
AJIL *American Journal of International Law*
All ER *All England Reports*
Aust YBIL Australian Year Book of International Law
Barberis, 'La Jurisprudencia' Julio A. Barberis, 'La Jurispruden-
cia Internacional como fuento de Derecho de Gentes según la
Corte de la Haya', *ZöV*, 31 (1971), pp. 641–670
Beckett 'Jurisprudence' W. E. Beckett, 'Les Questions d'Intérêt
général au point de vue juridique dans la Jurisprudence de la
Cour permanente de Justice internationale', *Hag R*, 39 (1932–
I), pp. 135–269
Brierly, 'Règles générales du droit de la paix' J. L. Brierly,
'Règles générales du droit de la paix', *Hag R*, 58 (1936–IV),
pp. 5–237
BYBIL *British Year Book of International Law*
Castberg, 'La Méthodologie' Frede Castberg, 'La Méthodologie
du droit international public', *Hag R*, 43 (1933–I), pp. 313–383
CLJ *Cambridge Law Journal*
Col LR *Columbia Law Review*
Condorelli, 'L'Autorité' Luigi Condorelli, 'L'Autorité de la
décision des juridictions internationales permanentes', in *La
Juridiction internationale permanente,* Colloque de Lyon (Paris,
1987), pp. 277–313
Cross and Harris, *Precedent* Rupert Cross and J. W. Harris, *Pre-
cedent in English Law,* 4th edn (Oxford, 1991)
De Visscher, *Theory and Reality* Charles De Visscher, *Theory and
Reality in Public International Law,* tr. P. E. Corbett, revised edi-
tion (New Jersey, 1968)

Documents Presented, 1920 Permanent Court of International Justice, Advisory Committee of Jurists, *Documents Presented to the Committee Relating to Existing Plans for the Establishment of a Permanent Court of International Justice*, HMSO (London, 1920)

Documents concerning the Action Taken by the Council of the League of Nations, 1921 League of Nations, *Documents concerning the Action taken by the Council of the League of Nations under Article 14 of the Covenant and the Adoption by the Assembly of the Statute of the Permanent Court* (Geneva, 1921)

ECHR European Court of Human Rights

EJIL *European Journal of International Law*

Fitzmaurice, *Law and Procedure* Sir Gerald Fitzmaurice, *The Law and Procedure of the International Court of Justice*, 2 vols. (Cambridge, 1986)

Germ YBIL *German Year Book of International Law*

Goodhart, 'Precedent' A. L. Goodhart, 'Precedent in English and Continental Law', *LQR*, 50 (1934), pp. 40–65

Hag R *Recueil des cours, Académie de Droit International de La Haye*

Hudson, *The Permanent Court* M. O. Hudson, *The Permanent Court of International Justice, 1920–1942, A Treatise* (New York, 1943)

ICJYB *International Court of Justice Yearbook*

ICLQ *International and Comparative Law Quarterly*

Indian JIL *Indian Journal of International Law*

ILR *International Law Reports*

Jennings, 'Collegiate Responsibility' Sir Robert Jennings, 'The Collegiate Responsibility and Authority of the International Court of Justice', in Yoram Dinstein (ed.), *International Law at a Time of Perplexity, Essays in Honour of Shabtai Rosenne* (Dordrecht, 1989), pp. 343–353

Jennings, 'General Course' R. Y. Jennings, 'General Course on Principles of International Law', *Hag R*, 121 (1967–II), pp. 323–606

Keith, *Advisory Jurisdiction* K. J. Keith, *The Extent of the Advisory Jurisdiction of the International Court of Justice* (Leiden, 1971)

Koopmans, '*Stare decisis* in European Law' T. Koopmans, '*Stare decisis* in European Law', in David O'Keefe and Henry G. Schermers (eds.), *Essays in European Law and Integration* (Deventer, 1982), pp. 11–27

Lauterpacht, *Collected Papers* E. Lauterpacht (ed.), *International Law, being the Collected Papers of Hersch Lauterpacht*, Vol. II, (Cambridge, 1975)

Lauterpacht, *Development* Sir Hersch Lauterpacht, *The Development of International Law by the International Court* (London, 1958)

Lauterpacht, 'Schools of Thought in International Law' H. Lauterpacht, 'The so-called Anglo-American and Continental Schools of Thought in International Law', *BYBIL*, 12 (1931), pp. 31–62

LQR *Law Quarterly Review*

MLR *Modern Law Review*

Oppenheim *Oppenheim's International Law*, 9th edn (London, 1992)

Procès-Verbaux, **1920** Permanent Court of International Justice, Advisory Committee of Jurists, *Procès-Verbaux of the Proceedings of the Committee, June 16th–July 24th 1920, with Annexes,* (The Hague, 1920)

RGDIP *Revue générale de droit international public*

RIAA *Reports of International Arbitral Awards*

Röben, 'Le précédent' Volker Röben, 'Le précédent dans la jurisprudence de la Cour internationale', *Germ YBIL*, 32 (1989), pp. 382–407

Rosenne, *Law and Practice* S. Rosenne, *The Law and Practice of the International Court*, 2 vols. (Leiden, 1965); second revised edition in one volume (Dordrecht, 1985)

Scelle, 'Les Sources des diverses branches du droit' Georges Scelle, 'Les Sources des diverses branches du droit, Essai sur les sources formelles du droit international', in *Recueil d'études sur les sources du droit en l'honneur de François Gény*, III (Paris, 1934)

Sørensen, *Les Sources* Max Sørensen, *Les Sources du Droit international* (Copenhagen, 1946)

UNCIO *Documents of the United Nations Conference on International Organization*, 22 vols. (London/New York, 1945)

Waldock, *Advisory Jurisdiction* Sir Humphrey Waldock, *Aspects of the Advisory Jurisdiction of the International Court of Justice* (Gilberto Amado Lecture, Geneva, 1976)

Waldock, 'General Course' H. Waldock, 'General Course on Public International Law', *Hag R*, 106 (1962–I) pp. 1–251

Wright, 'Precedents' Lord Wright, 'Precedents', *CLJ*, 8 (1942), pp. 118–145

YBILC *Yearbook of the International Law Commission*

ZöV *Zeitschrift für ausländisches öffentliches Recht und Völkerrecht*

1

Introduction

Decisional authority

'Judicial decisions', said Hersch Lauterpacht, 'particularly when published, become part and parcel of the legal sense of the community.'[1] Not everyone rejoices. Writing in 1942, Lord Wright remarked that one effect of the destruction inflicted during the war on 'law libraries has been to reduce the number of authorities quoted in arguments in Court. Professor Goodhart', he cheerfully added, 'has assured me that this will conduce to the improvement of the law.'[2] Drastic action is not yet needed at The Hague; but beyond that it would not be prudent to prophesy. 'The practising international lawyer of today', remarked O'Connell, '. . . selects as his sharpest and most valued tool the judicial decisions which will support his case.'[3] This monograph is devoted to the precedential aspects of the most important of these, namely, decisions of the World Court itself; the prominence of the role played by them is all the more striking when it is considered that, as compared with the situation at municipal law, the number of cases decided by the Court is small.[4]

Comparison may, of course, be made with several legal systems. If so wide an exercise is not undertaken, this is because, at the founding of the Permanent Court of International Justice, the

---

[1] E. Lauterpacht (ed.), *International Law, being the Collected Papers of Hersch Lauterpacht* (Cambridge, 1975), II, pp. 473–474.
[2] Lord Wright, 'Precedents', *CLJ*, 8 (1942), p. 145.
[3] D. P. O'Connell, *International Law* (London, 1970), I, p. 32.
[4] Max Sørensen, *Les Sources du Droit international* (Copenhagen, 1946), p. 174.

schools of thought which were influential with the framers of its
Statute were two, namely, the Continental and the common law
schools. In an effort to form a general view of the use to which
the Court puts its holdings, the practical course would be to limit
comparison, where necessary, to those two schools. But that, whenever it is done, is subject to the caution that, if in the end the
Court's approach appears to lie closer to one than to the other,
this is not because it has sought consciously to model its method
on one as against the other; it is the coincidental result of the
independent operation of the systems. There is no suggestion that
any particular legal tradition is superior to another. Each system
has its virtues.

There is no reason to believe that any lawyer from anywhere has
any special difficulty in coming to terms with the methods of
reasoning employed by the Court. It is possible, however, that a
lawyer formed in the traditions of the common law may feel rather
at home, if somewhat strangely so, in the way the Court has
recourse to its previous decisions in the process of determining the
law. The principal difference, he will be told, is that *stare decisis* does
not apply; and, indeed, largely because of this important fact, it is
sometimes said that it is not right to speak of 'precedents' in the
case of decisions of the Court. But the fact that the doctrine of
binding precedent does not apply means that decisions of the Court
are not binding precedents; it does not mean that they are not
'precedents'. The term occurs in the jurisprudence of the Court;[5]
it occurs also in the pleadings of counsel and in the writings of
publicists.[6]

Nor is this surprising, for the fact is that the Court seeks guidance from its previous decisions, that it regards them as reliable[7]

---

[5] *Interpretation of the Greco-Turkish Agreement of 1 December 1926 (Final Protocol, Article iv), 1928, PCIJ, Series B, No. 16*, p. 15, and *Factory at Chorzów (Merits), 1928, PCIJ, Series A, No. 17*, p. 7. And see *Certain Norwegian Loans, ICJ Rep 1957*, p. 60, Judge Lauterpacht; and *Namibia, ICJ Rep 1971*, p. 19, para. 9.

[6] See, for example, *Continental Shelf (Tunisia/Libyan Arab Jamahiriya), Application for Permission to Intervene, ICJ Rep 1981*, p. 11; and Shabtai Rosenne, 'Article 27 of the Statute of the International Court of Justice', *Virg JIL*, 32 (1991), pp. 230–231.

[7] It is not believed that, in this context, much violence is done to the distinction made by Fitzmaurice when he said that decisions of the Court may be cited '[a]s 'authority', but not necessarily as authoritative'. See Sir Gerald Fitzmaurice, *The Law and Procedure of the International Court of Justice* (Cambridge, 1986), I, p. xxxii, footnote 22. He went on, in the text, to say that 'even controversial [decisions]

expositions of the law, and that, though having the power to depart from them, it will not lightly exercise that power. In these respects, the submission is that the Court uses its previous decisions in much the same way as that in which a common law court of last resort will today treat its own previous decisions. Thus, the fact that decisions of the Court are not precedentially binding is not likely to interest the common lawyer very much, not at any rate in the period following the House of Lords Practice Statement of 1966.

A question which may be of some interest to him – and, contradictorily as it may seem, it may not be the same – is whether decisions of the Court create law. It is of course an old quarrel; it is not on that account irrelevant. If decisions of the Court can result in the creation of law, is this a sufficiently important matter to merit asking how, and at what point, is that law created? Does the phenomenon occur within the judicial process itself? Or outside of it?

These issues apart, opportunity has been taken to deal with connected elements in the hope of not putting forward too disjointed an account of the system, while not claiming to paint a full portrait. Thus, the question is considered whether the Court makes a distinction between *ratio decidendi* and *obiter dictum*. If it does, what is the measure of authority or persuasiveness that it assigns to each category? To what extent does it practise the art of distinguishing cases? Can it depart from its previous decisions? If so, in what circumstances? What is the impact of individual opinions – whether separate or dissenting – on the system? Has the Court developed rules on these matters? These questions are interrelated, and answers may overlap. It is sought to deal with them in the following pages.

The juridical basis of the Court's functions

The questions posed above, and the answers which they attract, assume a system of adjudication functioning on the basis of law. A preliminary word may be said on this.

To liken the Court to a municipal court is misleading; there are important organisational, jurisdictional and procedural differences.

tend in the course of years to be generally regarded as law'. It may be supposed that, at least when that result comes about, they may be taken to be 'authoritative'.

3

Yet, the similarities are greater than the differences. The fundamental nature is the same;[8] for the essential thing about the Court is that it is, of course, a court of justice.[9] That is the characteristic which distinguishes it from other mechanisms of peaceful settlement. There are several such mechanisms, and States are free to resort to any; but this freedom of recourse to other methods, or the utility of the solutions which they offer, should not obscure the special character of the Court as a court of justice.

There is a political aspect to a municipal court in the paradoxical sense that, to the extent that it delivers justice in accordance with strictly legal criteria, as it must, it is providing one of the services expected of a sound system of government broadly understood. However the global arrangements within which the Court functions may be characterised, there is a sense in which it may also be said of it that, if it is to satisfy the indispensable requirement of political credibility, it must act judicially, and only so.[10] Decisions of national courts, even the most circumspect of these, are sometimes followed by suspicions of political motivation. Decisions of the World Court have not been exempt from similar criticisms, as witness the controversies attendant on the decision of the Permanent Court of International Justice in *Customs Regime between Germany and Austria*.[11] But the criticisms presuppose that the Court operates on a judicial basis; though sometimes severe, they do not justify the view that it does not.[12] Needless to say, its functions can only be discharged on the basis of judicial independence. The concept is well understood in municipal law; but, in the age of communication, it is as well to recall Judge Tanaka's view that 'the judicial independence

---

[8] Gilbert Guillaume, 'L'administration de la justice internationale', *Revue française d'administration publique*, 57 (1991), p. 135.

[9] See, *inter alia*, *Fisheries Jurisdiction, ICJ Rep 1974*, pp. 23–24, para. 53; by the present writer 'The International Court of Justice: The Integrity of an Idea', in R. S. Pathak and R. P. Dhokalia (eds.), *International Law in Transition, Essays in Honour of Judge Nagendra Singh* (Dordrecht, 1992), p. 341; and, also by him, *First Taslim Elias Memorial Lecture* (Nigerian Institute of Advanced Legal Studies, Lagos, 1994).

[10] As to the sense in which a court may be said to fulfil a political purpose, see Francis Vallat, reviewing Shabtai Rosenne, *The Law and Practice of the International Court* (Leiden, 1965), in *BYBIL*, 43 (1968–69), pp. 322–323.

[11] *1931, PCIJ, Series A/B, No. 41*, p. 4.

[12] See answers to criticisms of bias given in Thomas M. Franck, 'Fairness in the International Legal and Institutional System', *Hag R*, 240 (1993–III), pp. 304, 307, 313, 340.

of courts and judges must be safeguarded not only from other branches of the government, that is to say, the political and administrative power, but also from any other external power, for instance, political parties, trade unions, mass media and public opinion'.[13]

Insistence on these normative bases does not, of course, mean that the Court is required to take a blinkered view of the reality of a situation; no more so than in the case of a municipal court. In the words of President Huber:

[I]l n'est pas douteux que tout législateur et tout juge, pour bien remplir ses fonctions, doive avoir une pleine compréhension des rapports de la vie sociale dans lesquels il intervient soit par une loi, soit par un jugement. De même, il est nécessaire que la Cour, en interprétant et en recherchant les règles de droit international, tienne compte de la nature spécifique des rapports entre Etats. La Cour n'a pas seulement besoin de la confiance de l'opinion publique, mais aussi de celle des gouvernements, et il est naturel que ceux-ci veuillent être assurés que la Cour a une véritable compréhension des problèmes qui sont à la base des différends qu'elle est appelée a trancher.[14]

However, marking the essential distinction between political decision-making and judicial decision-making, the same celebrated judge added:

Foncièrement différente est la Justice. Ici toute balance de forces, tout opportunisme, tout marchandage sont exclus. La décision judiciaire tire son autorité non pas du fait qu'elle s'adapte bien aux exigences d'une situation particulière et momentanée, mais de ce qu'elle repose sur des raisons qui ont une valeur générale en dehors du cas concret et une force conclusive pour tous. Les institutions judiciaires reposent toutes sur deux principes d'ordre spirituel: la logique juridique, élément rationnnel, et la justice, élément moral. Ces deux principes, ces deux piliers de la fonction judiciaire l'élèvent au dessus de la mêlée où s'affrontent les intérêts et

---

[13] *Barcelona Traction, Light and Power Company, Limited, ICJ Rep 1970*, p. 154.

[14] *PCIJ, Series C, No. 7–I*, p. 17. And see *ICJ Pleadings, Reparation for Injuries Suffered in the Service of the United Nations*, p. 46, President Basdevant; *Namibia, ICJ Rep 1971*, p. 23, para. 29; Charles De Visscher, *Theory and Reality in Public International Law*, tr. P. E. Corbett, revised edition (New Jersey, 1968), pp. 387–388; Rosenne, *Law and Practice* (1965), I, pp. 90–92; Sir Robert Jennings, in *Judicial Settlement of International Disputes* (Berlin, 1974), p. 37; and W. M. Reisman, 'International Politics and International Law-Making – Reflections on the so-called "Politicization" of the International Court', in Wybo P. Heere (ed.), *International Law and its Sources, Liber Amicorum Maarten Bos* (Deventer, 1981), p. 81.

les passions des hommes, des partis, des classes, des nations et des races.[15]

The jurisprudence of the Court is impressed with this emphasis on the juridical basis on which its functions are exercised; that in turn forms the foundation of its system of precedents.

The concept of precedents

As remarked by Lord Wright, 'Precedents are what they are because men faced with a problem ask "Have we not had this before or something like it?".'[16] The point is illustrated by the well-known words of James I, 'Reason is too large. Find me a precedent and I will accept it.'[17] In the dictionary definition of the term, the idea is followed by many legal systems, if not by all.[18] Goodhart recalls a suggestion by Sir Edward Coke that Moses was the first law reporter. The idea must have been sufficiently known to the Romans to move Justinian to limit it with the precept *non exemplis, sed legibus iudicandum est*.[19] That maxim, though the basis of the Continental approach, has not succeeded in altogether preventing the development of the precedential influence of decisions even in civil law systems. The phenomenon has of course been even more marked in common law systems.[20] Can it exist outside of the framework of a municipal legal system? It would seem so; it is noticeable in international law, particularly as applied by the International Court of Justice.

---

[15] *PCIJ, Series C, No. 7–I*, p. 18. For the distinction, in English law, between the administrator and the judge, see H. W. R. Wade, *Administrative Law*, 6th edn (Oxford, 1988), p. 46, and S. A. de Smith, *Judicial Review of Administrative Action*, 4th edn (London, 1980), pp. 48, 69, 77, 81–82, 101.

[16] Wright, 'Precedents', p. 144.

[17] Gerald J. Postema, 'Some Roots of our Notion of Precedent', in Laurence Goldstein (ed.), *Precedent in Law* (Oxford, 1987), p. 9.

[18] A. L. Goodhart, 'Precedent in English and Continental Law', *LQR*, 50 (1934), p. 41. Cf. Laurence Goldstein, *Precedent in Law* (Oxford, 1987), p. 1, stating that it is false to suggest 'that, in any legal system, a practice exists of deciding cases on the basis of decisions made in similar cases in the past'.

[19] Codex 7.45.13, cited in Goodhart, 'Precedent', p. 56.

[20] See C. K. Allen, *Law in the Making*, 7th edn (Oxford, 1964), pp. 187 ff. The phenomenon was already sufficiently prominent to rate a well-known reference in Shakespeare's *The Merchant of Venice*. See Goodhart, 'Precedent', p. 56, citing Act IV, Scene 1.

The use of precedents by the Court is governed primarily by Article 38, paragraph 1 (d), of its Statute, which of course goes back to the corresponding provision of the Statute of the Permanent Court of International Justice. The precise meaning of this provision, which will be considered later, lies at the root of the literature on the subject. Writing in 1933, Castberg considered that the provision presented no special difficulty of interpretation.[21] That view is not generally shared today. That author was right, however, in observing that no certain rules existed for attributing importance to precedents.[22] So too did Hudson, remarking in 1943 that in 'its jurisprudence to date, the Court has not evolved a definite principle as to the weight which it will attach to its earlier judgments'.[23] Although noticing the Court's 'consistent reference to its own judicial precedents', in 1964 Rosenne likewise considered that it was 'premature to deduce any definite concepts or rules or principles governing their use'.[24] That caution has not lost its force; it will not do to give the matter more system or shape than the facts will admit. Yet, some thirty years later, there may be reason to revisit the subject. Possibly, the need for rules is less felt in the case of a court which, like the World Court, does not operate as a tier within a judicial hierarchy. Where, as in a national system, a court operates as part of such a hierarchy, the need for clear principles is greater. In some parts of the Commonwealth, for example, it is important to be wary of the rules regulating the relative weight to be attached to a decision on the common law given by the House of Lords, as against one given by the Privy Council; counsel, who has got the rules wrong, could lose his client's case.[25] No similar risk is likely to ambush the practitioner at The Hague. He may yet share the surprise felt by Jennings when he remarked in 1967 that

[21] Frede Castberg, 'La Méthodologie du droit international public', *Hag R*, 43 (1933–I), p. 373.
[22] *Ibid.*, p. 367.
[23] M. O. Hudson, *The Permanent Court of International Justice, 1920–1942, A Treatise* (New York, 1943), p. 627.
[24] Rosenne, *Law and Practice* (1965), II, p. 612. And see, by him, 'Article 27 of the Statute of the International Court of Justice', *Virg JIL*, 32 (1991), pp. 230–231.
[25] See, generally, Taslim O. Elias, 'Judicial Process and Legal Development in Africa', in I. J. Mowoe and Richard Bjornson (eds.), *Africa and the West: The Legacies of Empire* (New York, 1986), p. 196; W. S. Clarke, 'The Privy Council, Politics and Precedent in the Asia–Pacific Region', *ICLQ*, 39 (1990), p. 741; and *De Lasala* v. *De Lasala* [1979] 2 All ER 1146, PC.

since 'judicial decision has become so important in the development of international law it is surprising that relatively so little has been done to elaborate principles governing the use of precedents in international law'.[26]

The surprise is understandable. In so far as the corpus of the law is based on decided cases, it is logical that there should be rules regulating the way in which previous cases are used for the purpose of determining the law. A system of precedents is thus the inevitable accompaniment of a body of law based on case law. The conditions required for its development have been considered by several writers.[27] In a valuable article Koopmans identified three. Condensing rather liberally, these are, first, that the main rules are unwritten; second, that the court should function as a unifying element in a legal system characterised by centrifugal forces; and, third, that there is something like the necessity of resorting to principles.[28]

Now, it is possible to say that, technically, some or all of those three conditions are not met in the case of the Court; but, if the matter is looked at in the broad sense appropriate to international law, a different conclusion is suggested. Despite the growing importance of 'law-making treaties', the main rules of international law are unwritten; further, as has been the experience of countries with written codes, even in relation to codified international law the development of a system of precedents is not excluded. The first of Koopmans's three conditions may be reasonably regarded as satisfied. Arguably, the second condition is also met, for, although there is no hierarchical judicial system in international law headed by a common superior organ, the various adjudicating bodies, with the International Court of Justice – a permanent global judicial institution – as their informally acknowledged summit of authority,[29] do exercise a unifying normative influence on the polycentric forces within the inter-

---

[26] R. Y. Jennings, 'General Course on Principles of International Law', *Hag R*, 121 (1967–II), p. 342.

[27] See *inter alia*, Goodhart, 'Precedent', *passim*, and John C. Gardner, *Judicial Precedent in Scots Law* (Edinburgh, 1936), pp. 19, 76–78.

[28] T. Koopmans, '*Stare decisis* in European Law', in David O'Keefe and Henry G. Schermers (eds.), *Essays in European Law and Integration* (Deventer, 1982), pp. 14–17.

[29] See C. F. Amerasinghe, *State Responsibility for Injuries to Aliens* (Oxford, 1967), p. 33.

national legal system.[30] The point is not free from controversy;[31] yet one can scarcely disagree with the remark made by Basdevant, speaking of the Permanent Court of International Justice, that 'la jurisprudence de cette Cour jouit d'une grande autorité auprès des autres tribunaux internationaux'.[32] Speaking of the present Court, Grisel has likewise observed, 'Seul tribunal vraiment universel et principal organe judiciaire des Nations Unies, la Cour rend des arrêts qui ont une autorité considérable'.[33] The third condition is also satisfied, there being clear necessity for legal issues arising within the international community to be resolved by recourse to general propositions of law if the solutions reached are to command some critical minimum level of supporting respect; all international tribunals recognise this.

Different ways in which a system of precedents may operate

A system of precedents may operate in one of several ways. At the risk of oversimplification, but, it is hoped, not of caricaturing, these may be summarised thus: such a system may authorise the judge to consider previous decisions as part of the general legal material from which the law may be ascertained; or, it may oblige him to decide the case in the same way as a previous case unless he can give a good reason for not doing so; or, still yet, it may oblige him to decide it in the same way as the previous case even if he can give a good reason for not doing so.[34] Continental systems are of the first kind; occasionally, they incline to the second, and in some areas to the third. A system of the last kind is said to be based on the

---

[30] Emmanuel Roucounas, 'Rapport entre 'moyens auxiliaires' de détermination du droit international', *Thesaurus Acroasium*, 19 (1992), pp. 264, 265, 267; but see, *ibid.*, p. 270, para. 26.

[31] See and compare Sørensen, *Les Sources*, p. 154; Sir Humphrey Waldock, *Aspects of the Advisory Jurisdiction of the International Court of Justice* (Gilberto Amado Lecture, Geneva, 1976), p. 92; Luigi Condorelli, 'L'Autorité de la décision des juridictions internationales permanentes', in *La Juridiction internationale permanente*, Colloque de Lyon (Paris, 1987), pp. 309–310; and Volker Röben, 'Le précédent dans la jurisprudence de la Cour internationale', *Germ YBIL*, 32 (1989), p. 382.

[32] Jules Basdevant, 'Règles générales du droit de la paix', *Hag R*, 58 (1936–IV), p. 511.

[33] Etienne Grisel, '*Res judicata*: l'autorité de la chose jugée en droit international', in Bernard Dutoit (ed.), *Mélanges Georges Perrin* (Lausanne, 1984), p. 142.

[34] Rupert Cross and J. W. Harris, *Precedent in English Law*, 4th edn (Oxford, 1991), p. 4.

doctrine of binding precedent. Common law courts are of this kind, but the highest courts, while generally following their previous decisions, reserve the right to depart from them; in this sense the view may be hazarded that, even where they aver that they are treating their former decisions as 'normally binding', their power to depart 'when it appears right to do so' means that they are not strictly bound.[35]

The development of the right of a common law court of last resort to depart from its own previous decision strengthens a tendency to narrow the differences between the two systems at the top.[36] In a general way, however, it may be said that the highest common law courts pay greater attention to particular cases than do their civil law counterparts; they are likelier to rely on a single case as sufficing to establish a principle of law. The Continental approach to precedent is, as the writer understands it, that, although the court in some circumstances follows a single decision,[37] particularly where, as in France, the decision has been given on a question of principle by l'Assemblée plénière du Conseil d'Etat or les chambres réunies de la Cour de Cassation, more normally, it tends to seek guidance from an accumulation of judicial responses to a particular legal problem.[38] The excellence of that approach is clear, involving, as it does, a certain suppleness in a process of trial and error, as contrasted with what may be thought of as an element of rigidity

---

[35] See the wording of the 1966 House of Lords Practice Statement, in Cross and Harris, *Precedent*, p. 104; and *A.–G. v. Reynolds*, (1979) 3 All ER 140.

[36] See, in the case of The Netherlands, Maarten Bos, 'The Interpretation of International Judicial Decisions', *Revista Española de Derecho Internacional*, 33 (1981), p. 16.

[37] Lazare Kopelmanas, 'Essai d'une théorie des sources formelles du Droit international', *Revue de Droit international*, 21 (1938), p. 126; and H. C. Gutteridge, *Comparative Law, An Introduction to the Comparative Method of Legal Study and Research*, 2nd edn (Cambridge, 1949), p. 90.

[38] Goodhart, 'Precedent', p. 42. For precedent in Continental systems, see, *inter alia*, W. S. Holdsworth, *A History of English Law*, 3rd edn (London, 1924), IV, pp. 220 ff; René David and H. P. de Vries, *The French Legal System, An Introduction to Civil Law Systems* (New York, 1958), Part 3, Chapter IV; H. C. Gutteridge, *Comparative Law, An Introduction to the Comparative Method of Legal Study and Research*, 2nd edn (Cambridge, 1949), pp. 90 ff; Koopmans, '*Stare decisis* in European Law', pp. 11 ff; Otto Kahn-Freund, Claudine Lévy and Bernard Rudden, *A Source-book on French Law* (Oxford, 1973), pp. 98 ff; and Roger Perrot, *Institutions judiciaires*, 5th edn (Paris, 1993), pp. 29–30, para. 26. For the position in the European Court of Justice, see Bernard Rudden, *Basic Community Cases* (Oxford, 1987), p. 39; and T. C. Hartley, *The Foundations of European Community Law*, 2nd edn (Oxford, 1988), pp. 75–76 .

in the common law system. In *Serbian Loans*, Judge Pessoa, dissenting in the Permanent Court of International Justice, gave expression to the Continental idea when he remarked, on the domestic question of currency laws, that 'the jurisprudence of the French courts in this matter has not as yet that continuous, uniform and fixed character which is required in order to make it binding'.[39] The World Court has never said that, or anything similar to it, in reference to its own case law.

The Court has indeed spoken of its 'settled jurisprudence',[40] as have individual judges; but the better view would appear to be that it does not act on the *jurisprudence constante* model of the Continent; at any rate, it does not use a line of cases as an undifferentiated pool of resource material evidencing the gradual emergence of a new principle by way of movement from non-law to law. The available decisions are not so numerous, anyhow. True, a particular decision may be regarded as consolidating the previous case law on a point. Judge Gros recognised this, although of the view that it had not happened on a particular point, when he said that a 'certain tendency has arisen to consider that the Orders of 17 August 1972 in the *Fisheries Jurisdiction* cases have, as it were, consolidated the law concerning provisional measures'.[41] But, even where there is no question of consolidating the previous case law, a particular decision may well be relied on.[42]

As pointed out by Sørensen, the disposition of the Court to follow a single decision is related to the authority of the tribunal by which the decision is rendered.[43] Obviously, and rightly, the Court regards its own authority, and that of its predecessor, as supreme in the field of international adjudication. Several cases may be cited, but often only as further illustrations of the principle decided in a particular case. In the presence of a clear precedent set by itself or its predecessor, the Court will not normally undertake fresh research.[44]

---

[39] *1929, PCIJ, Series A, Nos. 20/21*, p. 73, para. 21.

[40] *United States Diplomatic and Consular Staff in Tehran, ICJ Rep 1980*, p. 18, para. 33; and *Interpretation of the Agreement of 25 March 1951 between the WHO and Egypt, ICJ Rep 1980*, p. 87, para. 33.

[41] *Nuclear Tests (Australia v. France), Interim Protection, ICJ Rep 1973*, p. 122.

[42] See discussion in Sørensen, *Les Sources*, p. 155; and Suzanne Bastid, 'La Jurisprudence de la Cour internationale de Justice', *Hag R*, 78 (1951–I), p. 631.

[43] Sørensen, *Les Sources*, p. 165.

[44] Suzanne Bastid, 'La Jurisprudence de la Cour internationale de Justice', *Hag R*, 78 (1951–I), p. 631; and see Georges Scelle, 'Les Sources des diverses branches

As a general tendency, if no more, in a new case it will refer specifically to the earlier decision; but, in still later cases, the language is likely to reduce itself to a recital of the principle established by the decision, reference to the decision being now dispensed with or confined to parenthetical citation.[45]

As remarked above, although the Court does not regard its previous decisions as laying down the law with binding effect, for practical purposes it 'treats them as sufficient authority for the principle under consideration'.[46] It will consequently follow them unless they can be distinguished on valid grounds or shown to be clearly wrong, or, possibly, where they no longer meet the new conditions of the evolving international community. It will be convenient to return to some of these aspects after considering the growth which has taken place over the years in the Court's case law.

du droit, Essai sur les sources formelles du droit international', in *Recueil d'études sur les sources du droit en l'honneur de François Gény* (Paris, 1934), III, p. 427.

[45] See, generally, Julio A. Barberis, 'La Jurisprudencia Internacional como fuento de Derecho de Gentes según la Corte de la Haya', *ZöV*, 31 (1971), p. 661; and Röben, 'Le précédent', p. 395. Cf. Sørensen, *Les Sources*, p. 167. For a similar position in the common law, see Lord Macmillan, 'The Writing of Judgments', *Canadian Bar Review* (1948), p. 498: 'In the process of reaching a decision precedents are very properly read and studied as evidence of the law, but they should be used for the purpose of extracting the law from them. It is undesirable to cumber a judgment with all the apparatus of research which Bench and Bar have utilised in ascertaining the principle of law to be applied.'

[46] H. Waldock, 'General Course on Public International Law', *Hag R*, 106, (1962–I), p. 93.

2

The growth of the Court's case law

Increase in the relative importance of case law

The World Court, existing first as the Permanent Court of International Justice and currently as the International Court of Justice, has been in existence for nearly three-quarters of a century. The prospect of the Court building up its own case law and the practical implications of this for the international community had been the subject of early notice, going back to the period leading up to the establishment of the first Court. Following on its establishment, one finds that the precise extent of the possible precedential value of *Status of Eastern Carelia*[1] underlay much of the debate relating to the question of United States accession to the Protocol of Signature of the Statute of the Permanent Court of International Justice. Writing on the issue in 1926, Sir Cecil Hurst advised the British Secretary of State for Foreign Affairs as follows:

How far the rule embodied in this decision of the Court extends is a question which at the present time it is impossible to answer. All that it is possible to do, therefore, with regard to complying with the United States condition[2] is to refer to the Eastern Carelia case. The Court will gradually build up a rule of law on this point out of the decisions which it gives, as no doubt such successive decisions will constitute precedents in the same way that the successive decisions of the English courts in early times have built up the Common Law of England. It would be unwise

---

[1] *1923, PCIJ, Series B, No. 5.*

[2] This related to a requirement that the Court shall not, 'without the consent of the United States, entertain any request for an advisory opinion touching any dispute or question in which the United States has or claims an interest'. See the discussion in Hudson, *The Permanent Court*, pp. 219 ff.

to attempt to fetter the power of the Court to build up the rule in this way.[3]

From a practical point of view, these expectations about the growth of precedents in the jurisprudence of the Court proved to be largely right, even if equation with the technical basis of the common law model of development may be more debatable.

The published decisions of the Permanent Court of International Justice, as conveniently collected in a Kraus reprint edition, consist of nine volumes. Those of the International Court of Justice, as at the end of 1994, consist of forty-seven, of varying bulk. The law reports of the two Courts extend to about two metres of shelf space. Not a lot, the common lawyer may say; and, indeed, a somewhat slender basis for talk of precedents. But one does not judge with eyes trained on the mountains of case law dominating, and sometimes intimidating, the common law world. Speaking in 1925, President Huber had some words on the contrast:

Le nombre des affaires portées devant la Cour sera toujours relativement limité. Cela tient à la composition de la communauté internationale. C'est pourquoi la valeur de chaque arrêt que nous rendons exerce sur l'autorité de notre Cour une influence, tout autre que celle d'un jugement d'un tribunal national. En effet, un tribunal national rend par an des centaines de décisions; s'il s'en trouve quelques-unes de critiquables, la bonne moyenne qui résulte d'une jurisprudence longuement constituée n'en saurait cependant être modifiée. Pour nous, il n'en est pas de même: comme notre compétence est toujours basée en dernière ligne sur la libre volonté des Etats et partant sur le crédit moral dont nous jouissons, chaque arrêt et chaque avis consultatif comporte à notre égard un caractère de gravité – tout à fait indépendamment des intérêts en jeu.[4]

Thus, the very paucity of the Court's decisions highlights their jurisprudential worth. It is still a relatively exceptional thing for sovereign States to go to law; the oft-repeated idea that international litigation is merely another form of friendly settlement, though correct in theory and sometimes pleasantly true in practice, is not always a reflection of reality – no more so than in the case of municipal litigation.[5] In the 'Lotus', M. Basdevant told the Court

---

[3] *The Permanent Court of International Justice, Question of Accession of the United States of America to the Protocol of December 16, 1920*, HMSO, Cmd. 2776 (1926), p. 8, para. 26.

[4] *PCIJ, Series C, No. 7–I*, pp. 16–17.

[5] P. C. Jessup, 'International Litigation as a Friendly Act', *Col LR*, 60 (1960), pp. 24 ff, and Guy de Lacharrière, in Garry Sturgess and Philip Chubb, *Judging the*

that emotions, which had been aroused in France by the incident, had been entirely calmed when it was made known that the dispute would be submitted to the Court by the two sides.[6] But litigation can have the opposite effect of exacerbating tension; it is true also, as Judge Dillard remarked, that '[l]aw "goes on" every day without adjudication of any kind'.[7] Notwithstanding this, the growth of international case law has been marked. This is particularly apparent if one takes into account arbitral and national case law concerning international law issues. But, even excluding these sources, the case law produced by the World Court has been both substantial in volume and wide in range.

The result of the general expansion has, in the words of Lord McNair, 'completely transformed the international corpus juris from a system that rested very largely upon textbooks and diplomatic dispatches into a body of hard law, resembling the common law or equity of' the United States or England.[8] In the four decades which have elapsed since that observation was made, the transformation has continued unabated.[9] Evidence of this is to be found not only in the Court's own decisions, but in a sizeable literature which has sprung up around the subject of its jurisprudence.[10] Surveying the direction taken by developments, Judge Jennings, as Lord McNair had done earlier, has also spoken 'of a change in the sources of international law, which had already begun to be felt even in the early 1930s: international law has become a case law'.[11] The change had been foreshadowed by Lord Sumner as early as 1921. Delivering the judgment of the Privy Council, and speaking admittedly of the duty of British Prize Courts to follow 'the current of decisions' (presumably British ones), he remarked that the 'more

---

World: Law and Politics in the World's Leading Courts (Sydney, 1988), p. 455. Cf. Aegean Sea Continental Shelf, ICJ Rep 1978, p. 52, Judge Lachs, separate opinion.

[6] PCIJ, Series C, No. 13–II, p. 29.

[7] Namibia, ICJ Rep 1971, p. 168, separate opinion; and see Baron van Asbeck, 'Growth and Movement of International Law', ICLQ, 11 (1962), pp. 1054 ff.

[8] Sir Arnold Duncan McNair, The Development of International Justice (New York, 1954), p. 16. And see, also by him, 'La terminaison et la dissolution des traités', Hag R, 22 (1928–II), p. 463; The Expansion of International Law (Jerusalem, 1962), p. 54; and Lord McNair: Selected Papers and Bibliography (Leiden/Dobbs Ferry, 1974), pp. 213, 256.

[9] See Manfred Lachs, 'Le Droit international à l'aube du XXIe siècle', RGDIP, 96 (1992), p. 537.

[10] For a useful though unfortunately not up-to-date guide, see the eleven volumes of Edvard Hambro, The Case Law of the International Court (Leiden, 1952–1976).

[11] Robert Y. Jennings, 'An International Lawyer Takes Stock', ICLQ, 39 (1990), p. 519.

the field is covered by decided cases the less becomes the authority of commentators and jurists'.[12] That has been happening. In the result, the system seems to be moving, if cautiously, in the direction pointed out in another penetrating remark by Lord McNair to the effect that the 'value of Justinian's Digest lies in the fact that it is also based on case-law'.[13]

The experience of the Permanent Court of International Justice

The Permanent Court of International Justice, which formally convened on 30 January 1922, began its first ordinary session on 15 June 1922. Its first judicial pronouncement was made in the form of an advisory opinion given six weeks later, on 31 July 1922.[14] In the nature of things it would take some time before the Court could begin to refer to its previous decisions or opinions for their precedential worth; but the process began soon enough.[15] An early instance occurred in *Mavrommatis Palestine Concessions*[16] in which the Court, on 30 August 1924, referred to and distinguished *Nationality Decrees Issued in Tunis and Morocco*, an advisory opinion of 7 February 1923.[17] The art of distinguishing is of course the trademark of a system of precedents; non-anglophone lawyers are as good at it as any. More positive evidence of the operation of the system is to be found in the ninth advisory opinion, which was given on 4 September 1924, in the *Question of the Monastery of Saint-Naoum*. One of the issues concerned the legal status of a decision of the Conference of Ambassadors which had been instituted pursuant to certain post-War treaty arrangements. The question had received consideration in the Court's previous advisory opinion, relating to the *Jaworzina*. Consequently, the Court now limited itself to observing that in 'Advisory opinion No. 8 concerning the affair of Jaworzina, the Court, in a question closely resembling that of Saint-Naoum, states the general legal considerations determining the nature and effects

---

[12] *The Kronprincessan Margareta*, [1921] AC 486, 495, PC.
[13] Sir Arnold Duncan McNair, *The Development of International Justice* (New York, 1954), p. 17.
[14] *Designation of the Workers' Delegate for The Netherlands at the Third Session of the International Labour Conference, 1922, PCIJ, Series B, No. 1.*
[15] See, generally, Hudson, *The Permanent Court*, pp. 627–628.
[16] *1924, PCIJ, Series A, No. 2*, p. 16.
[17] *1923, PCIJ, Series B, No. 4.*

of a decision of this kind. The Court now refers to this opinion'.[18]

The working of the system was also apparent in the *'Lotus'*, in which the Court said that it 'must recall ... what it has said in some of its preceding judgments and opinions, namely, that there is no occasion to have regard to preparatory work if the text of a convention is sufficiently clear in itself'.[19] In its 1928 judgment in the *Factory at Chorzów*,[20] it drew upon its first judgment, rendered in the *SS 'Wimbledon'* in 1923, stating that the 'Court must ... draw attention ... to what it has already said in Judgment No. 1[21] to the effect that it neither can nor should contemplate the contingency of the judgment not being complied with at the expiration of the time fixed for compliance'.[22]

In *Readaptation of the Mavrommatis Jerusalem Concessions, Jurisdiction*, it said, 'The Court sees no reason to depart from a construction which clearly flows from the previous judgments the reasoning of which it still regards as sound'.[23] The precedential significance of that statement, though appearing to be somewhat qualified, was not much weakened by the additional words, 'more especially seeing that the two Parties have shown a disposition to accept the point of view adopted by the Court'; the construction adopted in one case of an instrument was being extended to another in which the same instrument was involved. The circumstance that the parties might be the same need not obscure the fact that the earlier case was operating precedentially in relation to the later.[24]

In *Minority Schools in Albania* the Court observed 'that in its Advisory Opinion of September 15th, 1923, concerning the question of the acquisition of Polish nationality (Opinion No. 7), the Court referred to the opinion which it had already expressed in Advisory Opinion No. 6 to the effect that "an interpretation which would deprive the Minorities Treaty of a great part of its value is

---

[18] *1924, PCIJ, Series B, No. 9*, p. 15.
[19] *1927, PCIJ, Series A, No. 10*, p. 16.
[20] *1928, PCIJ, Series A, No. 17*, p. 63.
[21] *PCIJ, Series A, No. 1*, p. 32.
[22] Followed by the present Court in *Military and Paramilitary Activities in and against Nicaragua, ICJ Rep 1984*, p. 437, para. 101, and in *Application for Revision and Interpretation of the Judgment of 24 February 1982 in the Case concerning the* Continental Shelf (Tunisia/Libyan Arab Jamahiriya) *(Tunisia v. Libyan Arab Jamahiriya), ICJ Rep 1985*, p. 229, para. 67.
[23] *1927, PCIJ, Series A, No. 11*, p. 18.
[24] Sørensen, *Les Sources*, p. 173.

inadmissible" '.[25] In *Electricity Company of Sofia and Bulgaria* it recalled 'what it said in the Judgment of June 14th, 1938 (Phosphates in Morocco, Preliminary Objection)' on the question of 'situation or facts' referred to in optional clause declarations.[26]

The idea of precedents applies not only to the substantive law, but also to procedural law. On procedural questions, the Court would consult its previous decisions, published or unpublished. In the *Borchgrave* case, the publications of the Court stated that the 'precedents were examined and it was found that in fixing "new time-limits", the Court had been guided by the circumstances in each particular case. The Court decided that in this case the time-limits should be as originally contemplated.'[27] The *Panevezys-Saldutiskis Railway* case is interesting. There the Court

considered the question whether the order made joining the preliminary objections to the merits should include a statement of the facts in the case. It was observed that only in one order relating to the joinder of preliminary objections to the merits of a case (the *Losinger* case, 1936) had a statement of the facts been included.

The Court came to the conclusion that in the present case such a statement was unnecessary, but it was agreed that this decision should not constitute a precedent and that the question whether a statement of the facts should be included in the Court's decision should be considered in each case as it arose.[28]

In agreeing (possibly because of the circumstances) that that particular 'decision should not constitute a precedent', the Court by implication accepted that a decision on procedural matters could constitute a precedent.

In matters relating to its work (in respect of which it has a separate rule-making competence), the Court, in deciding a given case, seems to have proceeded on the basis that it could issue something in the nature of a practice direction as to future cases. Thus, in *Free Zones of Upper Savoy and the District of Gex*, it considered that

it is important to set forth clearly that special agreements whereby international disputes are submitted to the Court should henceforth be formulated with due regard to the forms in which the Court is to express its

---

[25] *1935, PCIJ, Series A/B, No. 64*, p. 20.
[26] *1939, PCIJ, Series A/B, No. 77*, p. 82.
[27] *PCIJ, Series E, No. 16*, p. 190.
[28] *Ibid.*

opinion according to the precise terms of the constitutional provisions governing its activity, in order that the Court may be able to deal with such disputes in the ordinary course and without resorting, as in the present case, to a construction which must be regarded as strictly exceptional.[29]

Apart from instances referred to above, a sample of statements indicating that the Court was following its previous decisions might include the following: 'as the Court has had occasion to state in previous judgments and opinions . . .';[30] 'As the Court said in Judgment No. 12 . . .';[31] 'On this point the Court refers to its Advisory Opinion No. 15';[32] 'This is in conformity with the general principle of the international responsibility of States and with the decision given by the Court in the case concerning Certain German Interests in Polish Upper Silesia (Judgment No. 7)';[33] 'A similar view [on discrimination] has already been expressed by the Court in its Advisory Opinion No. 6 relating to German settlers in Poland.'[34]

Individual judges did not lag behind. In *Certain German Interests in Polish Upper Silesia, Jurisdiction*,[35] Judge Anzilotti, having cited a passage on the procedure relating to objections to jurisdiction from *Mavrommatis Palestine Concessions*,[36] said, 'I regard this passage as a very accurate statement of the principles of international law which govern the Court's jurisdiction, and I am very glad to note that its essential idea is restated on page 15 of the present Judgment'.[37]

In his dissenting opinion in *Certain German Interests in Polish Upper Silesia (supra)*, Judge Rostworowski, citing a passage from the opinion of Judge Moore in *Mavrommatis Palestine Concessions*,[38] described it as 'most judicious';[39] he at the same time cited three passages from the judgment of the Court in that case as giving a 'general idea of the great care taken by the Court before deciding on a

---

[29] *1929, PCIJ, Series A, No. 22*, p. 13.
[30] *Jurisdiction of the European Commission of the Danube, 1927, PCIJ, Series B, No. 14*, p. 36.
[31] *Factory at Chorzów, Merits, 1928, PCIJ, Series A, No. 17*, p. 37.
[32] *Treatment of Polish Nationals and Other Persons of Polish Origin or Speech in the Danzig Territory, 1932, PCIJ, Series A/B, No. 44*, p. 24.
[33] *Ibid.*, p. 25.
[34] *Ibid.*, p. 28.
[35] *1925, PCIJ, Series A, No. 6*, p. 30.
[36] *1924, PCIJ, Series A, No. 2*.
[37] *1925, PCIJ, Series A, No. 6*, p. 30.
[38] *1924, PCIJ, Series A, No. 2*, p. 60.
[39] *1925, PCIJ, Series A, No. 6*, p. 33.

similar point' relating to jurisdiction.[40] In 1932 Judge Negulesco, dissenting, remarked, 'The Court itself said as much in its Order of December 6th, 1930' as to the propriety of giving 'a judgment which either of the Parties may render inoperative'.[41]

By 1929 the position had become sufficiently clear for the Six Governments in the *Oder Commission* case formally to request the Court 'to follow its previous decisions in refusing to admit any recourse to . . . preparatory work for the purpose of putting upon a text an interpretation different from the plain meaning *(sens naturel)* of the language used'.[42] They might well have had in mind, in particular, a decision made two years earlier in which the Court stated that it 'adheres to the rule applied in its previous decisions that there is no occasion to have regard to the protocols of the conference at which a convention was negotiated in order to construe a text which is sufficiently clear in itself'.[43]

As the *Oder Commission* case shows, there was contemporary awareness of the precedential practice developing in the Court. Available publications promoted appreciation of the development. As early as 1927, one finds the *Third Annual Report* of the Permanent Court of International Justice stating, with reference to published cases, that the 'Court has in a number of its judgments and advisory opinions made references to or comparisons with earlier judgments or advisory opinions'.[44] These examples followed:

(1) In Judgment No. 2 (Series A, No. 2, p. 16) the Court refers to Advisory Opinion No. 4 (Series B, No. 4, p. 26) in order to show the connection between its arguments in the two cases.

(2) In the observations by a member of the Court attached to Judgment No. 6 (Series A, No. 6, p. 29) a passage in Judgment No. 2 (Series A, No. 2, p. 16) is quoted which is described as 'a very accurate statement of the principles of international law which govern the Court's jurisdiction'. The essential idea of this passage is restated in Judgment No. 6 (p. 15).

---

[40] *1925, PCIJ, Series A, No. 6*, p. 33.
[41] *Free Zones of Upper Savoy and the District of Gex, 1932, PCIJ, Series A/B, No. 46*, p. 192.
[42] *Territorial Jurisdiction of the International Commission of the River Oder, 1929, PCIJ, Series A, No. 23*, p. 39.
[43] *Jurisdiction of the European Commission of the Danube, 1927, PCIJ, Series B, No. 14*, p. 28.
[44] *PCIJ, Series E, No. 3* (15 June 1926–15 June 1927), p. 217.

(3) In Advisory Opinion No. 10 (Series B, No. 10, p. 21) a passage from Judgment No. 7 (Series A, No. 1, p. 25) is quoted and the principle therein contained is confirmed.

(4) In Advisory Opinion No. 13 (Series B, No. 13) the Court quotes (p. 17) from Advisory Opinion No. 2 (p. 27) and (p. 20) refers to Advisory Opinion No. 3 (pp. 53–55–57) using the reasoning employed therein to support the conclusions of Advisory Opinion No. 13.

(5) In Advisory Opinion No. 9, the Court (Series B, No. 9, pp. 14–15) cites and refers to the general legal considerations stated by it in Advisory Opinion No. 8 (Series B, No. 8, pp. 27–30) in connection with a question which is held to be similar to that dealt with in Opinion No. 9.

(6) In Advisory Opinions Nos. 11 (Series B, No. 11, pp. 27–31) and 12 (Series B, No. 12, p. 25) the Court implicitly refers to the principles previously stated in Advisory Opinions Nos. 8 (Series B, No. 8, pp. 27–30) and 9 (pp. 14–15) with regard to the arbitral nature of a decision accepted in advance by both Parties to a dispute.[45]

Surveying the situation in 1929, Beckett wrote:

In the publications of the Permanent Court of International Justice there are at the present moment to be found twenty-three judgments and interlocutory orders, and sixteen advisory opinions. With the obvious exception of the *Lotus* case (Series A, No. 10) and the perhaps less obvious exceptions of the *Irak-Turkish Frontier* case (Series B, No. 12), the *Eastern Carelia* case (Series B, No. 5), the case of the *Tunis and Morocco Nationality Decrees* (Series B, No. 4) and the case of the *Free Zones of Upper Savoy and Gex* (Series A, No. 22), all the cases submitted to the Court have related to the construction of complicated and obscure treaty or contract provisions of apparently no great general interest, and not directly to any question of general international law. For this reason it seems probable that it is not generally realized how many points of general application have already arisen incidentally in the cases submitted to the Court, or how many rulings by the Court on questions of general international law or procedure are to be found embedded in these necessarily long and complicated judgments...

The judgments and advisory opinions of the Permanent Court are, apart from general declarations or law-making conventions accepted by states, the most authoritative pronouncements on questions of international law and procedure that can be made while the family of nations remains as at present constituted. In view, moreover, of the rapidly increasing 'obligatory jurisdiction' now being conferred upon it by acceptances of the

---

[45] *Ibid.*, p. 218.

Optional Clause, it seems probable that the Court is likely in the future to play a rôle in the international community no less vitally important than that which the Supreme Court of the United States fills under the Federal Constitution. Consequently it may be of value to have the authority of the Permanent Court for even an elementary and obvious principle, and, in default of a decision on the point, even a dictum may be of some weight.[46]

Progress in the precedential tendencies noted by Beckett in 1929 has continued unaffected by disappointed expectations relating to 'the rapidly increasing "obligatory jurisdiction" ' which was then observable.

Continuity in the judicial system

The system begun under the Permanent Court of International Justice continued to operate under the International Court of Justice. It is tempting to say that this continuity occurred as a matter of course. It is useful, however, to note that in some national jurisdictions in which the common law doctrine of binding precedent prevails, a problem sometimes arises as to the continuance of the precedential value of a superior court's decisions when that court is later superseded by another court of coordinate status.[47] By contrast, although the International Court of Justice is institutionally distinct from the Permanent Court of International Justice, the continuity in the jurisprudence of the two bodies has always been clear. This had been visualised at San Francisco in 1945. The Report of the Rapporteur of Committee I of Commission IV on Judicial Organizations recorded that the '1945 Statute will garner what has come down from the past. To make possible the use of precedents under the old Statute the same numbering of the articles has been followed in the new Statute.'[48]

---

[46] W. E. Beckett, 'Decisions of the Permanent Court of International Justice on Points of Law and Procedure of General Application', *BYBIL*, 11 (1930), p. 1.

[47] See, for example, in the case of Ireland, J. M. Kelly, *Fundamental Rights in the Irish Law and Constitution*, 2nd edn (New York, 1968), pp. 31–32; and, in the context of a colony becoming independent, *Hanover* v. *Income Tax Commissioner* (1964), 7 *West Indian Reports* 300, Court of Appeal of Jamaica; *Sampson* v. *Glenn*, Court of Appeal of Guyana, 23 October 1972; and A. D. Burgess, 'Judicial Precedent in the West Indies', *Anglo-American Law Review*, 7 (1978), pp. 117–118.

[48] *Documents of the United Nations Conference on International Organisation* (London, 1945), XIII, p. 384.

The second sentence of that passage was cited in the joint dissenting opinion in *Aerial Incident of 27 July 1955*, which stressed the substantial identity of the two bodies notwithstanding the theoretical lack of it.[49] In 1984 the Court likewise observed that 'the primary concern of those who drafted the Statute of the present Court was to maintain the greatest possible continuity between it and its predecessor'.[50] True, that related to jurisdictional succession; but it was also consistent with jurisprudential continuity. The present Court makes no distinction between its own jurisprudence and that of its predecessor on the ground of the institutional distinction between the two bodies. In the view of Judge Read, 'The provisions of Article 92 of the Charter disclose the intention of the United Nations that continuity should be maintained between the Permanent Court of International Justice and this Court. There can be no doubt that the United Nations intended continuity in jurisprudence, as well as in less important matters.'[51] And in the words of President Winiarski:

The present Court has since the beginning been conscious of the need to maintain a continuity of tradition, case law and methods of work. Its first President was Judge Guerrero, the last President of the former Court. It adopted the rules of the former Court, with a few modifications of minor importance, and even its external forms. Above all, without being bound by *stare decisis* as a principle or rule, it often seeks guidance in the body of decisions of the former Court, and the result is a remarkable unity of precedent, an important factor in the development of international law.[52]

The passage from one Court to another does not, therefore, represent a jurisprudential break.

Reliance by the International Court of Justice on the practice of the Permanent Court of International Justice

The practice of the Permanent Court of International Justice was accordingly taken over and followed by the International Court of

---

[49] *ICJ Rep 1959*, pp. 158–159. And see *Barcelona Traction, Light and Power Company, Limited, Preliminary Objections, ICJ Rep 1964*, p. 69, separate opinion of Judge Tanaka.

[50] *Military and Paramilitary Activities in and against Nicaragua (Nicaragua v. United States of America), Jurisdiction and Admissibility, ICJ Rep 1984*, p. 407, para. 32.

[51] *Interpretation of Peace Treaties with Bulgaria, Hungary and Romania, Second Phase, ICJ Rep 1950*, pp. 232–233, dissenting opinion. See also *ibid.*, p. 240.

[52] *ICJ Pleadings, The Temple of Preah Vihear*, II, p. 122.

Justice; the latter has frequently relied on decisions of the former.[53] A good illustration is provided by the first *Admission* case, decided at the dawn of the life of the new Court. Moving on the well-trodden ground of the admissibility of preparatory work in construing the text of a convention, the opinion read, 'The Court considers that the text is sufficiently clear; consequently, it does not feel that it should deviate from the consistent practice of the Permanent Court of International Justice, according to which there is no occasion to resort to preparatory work if the text of a convention is sufficiently clear in itself.'[54]

In the *Reparation* case, the Court concluded that 'under international law, the Organization must be deemed to have those powers which, though not expressly provided in the Charter, are conferred upon it by necessary implication as being essential to the performance of its duties'.[55] In support of this important proposition, it said that this 'principle of law was applied by the Permanent Court of International Justice to the International Labour Organization in its Advisory Opinion No. 13 of July 23rd 1926 (Series B, No. 13, p. 18), and must be applied to the United Nations'.[56] Without any fresh inquiry into the juristic bases on which it rested, this principle, deriving from the jurisprudence of its predecessor, was simply reproduced by the Court in 1954 in support of the view that, although there 'is no express provision [in the Charter] for the establishment of judicial bodies or organs', the General Assembly had power to establish such a body for the purpose of adjudicating upon staff disputes arising out of contracts of service.[57]

In the second *Admission* case, in support of the principle relating to the ordinary and natural meaning of words, the Court thought it sufficient to say:

As the Permanent Court said in the case concerning the *Polish Postal Service in Danzig* (P.C.I.J., Series B, No. 11, p. 39): 'It is a cardinal principle of

---

[53] See *ICJYB 1947–1948*, p. 66; *ibid., 1948–1949*, p. 74; *ibid., 1950–1951*, p. 108.

[54] *Conditions of Admission of a State to Membership in the United Nations (Article 4 of Charter)*, *ICJ Rep 1948*, p. 63.

[55] *Reparation for Injuries Suffered in the Service of the United Nations*, *ICJ Rep 1949*, p. 182.

[56] *Ibid.*, pp. 182–183.

[57] *Effect of Awards of Compensation Made by the United Nations Administrative Tribunal*, *ICJ Rep 1954*, p. 56.

interpretation that words must be interpreted in the sense which they would normally have in their context, unless such interpretation would lead to something unreasonable or absurd.'[58]

In 1952, on the question of the distinction between consumption taxes and customs duties, it cited the *Free Zones* case[59] in recalling 'that the Permanent Court of International Justice recognized that fiscal duties collected at the frontier on the entry of certain goods were not to be confused with customs duties'.[60]

In *Nottebohm, Second Phase*, the Court referred to Guatemala's statement of 'a well established principle of international law ... that "it is the bond of nationality between the State and the individual which alone confers upon the State the right of diplomatic protection" ', and observed, 'This sentence is taken from a Judgment of the Permanent Court of International Justice (Series A/B, No. 76, p. 16), which relates to the form of diplomatic protection constituted by international judicial proceedings.'[61] In the same case it stated that diplomatic 'protection and protection by means of international judicial proceedings constitute measures for the defence of the rights of the State', and thought it sufficient to support this proposition by saying:

As the Permanent Court of International Justice has said and has repeated, 'by taking up the case of one of its subjects and by resorting to diplomatic action or international judicial proceedings on his behalf, a State is in reality asserting its own rights – its right to ensure, in the person of its subjects, respect for the rules of international law' (PCIJ, Series A, No. 2, p. 12, and Series A/B, Nos. 20–21, p. 17).[62]

In *Anglo-Iranian Oil Company* the judgment stated: 'As the Iranian Declaration is more limited in scope than the United Kingdom Declaration, it is the Iranian Declaration on which the Court must base itself.'[63] Tracing the pedigree of the statement, in *Certain Norwegian Loans* the Court observed that it was made '[f]ollowing ... the jurisprudence of the Permanent Court of International Justice. (Phosphates in Morocco case, Judgment of

---

[58] *Competence of the General Assembly for the Admission of a State to the United Nations*, *ICJ Rep 1950*, p. 8.
[59] *1932, PCIJ, Series A/B, No. 46*, p. 172.
[60] *Rights of Nationals of the United States of America in Morocco, ICJ Rep 1952*, p. 206.
[61] *ICJ Rep 1955*, p. 13.
[62] *Ibid.*, p. 24.
[63] *ICJ Rep 1952*, p. 103.

June 14th, 1938, PCIJ, Series A/B, No. 74, p. 22; Electricity Company of Sofia and Bulgaria case, Judgment of April 4th, 1939, PCIJ, Series A/B, No. 77, p. 81)'.[64]

Another example of reliance placed by the present Court on the case law of the Permanent Court is provided by *Barcelona Traction, Light and Power Company, Limited, Preliminary Objections*. There, on a question of joinder to the merits, the Court said it

> will ... content itself by saying that it decides to join this objection to the merits because – to quote the Permanent Court in the *Pajzc, Csáky, Esterházy* case (*PCIJ, Series A/B, No. 66*, at p. 9) – 'the ... proceedings on the merits ... will place the Court in a better position to adjudicate with a full knowledge of the facts'; and because 'the questions raised by ... these objections and those arising ... on the merits are too intimately related and too closely interconnected for the Court to be able to adjudicate upon the former without prejudging the latter'.[65]

No further examination of the law was undertaken, the reasoning and conclusions of the Permanent Court of International Justice being considered enough.

Likewise, in *Nuclear Tests (Australia v. France)*, the Court said, 'It is true that "the Court cannot take into account declarations, admissions or proposals which the Parties may have made during direct negotiations between themselves, when such negotiations have not led to a complete agreement" (*Factory at Chorzów (Merits), PCIJ, Series A, No. 17*, p. 51).'[66] It was only after conceding the principle on the basis of the cited authority of its predecessor that the Court proceeded to distinguish the case before it, stating: 'However, in the present case, that is not the situation before the Court.'[67]

Reliance by the International Court of Justice on its own case law

It is scarcely necessary to state that the Court also follows its own case law. Where no particular discussion is called for, like its predecessor, it frequently makes use of short phrases to show that it is following the previous case. In 1951, on the question whether it

---

[64] *ICJ Rep 1957*, pp. 23–24.
[65] *ICJ Rep 1964*, p. 46.
[66] *ICJ Rep 1974*, p. 270, para. 54.
[67] *Ibid.*

should decline a request for an advisory opinion, it simply observed, 'In this connection, the Court can confine itself to recalling the principles which it laid down in its Opinion of March 30th, 1950 (ICJ Reports 1950, p. 71). A reply to a request for an Opinion should not, in principle, be refused.'[68] In 1952 the Court held that it could not adopt a construction of a convention which would involve radical changes or additions to its provisions. In support, it merely recalled that the 'Court, in its Opinion – Interpretation of Peace Treaties (Second Phase) (*ICJ Reports 1950*, p. 229) – stated: "It is the duty of the Court to interpret the Treaties, not to revise them".'[69] In the same case,[70] on the question of proof of custom, it recited what it had said on the point in the *Asylum* case.[71]

Barcelona Traction, Light and Power Company, Limited, Second Phase, is one of many cases in which a principle was stated and simply followed by the citation of a relevant precedent set by the Court itself. There, in discussing the possibility of there being a dual basis of diplomatic protection, the Court said, 'This however is a case of one person in possession of two separate bases of protection, each of which is valid (*Reparation for Injuries Suffered in the Service of the United Nations, Advisory Opinion, ICJ Reports 1949*, p. 185).'[72] Likewise, in *Application for Revision and Interpretation of the Judgment of 24 February 1982 in the Case concerning* the Continental Shelf (Tunisia/Libyan Arab Jamahiriya) *(Tunisia/Libyan Arab Jamahiriya)*[73] the Court, in referring to 'the exercise of its "freedom to select the ground upon which it will base its judgment" ', merely followed this statement with the citation of '*Application of the Convention of 1902 Governing the Guardianship of Infants, ICJ Reports 1958*, p. 62'. A more recent example of a principle of law simply followed by a citation is provided by *Land, Island and Maritime Frontier Dispute (El Salvador/ Honduras), Application for Permission to Intervene*, in which the Order read: 'Whereas the rule of law that "every intervention is incidental to the proceedings in a case" (*Haya de la Torre, ICJ Reports 1951*, p. 76) applies . . .'[74]

---

[68] *Reservations to the Convention on the Prevention and Punishment of the Crime of Genocide*, *ICJ Rep 1951*, p. 19.
[69] *Rights of Nationals of the United States of America in Morocco, ICJ Rep 1952*, p. 196.
[70] *Ibid.*, p. 200.
[71] *ICJ Rep 1950*, pp. 276–277.
[72] *ICJ Rep 1970*, p. 38, para. 53.
[73] *ICJ Rep 1985*, p. 207, para. 29.
[74] *ICJ Rep 1990*, p. 4.

In just a little over two pages Hersch Lauterpacht gave a concise but complete classification of the various ways in which the Court has recourse to its previous decisions.[75] The key sentence reads to the effect that the Court's practice 'ranges from mere illustration and "distinguishing" to a form of speech apparently indicating the authoritative character of the pronouncement referred to'.[76] He gave examples of each category and sub-category. Sometimes, as was pointed out by Sørensen, the Court would employ the language of a precedent, without citing the case.[77] In the words of Fitzmaurice:

> It is . . . evident that the phraseology of certain passages in the statements of the Court, and of individual Judges, is not infrequently taken from, or reflects, language used in previous decisions that are not actually mentioned, and in these cases it is usually clear that something like a constant practice (a *jurisprudence constante*') exists, by which the Court regards itself as *de facto* bound.[78]

This does not mean that the Court has adopted a Continental conception of the subject; but it is obvious that the drafting of many decisions studiously reproduces what is regarded as the settled language of earlier ones.

Making the point that it is a legitimate course of all judicial activity to cite any precedent relied on and to show that the decision reached is as well founded as possible, Sørensen considered it normal for the Court to refer expressly to a precedent which it is following, and only exceptional for it to rely on the principle established by the precedent without express citation.[79] However, where it takes the latter course, the Court itself does not appear to think it is acting exceptionally; it is flexible in the way in which it considers it appropriate in particular circumstances to have recourse to a precedent. Many are the instances in which it is relying on the principle of a decided case without specific citation.

It is possible to multiply illustrations of the ways in which the Court makes use of its own decisions as precedents. From the point

---

[75] Sir Hersch Lauterpacht, *The Development of International Law by the International Court* (London, 1958), pp. 9–11.

[76] *Ibid.*, p. 9.

[77] Sørensen, *Les Sources*, pp. 167–168.

[78] Fitzmaurice, *Law and Procedure*, II, p. 583.

[79] Sørensen, *Les Sources*, p. 167.

of view of analysis, there is not much to be gained; but there is a connected aspect to which one may now pass.

The importance which the Court attaches to its case law

The cumulative effect of these and other instances is to establish, first, the existence of a case law of the Court, and second, the practical importance which the Court attaches to the maintenance of consistency in its holdings. As to the first point, the Court is itself on record as treating its previous decisions as constituting 'the case-law of the Court'. In 1982, in its opinion in the case of *Application for Review of Judgment No. 273 of the United Nations Administrative Tribunal*, it was concerned *inter alia* with the question of its proper role when asked for an advisory opinion in respect of the ground of objection that the Tribunal 'erred on a question of law relating to provisions of the Charter'. It observed:

The answer to this question must depend not only upon the terms of Article 11, but also upon several other factors including, first of all, the Court's Statute, *the case-law of the Court*, the general requirements for the exercise of the judicial function; and . . . upon the terms of the particular question asked of the Court by the Committee.[80]

As to the second point, remarks by the Court evidencing the importance which it attaches to precedential consistency occur in a number of cases. In 1953 it reaffirmed its respect for its own jurisprudence as well as for that of its predecessor, stating, 'The Court is not departing from the principle, which is well-established in international law and accepted by its own jurisprudence as well as that of the Permanent Court of International Justice, to the effect that a State may not be compelled to submit its disputes to arbitration without its consent.'[81] In *Nottebohm, Second Phase*, it observed that the 'same issue is now before the Court: it *must* be resolved by applying the same principles'.[82] In *Nuclear Tests* (*Australia* v. *France*), in holding that in deciding preliminary questions it must

---

[80] *ICJ Rep 1982*, p. 355, para. 57; emphasis added.
[81] *Ambatielos, Merits, ICJ Rep 1953*, p. 19.
[82] *ICJ Rep 1955*, p. 22, cited by Judge Armand-Ugon in his dissenting opinion in *Barcelona Traction, Light and Power Company, Limited, Preliminary Objections, ICJ Rep 1964*, p. 136; emphasis added.

avoid making any pronouncements which might prejudice the eventual decision on the merits, it considered it 'appropriate to recall that its approach to a phase of this kind *must* be, as it was expressed in the *Fisheries Jurisdiction* cases, as follows . . .'.[83] Speaking in 1982 of its functions in administrative review proceedings, it emphasised that its 'proper role is not to retry the case and to attempt to substitute its own opinion on the merits for that of the Tribunal';[84] in 1987 it remarked, 'That principle *must* continue to guide the Court in the present case.'[85]

The imperative character of the language used by the Court itself in these and other cases has often been mirrored in individual opinions. This is all the more striking when it is a non-common law member of the Court who is speaking, as in the case of Judge Ehrlich's statement that 'a rule of law applied as decisive by the Court in one case, should, according to the principle *stare decisis*, be applied by the Court as far as possible in its subsequent decisions'.[86] In 1966 Judge Koretsky expressed the position thus:

[I]t cannot be said that what today was for the Court a *veritas*, will tomorrow be a *non-veritas*. A decision binds not only the parties to a given case, but the Court itself. *One cannot forget that the principle of immutability, of the consistency of final judicial decisions, which is so important for national courts, is still more important for international courts.* The practice of the Permanent Court and of this Court shows the great attention they pay to former judgments, their reasons and opinions. Consideration must be given even to the question whether an advisory opinion of the Court, which is not binding for the body which requested it, is binding for the Court itself not only *vi rationis* but *ratione vis* as well.[87]

The position taken by Judge Gros in 1970 was not very different. In his view, 'Although the force of *res judicata* does not extend to the reasoning of a judgment, it is the practice of the Court, as of arbitral tribunals, to stand by the reasoning set forth in previous decisions.'[88]

---

[83] *ICJ Rep 1974*, pp. 257–258, para. 16; emphasis added.
[84] *Application for Review of Judgment No. 273 of the United Nations Administrative Tribunal, ICJ Rep 1982*, p. 356, para. 58.
[85] *Application for Review of Judgment No. 333 of the United Nations Administrative Tribunal, ICJ Rep 1987*, p. 33, para. 27; emphasis added.
[86] *Factory at Chorzów, Merits, 1928, PCIJ, Series A, No. 17*, p. 76, dissenting opinion.
[87] *South West Africa, Second Phase, ICJ Rep 1966*, pp. 240–241; emphasis added.
[88] *Barcelona Traction, Light and Power Company, Limited, Second Phase, ICJ Rep 1970*, p. 267.

For a matching observation by a common law judge, one may turn to the dissenting opinion of Judge Read in the *Peace Treaties* case. After referring to the policy of jurisprudential continuity as between the Permanent Court of International Justice and the existing Court, he said, 'While this does not make the decisions of the Permanent Court binding, in the sense in which decisions may be binding in common-law countries, it does make it necessary to treat them with the utmost respect, and to follow them unless there are compelling reasons for rejecting their authority.'[89] The present Court could scarcely be under a lower duty to follow its own decisions 'unless there are compelling reasons for rejecting their authority'. Judge Lauterpacht would not have thought so. In *Certain Norwegian Loans* he distinguished *Rights of Nationals of the United States of America in Morocco*.[90] Having done so, he added, 'I need not discuss the question as to the extent to which the Court would be bound by the precedent of the case of the *United States Nationals in Morocco*, if that case were relevant to the issue now before the Court.'[91] There seems to be a suggestion here – no more than a suggestion, but a significant one – that in Judge Lauterpacht's view, unless the earlier case could be distinguished, the Court would, to some 'extent' at any rate, be 'bound' by it as a 'precedent' if it was relevant to the issue then being considered. But, to return to a non-common law judge, it is useful to conclude with Judge Ago's complaint in *Military and Paramilitary Activities in and against Nicaragua*: 'I can only regret that the Court has not seized the opportunity to emphasize, by appropriate references, a confirmation of the position it took before and of the theoretical reasoning developed in support, so as to underline the continuity and solidity of the jurisprudence.'[92]

These arresting remarks by judges from different legal cultures may well be taken as indicative of the Court's own preoccupation to perceive itself and to be in turn perceived as pursuing a constant judicial policy of precedential consistency. The understanding is clear that the Court would normally follow its previous decisions where applicable. It is right that the Court should not regard itself as subject to any doctrine of binding precedent; it is remarkable that it has never rested a new holding on the non-applicability of the doctrine.

[89] *Peace Treaties, ICJ Rep 1950*, p. 233.
[90] *ICJ Rep 1951*, p. 109, and *ICJ Rep 1952*, p. 176.
[91] *ICJ Rep 1957*, p. 60.
[92] *ICJ Rep 1986*, p. 190, para. 19.

3

Range of precedential resources

Accessibility

Building up the law through the use of precedents naturally depends on the accessibility of decisions. As remarked by Hersch Lauterpacht, and recalled above, 'judicial decisions, particularly *when published*, become part and parcel of the legal sense of the community'.[1] Decisions which remain unpublished can scarcely release their full precedential force. By way of analogy, one may contrast the several references in the jurisprudence to the published rule-making proceedings of the Permanent Court of International Justice with the absence of similar references to the unpublished rule-making proceedings of the present Court. In relation to arbitral decisions, Jennings recalls a series of lectures delivered by Henry Maine in 1887. In the course of 228 pages, the lecturer, though nurtured in the most notable of all case law systems, referred to but one decided case – the *Alabama Claims* – even though 'there *were* quite a lot of decided cases on international law at the time'. Why so sparing in the use of this valuable resource? The reason was that 'there was until relatively recent times no international lawyers' *apparatus technicus* to make cases easily accessible as material for argument'.[2] So publication is important.[3] It has

---

[1] Lauterpacht, *Collected Papers*, II, pp. 473–474; emphasis added.
[2] Jennings, 'General Course', p. 342, referring to Henry Sumner Maine, *International Law, A Series of Lectures delivered before the University of Cambridge* (London, 1887), (2nd ed., 1915).
[3] For the relevance of publication to the development of the English rules of precedent, see Cross and Harris, *Precedent*, pp. 6, 24–25.

been undertaken continuously from the commencement of the Permanent Court of International Justice, each decision being made publicly available in printed form as soon as possible after delivery. The importance of this for scientific study is obvious. But the purpose is not only to minister to scholarly interest, natural and useful as that is; a more practical object is to facilitate recourse by practitioners to the precedential value of the Court's decisions.

As mentioned at p. 20 above, in 1927 the *Third Annual Report* of the Permanent Court of International Justice referred to a number of decisions.[4] Other examples were added in later *Annual Reports* of the Court.[5] These compilations appeared in a section of a digest of decisions given under the heading of 'Article 59' of the Statute, an aspect to be considered later. More generally, it may be observed that the annual reports of the first Court and the yearbooks of the second include material in the nature of a digest of decisions taken in application of the Statute and Rules.[6] Unofficial collections, at least of relevant passages, were also made, as in the *Annual Digest of Public International Law Cases*;[7] the general heading reads interestingly, 'Binding Force of the Court's own Judgments'. Extracts also appeared in *Fontes Juris Gentium*.[8]

Decisions of the Court are issued with headnotes, in the nature of catchwords, designed to facilitate identification of issues.[9] The headnotes have no authority, but indicative of the precedential value which the Court attaches to its decisions is the fact that they are settled by the Court itself, immediately before the final vote is taken.[10] The index of each volume of the Court's reports also has an extensive item relating to 'Decisions' of the Court and of its predecessor. A press release is issued by the Registry on the delivery of each judgment, opinion or major order. It gives an unofficial

[4] *PCIJ, Series E, No. 3*, pp. 217–218, 226.
[5] *PCIJ, Series E, No. 4*, pp. 292–293, 300; *Series E, No. 6*, p. 300; *Series E, No. 7*, p. 299; and *Series E, No. 8*, pp. 271–272.
[6] *PCIJ, Series E, No. 4*, pp. 292–293, 300; *Series E, No. 6*, p. 300; *Series E, No. 7*, p. 299; and *Series E, No. 8*, pp. 271–272.
[7] New title, *Annual Digest and Reports of Public International Law Cases* (London), as from VII (1933–1934); further renamed *International Law Reports* as from the volume for 1950.
[8] *Series A, Section 1* (Berlin), Vols. I, III and IV.
[9] Starting from around 1932; see, for example, *Interpretation of the Statute of the Memel Territory, PCIJ, Series A/B, No. 49*, p. 294.
[10] See *ICJYB, 1947–1948*, p. 68.

summary of the decision taken by the Court, which is prepared by the Registry, as well as a summary of each appended declaration or opinion, which is prepared by the judge concerned.

Originally, access to the Great Hall of Justice, in which the oral proceedings are held, was not quite as open as it now is. According to Jessup, 'There was a time when the dominant attitude in the Court was that cases were in effect private affairs between the Court and the sovereign parties; they were no concern of other States or of scholars and the public. It was even made difficult for the public to obtain entrance to the Great Hall of Justice to hear the arguments.'[11] But the way has long since been clear. Since March 1992 television cameras have been allowed to film the whole of the proceedings. The speeches of counsel are public.[12] Release of the written pleadings and annexed documents before conclusion of the case is dependent on the consent of the parties;[13] but, subject to a time-lag (understandable but now perhaps too long), the material is regularly published after the conclusion of each case. The published pleadings (which include the oral arguments) are usually more extensive than the decisions, and are always informative. It is normal to publish the full documentation; however, and more especially where the material is excessively voluminous, elements not relevant to an understanding of the issues raised in the case could be, and have been, excluded from publication.[14] Also, in 1967 the Court decided 'that the annexes to the pleadings would no longer be printed in cases which had been removed from the General List either because the application instituting proceedings disclosed that the other side had not accepted the jurisdiction of

[11] See Durward V. Sandifer, *Evidence Before International Tribunals* (New York, 1975), foreword by Jessup, p. x.

[12] See *PCIJ, Series E, No. 9*, p. 280.

[13] *Ibid.; PCIJ, Series E, No. 6*, p. 284; *PCIJ, Series D, No. 2, 2nd Addendum*, pp. 173, 124, 296; Rules of Court, 1978, Article 53, paragraph 1; Rosenne, *Law and Practice*, (1965) II, pp. 566–567; and Geneviève Guyomar, *Commentaire du Règlement de la Cour internationale de Justice* (Paris, 1983), pp. 343–346.

[14] Mohammed Bedjaoui, 'La 'Fabrication' des arrêts de la Cour internationale de Justice', in *Le Droit international au service de la Paix, de la Justice et du Développement, Mélanges Michel Virally* (Paris, 1991), p. 92, where reference is made to *Barcelona Traction, Western Sahara* and the *Gulf of Maine* as cases in which material was omitted from the published pleadings. The necessity for selective exclusion arises also from the fact that parties are required to deposit the whole of a document in the Registry although only the relevant parts need be annexed to the pleadings. See Rules of Court, 1978, Article 50, para. 3.

the Court or because there had been a settlement or a discontinuance of the case'.[15] These cases apart, a question might arise, after the close of the proceedings, as to whether a party is entitled to have some particular material excluded from publication. The position is not altogether clear; but it is submitted that the guiding principle is that the Court, as a court of justice, operates in public, and that consequently its proceedings must be made available to the public except during such time when publication or release might prejudice the good administration of justice. The importance of consulting the pleadings in using precedents has been repeatedly stressed.

Range of admissible precedents

There has been some argument as to whether arbitral decisions are included in the reference to 'judicial decisions' in Article 38, paragraph 1 (d), of the Statute. Sørensen is hesitant;[16] Waldock thinks they are included;[17] Barberis thinks they are not.[18] In practice they are considered by the Court. Generally speaking, however, specific, as distinguished from generalised, references to this and other non-World Court material are avoided in the Court's own decisions.[19] This tendency, for which various reasons have been given, is still strong, but signs of attenuation are appearing, at any rate in the case of arbitral awards.

The *Jaworzina* case was an early one in which an arbitral decision was referred to by the Permanent Court of International Justice, its opinion reading:

In the opinion of the Court, which differs from that adopted by the Delimitation Commission on September 25th, 1922, the frontier between

---

[15] *ICJYB, 1993–1994*, p. 225.
[16] Sørensen, *Les Sources*, p. 162.
[17] Waldock, 'General Course', pp. 88 and 92.
[18] Barberis, 'La Jurisprudencia', p. 643.
[19] See, generally, Hudson, *The Permanent Court*, pp. 613–615; Sir Arnold Duncan McNair, *The Development of International Justice* (New York, 1954), pp. 12–13; C. W. Jenks, *The Common Law of Mankind* (London, 1958), p. 438; Lauterpacht, *Development*, p. 15; Waldock, 'General Course', pp. 92–93; W. W. Bishop, 'General Course of Public International Law 1965', *Hag R*, 115 (1965–II), p. 232; De Visscher, *Theory and Reality*, pp. 390–391; Judge P. C. Jessup, letter dated 16 August 1979, *Annuaire de l'Institut de droit international*, 61 (1985–I), p. 253; Rosenne, *Law and Practice* (1965), II, p. 614; Fitzmaurice, *Law and Procedure*, II,

Hungary and Galicia was in August 1914 an international frontier, Galicia being then part of the Austrian Monarchy. This is proved, e.g. by the Arbitration Award of September 13th, 1902, with regard to the 'Meerauge' question.[20]

There, the arbitral decision was cited for its evidential value rather than for its jurisprudential worth. However, in *Polish Postal Service in Danzig* recourse to the decision of the Permanent Court of Arbitration in *Pious Funds of California* was clearly made for the precedential value of the decision.[21] In the *'Lotus'*, reference was likewise made to the arbitral decision in *Costa Rica Packet* as a precedent, if only for the purpose of distinguishing it.[22]

In *Nottebohm, Second Phase*, referring to issues of nationality, the present Court said, 'In order to decide this question arbitrators have evolved certain principles for determining whether full international effect was to be attributed to the nationality invoked. The same issue is now before the Court: it must be resolved by applying the same principles.'[23] There the Court made a general reference to arbitral jurisprudence. But, on the question of *compétence de la compétence*, it had, at the preliminary objection stage, made a specific reference to the *Alabama* in these words: 'Since the *Alabama* case, it has been generally recognized, following the earlier precedents, that, in the absence of any agreement to the contrary, an international tribunal has the right to decide as to its own jurisdiction and has the power to interpret for this purpose the instruments which govern that jurisdiction.'[24] Whether the *Alabama* supported that view is an interesting question.[25] Be that as it may, that passage from *Nottebohm* was cited by Judge Onyeama in the *ICAO* case;[26] it was later recalled by the Court itself in the case of the *Arbitral Award of 31 July 1989*.[27] A reference to the *Alabama* was also made by the Court in its advisory opinion in *Applicability of the Obligation*

p. 583; and *Applicability of Article VI, Section 22, of the Convention on the Privileges and Immunities of the United Nations, ICJ Rep 1989*, p. 220.

[20] *Jaworzina, 1923, PCIJ, Series B, No. 8*, pp. 42–43.
[21] *1925, PCIJ, Series B, No. 11*, p. 30.
[22] *'Lotus', 1927, PCIJ, Series A, No. 10*, p. 26.
[23] *ICJ Rep 1955*, p. 22.
[24] *Nottebohm, Preliminary Objection, ICJ Rep 1953*, p. 119.
[25] See Georg Schwarzenberger, *International Law as Applied by International Courts and Tribunals* (London, 1986), IV, pp. 50–56.
[26] *ICJ Rep 1972*, p. 88, note 1.
[27] *ICJ Rep 1991*, pp. 68–69, para. 46.

to Arbitrate under Section 21 of the United Nations Headquarters Agreement of 26 June 1947;[28] it was mentioned earlier, but on a different aspect, in the separate (but dissenting) opinion of Judge van Eysinga in *Oscar Chinn.*[29]

In the *Continental Shelf (Tunisia/Libyan Arab Jamahiriya)*,[30] the Court referred to the decision of the Anglo-French Court of Arbitration of 30 June 1977;[31] opinions appended to the judgment of the Court did likewise.[32] Speaking of the purpose of the proportionality factor in the field of maritime delimitation, in 1985 the Court found it supportive to say, 'Its purpose was again made very clear in the Decision' of the Court of Arbitration;[33] the arbitral decision was also cited in individual opinions appended to the judgment of the Court. References to it and to other arbitral decisions were made more recently in the case of *Maritime Delimitation in the Area between Greenland and Jan Mayen (Denmark v. Norway)*.[34] In other cases the Court has referred generally to arbitral jurisprudence.[35]

As has been seen, opinions appended to judgments of the Court have also referred to arbitral decisions.[36] Judge Altamira, dissenting, did so in the *'Lotus'*.[37] In the *Factory at Chorzów, Merits*, Judge Ehrlich, dissenting, said, 'The Parties are agreed, and moreover it follows from the principles generally applied by arbitral tribunals, that in cases like the present the basis of the award must be found, not in the enrichment of the Respondent, but in the loss suffered by the individuals concerned.'[38] In the *Temple of Preah Vihear, Merits*, Judge Fitzmaurice relied on the *Island of Palmas* in support of the proposition that 'the existence of a state of fact, or of a situation, at a later date, may furnish good presumptive evidence of its

---

[28] *ICJ Rep 1988*, p. 34, para. 57.
[29] *1934, PCIJ, Series A/B, No. 63*, p. 135.
[30] *ICJ Rep 1982*, pp. 38, 57, 79.
[31] 18 *RIAA*, p. 3.
[32] See, for example, Judge Jiménez de Aréchaga, separate opinion, *ICJ Rep 1982*, pp. 104–106.
[33] *ICJ Rep 1985*, p. 44, para. 57.
[34] *ICJ Rep 1993*, p. 38.
[35] See *Factory at Chorzów, Jurisdiction, 1927, PCIJ, Series A, No. 9*, p. 31; *Factory at Chorzów, Merits, 1928, PCIJ, Series A, No. 17*, p. 31; *Constitution of the Maritime Safety Committee of the Inter-Governmental Maritime Consultative Organisation, ICJ Rep 1960*, p. 169; and Lauterpacht, *Development*, p. 15.
[36] See, generally, Barberis, 'La Jurisprudencia', pp. 645–646.
[37] *1927, PCIJ, Series A, No. 10*, p. 97.
[38] *1928, PCIJ, Series A, No. 17*, p. 75.

existence at an earlier date also, even where the later situation or state of affairs has in other respects to be excluded from consideration'.[39] In *Barcelona Traction, Light and Power Company, Limited, Preliminary Objections*, Judge Koo, if only to distinguish them, referred to 'the cases of arbitral awards examined by the Parties' on the subject of the right of protection of the interests of the nationals of a State as shareholders in a foreign company.[40] In the same case, *Second Phase*, Judge Gros coupled the practice of arbitral tribunals with that of the Court in stating that 'it is the practice of the Court, as of arbitral tribunals, to stand by the reasoning set forth in previous decisions';[41] Judge Fitzmaurice cited the arbitral awards in the *Cayuga Indians* case and the *Ziat, Ben Kiran* case,[42] while Judge Padilla Nervo cited the opinion of the President of the arbitration commission in the *Rosa Gelbtrunk* case.[43] The arbitral award of 14 February 1985 relating to the *Delimitation of Maritime Boundaries between Guinea and Guinea-Bissau* was cited in the separate opinion of Vice-President Sette-Camara in *Continental Shelf (Libyan Arab Jamahiriya/Malta)*,[44] as well as in the joint separate opinion given in the same case.[45]

Speaking of Mixed Arbitral Tribunals, Judges Winiarski and Badawi Pasha, dissenting, thought that 'these Tribunals, as joint organs of two States, differ both as to their character and as to their procedure from an international tribunal, and, therefore, from the International Court of Justice, and there is, consequently, nothing to be learned from their precedents'.[46] The somewhat dismissive conclusion that there is 'nothing to be learned from their precedents' was no doubt attributable to the particular question under discussion, namely, the relationship between jurisdiction over the merits and the power to indicate interim measures of protection.

Apart from arbitral decisions, the Court has also referred to national decisions.[47] So too have individual judges; less frequently,

[39] *ICJ Rep 1962*, p. 61, citing Judge Huber's opinion in the *Island of Palmas*, 2 *RIAA*, p. 866.
[40] *ICJ Rep 1964*, p. 57, separate opinion.
[41] *ICJ Rep 1970*, p. 267, para. 1.
[42] *Ibid.*, pp. 84–85, para. 35.
[43] *Ibid.*, pp. 248–249.
[44] *ICJ Rep 1985*, pp. 73–74.
[45] *Ibid.*, p. 88.
[46] *Anglo-Iranian Oil Co., Interim Protection, ICJ Rep 1951*, p. 97.
[47] *'Lotus'*, 1927, *PCIJ*, Series A, No. 10, pp. 28–30.

they have also made use of decisions of international or regional courts other than the Court or its predecessor. A decision of the European Court of Human Rights was referred to in an individual opinion in 1966; that happened also in 1989.[48] In 1992, a 1917 judgment of the short-lived but important Central American Court of Justice was cited by a chamber of the Court thus:

> The position, therefore, is that the Chamber should take the 1917 Judgement into account as a relevant precedent decision of a competent court, and as, in the words of Article 38 of the Court's Statute, 'a subsidiary means for the determination of rules of law'. In short, the Chamber must make up its own mind on the status of the waters of the Gulf, taking such account of the 1917 decision as it appears to the Chamber to merit.[49]

That and another decision of the Central American Court of Justice were also before the Court in 1995 and were referred to in individual opinions.[50]

The range of admissible precedential material is wide. However, as has been pointed out in the first paragraph of chapter 1, these lectures treat only of the precedential value of decisions of the Court and of its predecessor.

[48] *South West Africa, Second Phase, ICJ Rep 1966*, p. 438, Judge Jessup, dissenting opinion, referring to the *Lawless* case (1961); and *Applicability of Article VI, Section 22, of the Convention on the Privileges and Immunities of the United Nations, ICJ Rep 1989*, p. 221, Judge Shahabuddeen, separate opinion, referring to the *Golder* case (1975).

[49] *Land, Island and Maritime Frontier Dispute (El Salvador/Honduras: Nicaragua Intervening), ICJ Rep 1992*, p. 601, para. 403.

[50] *East Timor (Portugal v. Australia), ICJ Rep 1995*, p. 90, separate opinion of Judge Shahabuddeen at pp. 124–126, and dissenting opinion of Judge Weeramantry at pp. 160 and 169. And see *Costa Rica* v. *Nicaragua* and *El Salvador* v. *Nicaragua*, *AJIL*, 11 (1917), at pp. 181 and 674 respectively.

4

The bases of the system

Introductory remarks

The Court's position as the principal judicial organ of the United Nations has been mentioned in explanation of its use of precedents. The argument is that, as such an organ, the Court shares in the responsibility of the United Nations to maintain peace, and that, in order to do so, it has an implied power to ensure consistency in decisions, lest inconsistencies should create tension within the international community.[1] That is a good reason for adhering to the practice; it is less clear that it is the juridical basis. The practical position of the Permanent Court of International Justice did not always coincide with the theory that it was separate from the League of Nations. It was referred to by no less an authority than President Loder in his inaugural speech as 'one of the principal organs of the League';[2] others have thought likewise.[3] There can be no doubt, however, that it was constitutionally not part of the League. Yet it observed the same practice. What is the basis of the practice?

The general jurisprudential basis

There are two bases on which the Court's use of precedents rests. The Court itself being a creature of the Charter and its Statute,

---

[1] See, Röben, 'Le précédent', pp. 403 ff.

[2] *PCIJ, Series D, No. 2*, p. 326.

[3] See N. Politis, *La Justice internationale* (Paris, 1924), p. 166; Hudson, *The Permanent Court*, pp. 111–112; Rosenne, *Law and Practice* (1965), I, pp. 61–63; Sir Muhammad Zafrulla Khan, 'The Contribution of the Principal Judicial Organ of the United Nations to the Achievement of the Objectives of the Organisation',

its use of precedents must likewise find its authority in these instruments. But these speak both expressly and impliedly; it is important to bear this in mind when estimating the legal character of the great judicial institution established by them. The implications of the fact that the Court has been constituted as a court of justice may operate to impose 'inherent limitations' on it, as would appear from *Northern Cameroons*;[4] but they may equally operate to endow its activities with an effect not apparent on first reading of the Statute. On a first reading, one encounters the well-known provisions of Article 38, paragraph 1 *(d)*, of the Statute, to which reference will be made later. Those provisions obviously furnish a basis of the Court's system of precedents; but, the Court having been set up as a court of justice, it is legitimate to construe the Charter and the Statute as also accepting, if only by implication and subject to any specific provisions, that the decisions of the Court would, in some measure, inevitably have the precedential effect normally associated with judicial decisions, the question whether that effect would be binding being another matter.

The principle involved is a broad one concerning the administration of justice. Speaking generally, Judge Alvarez remarked that legal 'texts can be interpreted by anyone; but when such an interpretation is made by an authorized organ, such as the General Assembly of the United Nations or the International Court of Justice, it presents a great practical value and creates precedents'.[5] In the case of a court of justice, according to L. N. Brown and F. G. Jacobs:

It is a fundamental principle of the administration of justice that like cases should be decided alike. Inconsistency in judicial decisions affronts even the most elementary sense of justice. In this sense the principle of *stare decisis*, of abiding by previous decisions, figures prominently in most legal systems, including those of all the Member States of the [European] Communities.[6]

Annual Review of UN Affairs (1969–1970), p. 42; and Leo Gross, *Essays on International Law and Organization* (The Hague, 1984), II, p. 855.

[4] *ICJ Rep 1963*, p. 30.

[5] *Competence of the General Assembly for the Admission of a State to the United Nations, ICJ Rep 1950*, p. 15, Judge Alvarez, dissenting opinion. The tendency is a general one; there is, for example, increasing use of material in the nature of precedents by United Nations legal advisers and others. See S. Rosenne, *Developments in the Law of Treaties 1945–1986* (Cambridge, 1989), p. 243.

[6] L. N. Brown and F. G. Jacobs, *The Court of Justice of the European Communities*, 3rd edn (London, 1989), p. 311.

For this reason, as it was put by Brierly:

Precedents are not therefore binding authorities in international law, but the English theory of their binding force merely elevates into a dogma a natural tendency of all judicial procedure. When any system of law has reached a stage at which it is thought worth while to report the decisions and the reasoning of judges, other judges inevitably give weight, though not necessarily decisive weight, to the work of their predecessors.[7]

Judicial decisions are also expressions of legal opinion, but they are more than mere academic views. Fitzmaurice compared them as follows:

No one who has been engaged in any international proceedings can doubt that the parties, their advocates and the tribunal itself, view in quite a different light such (material) sources of law as, for instance, the opinions of jurists (however eminent) and a *decision*, even if the tribunal giving it is composed of less eminent persons. No want of respect to the eminent jurist is involved in this; it is simply that a decision, if relevant to the case under discussion, has an actuality and a concrete character that causes it to impinge directly on the matters at issue, in a way that an abstract opinion, however good, can never do. This is easily seen in the attitude of both courts and advocates. When an advocate before an international tribunal cites juridical opinion, he does so because it supports his argument, or for its illustrative value, or because it contains a particularly felicitous or apposite statement of the point involved, and so on. When he cites an arbitral or judicial decision he does so for these reasons also, but there is a difference – for, additionally, he cites it as something *which the tribunal cannot ignore*, which it is bound to take into consideration and (by implication) which it ought to follow unless the decision can be shown to have been clearly wrong, or distinguishable from the extant case, or in some way legally or factually inapplicable. Equally the tribunal, while it may well treat juridical opinion as something which is of interest but of no direct authority, and which the tribunal is free to disregard, will not usually feel free to ignore a relevant decision, and will normally feel obliged to treat it as something that must be accepted, or else – for good reason – rejected, but which must in any event be taken fully into account.[8]

---

[7] J. L. Brierly, 'Règles générales du droit de la paix', *Hag R*, 58 (1936–IV), p. 64.

[8] Sir Gerald Fitzmaurice, 'Some Problems Regarding the Formal Sources of International Law', in *Symbolae Verzijl* (The Hague, 1958), pp. 171–172, footnote omitted.

As Fitzmaurice added: 'A decision is a *fact*; an opinion, however cogent, remains an opinion.'[9] McNair had spoken similarly four years earlier.[10] It was in this context that Hersch Lauterpacht criticised 'the habit, which is objectionable and a potential source both of abuse and embarrassment, of referring – with some hopeful emphasis – to previous expressions of opinions by adjudicating Judges themselves'.[11] These reflections explain the circumstance that the reference in Article 38, paragraph 1 *(d)*, to 'judicial decisions and the teachings of the most highly qualified publicists' does not mean that these two categories exert the same level of authority, not, at any rate, where decisions of the Court or of its predecessor are concerned.

Thus, there is an inevitable sense in which precedents are always used, even where the specific common law doctrine of *stare decisis* does not prevail. This is because, although any given international tribunal is adjudicating only as between the parties before it, it is at the same time functioning as an expression of the legal norms of the larger international community; it is these norms which ultimately assign legal value to the decision of the tribunal.[12] Sørensen expressed it this way:

L'autorité du précédent réside dans le fait que c'est une décision par un organe compétent à définir, avec force obligatoire pour les parties, leurs rapports juridiques.

Cette décision engendre parmi les membres de la communauté soumis à une juridiction internationale, la conviction qu'une question analogue sera décidée d'une manière analogue en vertu des considérations objectives sur lesquelles sont fondés les jugements, sans aucun

---

[9] *Ibid.*, p. 172.
[10] Sir Arnold Duncan McNair, *The Development of International Justice* (New York, 1954), pp. 16–17.
[11] Lauterpacht, *Development*, p. 25, note 82, adding: 'For these may, without any legitimate imputation of inconsistency, undergo a change in the light of the argument and information supplied by the parties or of the deliberations of the Court. In *McGrath* v. *Kristensen* (1950) 340 US 162, 176–178, Mr. Justice Jackson, confronted with an opinion previously given by him as Attorney-General, said: "I am entitled to say of that opinion what any discriminating reader must think of it – that it was as foggy as the Statute the Attorney-General was asked to interpret ..." He referred to Lord Westbury who, it is said, rebuffed, in the following words, a barrister's reliance upon an earlier opinion of his Lordship: "I can only say that I am amazed that a man of my intelligence should have been guilty of giving such an opinion." '
[12] See, in these respects, Condorelli, 'L'Autorité', pp. 306–312.

égard à la mesure où le tribunal se sentira lié par une décision antérieure.[13]

This process, through which decisions of international tribunals tend to be followed in later decisions, did not require the sanction of any specific treaty provision. As has so often been remarked, international law has developed and can develop without the need for courts.[14] However, there comes a point when the development of a normative system of relations between the subjects of the law ensues in the need for the establishment of some system of third-party adjudication. The idea of precedents now takes clearer shape. Not surprisingly, the idea antedated the establishment of the Permanent Court of International Justice. In 1904, while noting the difference between a permanent court and an arbitral tribunal, Louis Renault recognised that even decisions of the latter were not without precedential influence. Referring to such decisions, he said:

En droit, il est vrai que la chose jugée n'a qu'une autorité toute relative; mais en fait, qui pourrait nier l'influence des précédents? Je ne veux pas dire qu'en dehors du litige qu'elles auront terminé, les sentences arbitrales n'auront aucune valeur. Elles en auront une certainement, mais un tribunal nouveau, composé d'éléments tout différents, de juges d'autres nationalités, pourra, en toute liberté, en tenir tel compte que de raison. Lorsqu'une question controversée aura été tranchée de la même façon par plusieurs tribunaux d'arbitrage, on comprend quelle autorité aura une solution donnée à diverses reprises dans des conditions de complète indépendance par des juges d'une grande valeur appartenant à divers pays. On ne pourra reprocher à une pareille solution d'être inspirée par des vues étroites, des préjugés ou des intérêts nationaux. Elle entrera dans le corps du droit international à titre de raison écrite comme répondant à la justice et aux intérêts généraux de l'humanité.[15]

The transient nature of arbitral tribunals has however worked against the emergence of a smooth process of development. The problem was not solved by the establishment of the Permanent Court of Arbitration. Speaking of this body, De Martens asked,

---

[13] Sørensen, *Les Sources*, p. 175.

[14] See Baron van Asbeck, 'Growth and Movement in International Law', *ICLQ*, 11 (1962), pp. 1054 ff.

[15] A. de Lapradelle and N. Politis, *Recueil des arbitrages internationaux*, I (1798–1855), (Paris, 1905), p. vii, preface by Louis Renault. And see Madame Suzanne Bastid's foreword to Vincent Coussirat-Coustère and Pierre Michel Eisemann (eds.), *Repertory of International Arbitral Jurisprudence, 1794–1918* (Dordrecht, 1989), I, p. vii.

'What, then, is this court whose judges do not even know each other? The Court of 1899 is only an idea which sometimes takes the form of body and soul and then disappears again.'[16] Once standing judicial bodies have come into existence, they provide an additional mechanism for the further development of the law. Hudson put it this way:

Permanent tribunals usually show themselves disposed to shape their decisions into a consistent body of case-law. In the past the absence of permanent tribunals has delayed such a development in the field of international jurisprudence. The Court has not expressly been given the function of developing international law; yet if it holds the respect of Governments and of the legal profession, that must be an inevitable by-product of its functioning over a long period of time.[17]

The connection thus drawn between the permanent institutional character of the Court and the continuity of its contribution to the formulation and development of international legal principles is well known and has often been commented on. In the words of President Winiarski, 'The originality and importance of the element of permanency cannot be overstressed; to it is owed the fact that the Permanent Court of International Justice became an institution in the real sense of the term.'[18] He might well have called to witness the word 'Permanent' in the title of the Court. In the *Factory at Chorzów*, M. Kaufmann was soon to tell the Court 'c'est le sens et l'importance de la permanence de la Cour de Justice qu'elle crée et développe une jurisprudence constante en matière de droit international'.[19] So too with the word 'Court'; the term was not a misnomer: the 'Court' was intended to be a real court, as distinguished from arbitral tribunals.[20] Hence the remark by Lindsey that 'the constitution of the Court as a continuous permanent body the personnel of which will change but slowly strongly tends

---

[16] Hague Court Reports, 1916, Introduction, pp. xvii and xviii, cited in Permanent Court of Arbitration, *First Conference of the Members of the Court, 10 and 11 September 1993* (The Hague, 1993), p. 57. And see J. W. Garner, *Recent Developments in International Law* (Calcutta, 1925), pp. 661–662.

[17] Hudson, *The Permanent Court*, p. 628, para. 557.

[18] *ICJ Pleadings, Temple of Preah Vihear*, II, p. 121. And see, earlier, the argument of M. Kaufmann, *Factory at Chorzów*, PCIJ, Series C 13–I, p. 102.

[19] *PCIJ, Series C, No. 13–I*, p. 102.

[20] See, by the present writer, 'The International Court of Justice: the Integrity of an Idea', in R. S. Pathak and R. P. Dhokalia (eds.), *International Law in Transition, Essays in Honour of Judge Nagendra Singh* (Dordrecht, 1992), p. 341.

to ensure a continuity of formulation and enunciation of international legal principles'.[21] That, indeed, was a major consideration leading up to the establishment of the Court.[22] Almost certainly, it was one of the reasons underlying support of possible United States accession to the Statute of the Court, Secretary of State Stimson stating that never 'before was the world in greater need of the orderly development of international rules of conduct by the wise method of judicial decision.'[23]

The development of the law was an equally powerful factor in the establishment of the present Court.[24] Coherence, consistency and predictability, which are at the root of the idea of precedents, are obviously advanced through the functioning of a centralised piece of global judicial equipment. De Visscher's conception of the process at work in the case of the Court is pertinent. It reads:

Much more than the establishment of peace, the development of international law is the essential function of the judicial settlement by a permanent and institutionalized tribunal. The gradual elaboration of the law through the accumulation of a body of homogeneous decisions is a condition of order and stability. A more precise knowledge of the law enlightens States in the daily conduct of their mutual relations; promotes their recourse to justice; and may facilitate acceptance of compulsory jurisdiction.

As a judicial organ called upon to declare, clarify and develop the law, the International Court of Justice, like its predecessor the Permanent Court, has justified the hopes entertained of it. Though Article 59 of its Statute frees it from any strict obligation to follow precedents,[25] the concern to ensure continuity in its decisions is apparent in all of them. As they increase in number, the Court invokes them more and more, now to corroborate the decision it is about to render, by comparing it with its previous judgments or opinions, now, on the contrary, to distinguish the case and to forearm itself against the reproach of illogicality or contradic-

---

[21] Edward Lindsey, *The International Court* (New York, 1931), p. 268.

[22] Hudson, *The Permanent Court*, p. 630; H. Lauterpacht, *The Development of International Law by the Permanent Court of International Justice* (London, 1934), p. 3; Lauterpacht, *Development*, p. 8; and R. P. Anand, *Studies in International Adjudication* (Delhi, 1969), p. 171.

[23] Henry L. Stimson to Senator Borah, 22 March 1932, *PCIJ, Series E, No. 8*, p. 128.

[24] *Report to the President on the Results of the San Francisco Conference by the Chairman of the United States Delegation, the Secretary of State* (Washington, 26 June 1945), p. 138.

[25] This aspect is considered elsewhere in this work. See chapters 6–8.

tion. In one case it consults its previous decisions in order to find the elements of a legal construction that it is developing, in another, and with greater firmness, to present these as a doctrine that it does not intend to abandon.[26]

The specific statutory basis

The second basis on which the Court's system of precedents rests is Article 38, paragraph 1 *(d)*, of the Statute, which provides that the 'Court ... shall apply ... subject to the provisions of Article 59, judicial decisions and the teachings of the most highly qualified publicists of the various nations, as subsidiary means for the determination of rules of law'. Thus, the Court has to consider any relevant judicial decisions. By contrast, in France a judge is not obliged to consider case law.[27] And, though it seems scarcely necessary to do so, it may be added that the 'expression "judicial decisions" [in Article 38, paragraph 1 *(d)*, of the Statute] certainly includes the jurisprudence of this Court and of the Permanent Court';[28] if it did not, the prefatory words 'subject to the provisions of Article 59' would be pointless. It would, however, be convenient to return to these and other aspects of the meaning of Article 38, paragraph 1 *(d)*, after considering the course of the proceedings in the 1920 Advisory Committee of Jurists by which the Statute of the Permanent Court of International Justice was drafted.

---

[26] De Visscher, *Theory and Reality*, p. 390.
[27] Cross and Harris, *Precedent*, p. 10.
[28] *Anglo-Iranian Oil Co., ICJ Rep 1952*, p. 143, Judge Read, dissenting opinion.

5

The Advisory Committee of Jurists

Ambivalence in the work of the Committee

As was observed by Hersch Lauterpacht, 'the necessity of providing for a tribunal developing international law by its own decisions had been the starting-point for the attempts to establish a truly permanent international court as distinguished from the Permanent Court of Arbitration'.[1] Yet, the extent to which the founders of the Permanent Court of International Justice foresaw the development of the system of precedents might not have been altogether clear. As the same writer later observed:

Although the need for a tribunal ensuring, through its continuity, the development of international law was one of the main reasons for the creation of a permanent court of international justice, it is possible that the lawyers and statesmen who in 1920 drafted the Statute of the Court did not fully appreciate all the possibilities, in this direction, of the activity of the Court about to be established.[2]

There seems, in particular, to have been some ambivalence in the work of the Advisory Committee of Jurists, by which the Statute of the Permanent Court of International Justice was drafted in 1920, in the sense that, while there were assertions, forceful enough, to the effect that judges only declared the law, the objective drift of some of the material was in the opposite direction.

[1] Lauterpacht, 'The so-called Anglo-American and Continental Schools of Thought in International Law', *BYBIL*, 12 (1931), p. 59.
[2] Lauterpacht, *Development*, p. 8.

Reflecting the view that judges only declared the law as it stood, and did not make law, Professor de Lapradelle proposed that 'it would be useful to specify that the Court must not act as a legislator . . . . The reproach which had been levelled in this respect against the Court of Arbitration must not be allowed to apply to the new Court.'[3] In remarking that the Permanent Court of Arbitration had been reproached for acting as a legislator, Professor de Lapradelle no doubt also appreciated the difficulty that would be involved in attempting to prevent the new Court from creating law; his proposal to prevent that by specifying that the Court must not act as a legislator was not implemented. The later evolution of Continental jurisprudence has been more open in its acknowledgment of the impossibility of a judge not creating some law. This is even truer of Anglo-Saxon jurisprudence. When Lord Phillimore remarked in the Advisory Committee that 'judicial decisions state, but do not create, law',[4] he was probably out of date in his theoretical understanding of the real nature of the processes at work in the course of judicial decision-making. How far the articulation of these obsolescent positions meshed with the actual product of the labours of the Advisory Committee is an open question.

Some draft schemes assumed that the Court would make law

Some of the draft schemes presented to the Advisory Committee of Jurists exhibited an awareness by members of the international community that, one way or another, the new Court would inevitably make some law. Among the documents presented for the consideration of the Committee was a draft scheme prepared on behalf of Denmark, Norway and Sweden. Article 27 of this read in part, 'In default of generally recognised rules, the Court shall base its decision upon the general principles of Law.'[5] An alternative to this read, 'If no such provision exist, the Court shall decide the case

---

[3] Permanent Court of International Justice, Advisory Committee of Jurists, *Procès-Verbaux of the Proceedings of the Committee, June 16th–July 24th 1920, with Annexes*, (The Hague, 1920), p. 296.

[4] *Ibid.*, p. 584.

[5] Permanent Court of International Justice, Advisory Committee of Jurists, *Documents Presented to the Committee Relating to Existing Plans for the Establishment of a Permanent Court of International Justice*, HMSO (London, 1920), p. 179.

according to the established rules of International Law; or, if rules of this kind do not exist, the Court will decide according to what, in its opinion, should be the rules of International Law'.[6]

Article 15 of a draft scheme submitted on behalf of Denmark read:

When the question of law to be decided is covered by a Treaty in force between the two Parties, judgment is to be given on the basis of this Treaty.

In the absence of such arrangements, the Court shall apply the rules of international law then in force, or if such rules do not exist to cover the question under consideration, the Court shall give judgment according to what in its opinion should be the rule for international law.[7]

Article 15 of a Norwegian draft scheme read:

If a question of law to be decided be covered by a treaty in force, the Court must apply the provisions of the treaty.

In absence of such provisions, the Court must apply the rules of International Law; if such rules do not exist, application is made of what ought to be the law, according to the considered opinion of the Tribunal.[8]

Article 17 of a Swedish draft scheme read:

If the legal point at issue that is to be decided has been foreseen and provided for by an agreement drawn up between the parties, which is still in force, such agreement shall be made the basis of the decision to be arrived at.

If no such provision exists, the Court shall decide the case according to the established rules of the law of nations; or, if such rules yield no guidance for the decision, in accord with what in the considered judgment of the Court ought to be the international law upon the point at issue.[9]

Sweden also indicated a prospect

that such a permanent Court of Justice, constituted of professionally trained judges, will be able, with its experience acquired in the continuous exercise of its functions, to contribute effectively to the further development of the principles of the law of nations and thereby promote the interests of international law and procedure.[10]

---

[6] *Documents Presented*, 1920, p. 179.
[7] *Ibid.*, p. 205.
[8] *Ibid.*, p. 233.
[9] *Ibid.*, p. 241.
[10] *Ibid.*, p. 247.

Article 2 of a plan submitted by the five neutral powers (Denmark, The Netherlands, Norway, Sweden and Switzerland) read:

1. Whenever the point of law to be decided by the Court, is provided for directly or indirectly by any Treaty in operation between the contesting parties, such Treaty shall form the basis of the judgment.

2. In the absence of such treaty provisions, the Court shall apply the recognised rules of international law, or, should no rules applicable to the case exist, shall enter judgment according to its own opinion of what the rule of international law on the subject should be.[11]

A document submitted by the Brazilian jurist M. Bevilaqua (who unfortunately was unable to be present at the meetings, his place being taken by M. Fernandez)[12] included the following passages:

By pronouncing a succession of verdicts with a common purpose of establishing law and of conciliating interests justly and equitably, by creating an international Common Law, the judiciary power of the League of Nations will exercise a profound and beneficial influence on the individual conscience. It will lend greater clearness and strength to the idea of the unity of international law, and that idea, strengthened by the confidence inspired by the Tribunal, will create a moral atmosphere unfavourable to the development of motives for war.

'The American judiciary power has shown that Tribunals necessarily tend to develop law, to the benefit of society,' says Joseph Davis...

The various forms assumed by the law – usages of the parties, judicial decisions, customs resulting from these decisions, and written law – still exist, but without the written law, the most precise, the surest and strongest safeguard against arbitrary decisions, having as yet acquired the preponderance which it already enjoys in the national law systems of the western world. Now that the League of Nations has assumed a precise and effective shape, the decisions arrived at by its judiciary power will better adapt international law to the needs created by the relations between nationalities, will remove whatever may be artificial and incomplete in its character, and will endow it with elasticity and vitality.[13]

In fact, Article 24 of M. Bevilaqua's draft read in part:

[11] *Ibid.*, p. 301.
[12] M. Fernandez was himself described as 'a man of considerable ability and thoughtfulness'. See Lord Phillimore, 'Scheme for the Permanent Court of International Justice', *Transactions of the Grotius Society*, 6 (1920), p. 89.
[13] *Documents Presented*, 1920, pp. 359–361.

If there is a written law which governs the matter under litigation, the International Judicial Power, as well as the Judicial Power in each country, shall apply it, because that is precisely its duty.

If there is no *jus scriptum*, the generally accepted doctrine will replace it; because that is one of the means by which the legal consciousness expresses itself. The doctrine is the scientific statement of customary law.

If there is no doctrine, or if it is doubtful what the doctrine is, the Tribunal will fill that lacuna in the positive law; in doing this it will be guided by the high principles, which constitute the basis of international judicial order.[14]

Several of these drafts referred to 'the general principles of law'.[15] This apart, it seems reasonably clear, however, that it was assumed that the Court would inescapably have the duty of creating some law for the purpose of disposing of particular cases; the object of the various formulations was accordingly directed to guiding the Court to the material or broad principles from which it would fashion the required rule.

The drafting of Article 38 of the Statute

Against this background, one may now move on to consider briefly the drafting of Article 38 of the Statute (then draft Article 35). A text proposed by President Descamps read:

The following rules are to be applied by the judge in the solution of international disputes; they will be considered by him in the undermentioned order:

1. conventional international law, whether general or special, being rules expressly adopted by the States;
2. international custom, being practice between nations accepted by them as law;
3. the rules of international law as recognised by the legal conscience of civilised nations;
4. international jurisprudence as a means for the application and development of law.[16]

---

[14] *Documents Presented*, 1920, p. 371.
[15] The concept of 'general principles' was familiar to many municipal systems. See Bin Cheng, *General Principles of Law as Applied by International Courts and Tribunals* (London, 1953), pp. 16 and 19.
[16] *Procès-Verbaux*, 1920, p. 306.

Mr Root and Lord Phillimore later proposed a substitute text reading:

The following rules are to be applied by the Court within the limits of its competence, as described above, for the settlement of international disputes; they will be considered in the undermentioned order:

1. conventional international law, whether general or special, being rules expressly adopted by the States which are parties to a dispute;
2. international custom, being recognised practice between nations accepted by them as law;
3. the general principles of law recognised by civilised nations;
4. the authority of judicial decisions and the opinions of writers as a means for the application and development of law.[17]

After some discussion, including Lord Phillimore's remark 'that judicial decisions state, but do not create, law',[18] the wording of subparagraph 4 was amended to read, 'The Court shall take into consideration judicial decisions and the teachings of the most highly qualified publicists of the various nations as subsidiary means for the determination of rules of law.'[19]

It is useful also to bear in mind Article 1 of the draft Statute. As prepared by President Descamps, this read:

Independently of the Permanent Court of Arbitration organised by the Conventions of 1899 and 1907, and of the special Tribunals of Arbitrators which the States are free to establish for the settlement of their disputes, a Permanent Court of International Justice, which will always be available to States, and have for its purpose to assure the continuity and progress of international jurisprudence based on judgments, is hereby established in accordance with Article 14 of the Treaty of Versailles of June 28th 1919.[20]

The final draft retained the reference to the continuance of the Permanent Court of Arbitration, whose awards had been already modifying and developing the law. The reference to the purpose of the new Court being 'to assure the continuity and progress of international jurisprudence based on judgments' did not survive, but it is difficult to accept that the deletion made much difference.

---

[17] *Ibid.*, p. 344.
[18] *Ibid.*, p. 584.
[19] *Ibid.*, p. 620. See also pp. 294, 296, 307, 311, 317, 331, 334, 336, 337, 344, 584, 730.
[20] *Ibid.*, p. 373.

In explaining the draft on this point, President Descamps said that 'these last words had been added in view of the difference between the meaning of the word jurisprudence in English and French'.[21] The difference did not quite conceal the fact that judge-made law was possible under both systems; it has long been recognised that it is erroneous to exaggerate the differences between the two systems.[22]

There is agreement on all hands that *stare decisis* is not applicable to the Court. Also, the prevailing view within the Advisory Committee of Jurists was that judicial decisions would enable the Court to find the existing law, and not to create new law. Could this expectation control the objective character of the institution? It is clear that the Committee itself intended that judicial decisions should be used by the Court for their jurisprudential value. But precisely in what way? Two questions suggest themselves. First, would recourse to the jurisprudential value of judicial decisions extend to the point of affecting the development of international law? Second, if so, could that development result in some new law being created by the Court? Subject to some overlapping, the first question is considered in chapter 6; the second in chapter 7.

[21] *Procès-Verbaux*, 1920, p. 354. As to the difference in meaning of the word 'jurisprudence' in German, French and English law, see Gustav Radbruch, 'Anglo-American Jurisprudence through Continental Eyes', *LQR*, 52 (1936), p. 530: 'Jurisprudence means for the German the totality of legal sciences, for the Frenchman the precedent-making decisions of the law Courts and, therefore, the most concrete part of legal work – the English jurist on the other hand has reserved this very expression for the most general branch of the law.' The dictionary meaning in France is 'l'ensemble de décisions rendues par les tribunaux sur une même question ou sur des questions analogues'. See *Dictionnaire de droit* (ed. S. Corniot), 2nd revised edn (Paris, 1966), II, p. 23.

[22] C. K. Allen, *Law in the Making*, 7th edn (Oxford, 1964), pp. 178–187.

6

The view taken by the
League of Nations

Introductory remarks

Whatever the position taken in the Advisory Committee of Jurists on the question whether decisions of the Court could lead to the creation of new law, it is clear that the understanding of the Council of the League of Nations, by which the draft Statute was amended, and of the Assembly, by which it was ultimately adopted (with further amendments), was that decisions of the Court could at least affect the development of international law.

In considering the positions taken by the League of Nations and by the Advisory Committee of Jurists, it is right to bear in mind that, as was pointed out by M. Léon Bourgeois, the members of the Committee were all jurists. Hence, 'in purely technical matters' their views would command greater respect than those of the Council and the Assembly of the League of Nations, not all of whom were lawyers.[1] But this does not suffice to outweigh the consideration that the substantive decisions were made by the Council and the Assembly of the League. This is relevant in view of different currents of thinking implicit in the material presented to the Advisory Committee of Jurists.

The right of intervention

It is difficult to understand the view taken by some delegates on the right of intervention except on the basis that they assumed,

---

[1] League of Nations, *Documents concerning the Action taken by the Council of the League of Nations under Article 14 of the Covenant and the Adoption by the Assembly of the Statute of the Permanent Court* (Geneva, 1921), p. 46.

and assumed correctly, that the decisions of the Court could affect the development of international law. M. Bourgeois had invited the Council of the League of Nations to consider *inter alia*:

The right of intervention in its various aspects, and in particular the question whether the fact that the principle implied in a judgment may affect the development of international law in a way which appears undesirable to any particular State may constitute for it a sufficient basis for any kind of intervention in order to impose the contrary views held by it with regard to this principle.[2]

Thus, M. Bourgeois regarded it as a 'fact that the principle implied in a judgment may affect the development of international law'; he did not appear to think that there would be any dispute in the Council about this. The issue on which he was inviting discussion was not whether 'the principle implied in a judgment may affect the development of international law', but whether a State should have a right of intervention where the way in which a judgment might affect the development of international law appeared to it to be undesirable.

This also was how the matter was understood by Mr Balfour in a note submitted by him to the Council of the League of Nations in Brussels in October 1920. It read in part:

There is another point on which I speak with much diffidence. It seems to me that the decision of the Permanent Court cannot but have the effect of gradually moulding and modifying international law. This may be good or bad; but I do not think this was contemplated by the Covenant; and in any case there ought to be some provision by which a State can enter a protest, *not* against any particular decision arrived at by the Court, but against any ulterior conclusions to which that decision may seem to point.[3]

At the stage at which Mr Balfour presented his note, the draft Statute of the Court, as prepared by the Advisory Committee of Jurists, did not, of course, have Article 57*bis* (now Article 59); and Article 35, paragraph 4 (now Article 38, paragraph 1 (*d*)), did not have the prefatory words 'Subject to the provisions of Article 57*bis*'. So, looking at the position as it stood in the Committee's draft, Mr

---

[2] *Documents concerning the Action Taken by the Council of the League of Nations*, 1921, p. 46.
[3] *Ibid.*, p. 38.

Balfour very probably took the view that decisions of the proposed Court could lead to the creation of new law: however gradual the process, decisions of the Court could not have the effect of 'moulding and *modifying* international law' without in some way changing it; whatever may be said of 'moulding', to modify international law is certainly to change it; to change it would necessarily involve creating new law.

The creation of new law by the Court, however imperceptibly, would impair the preponderant influence which the major Powers had been previously exercising in framing rules of international law.[4] Speaking of that influence, in *Barcelona Traction* Judge Ammoun would later say:

Among the treaties which have been in question, it is necessary to go back to those which organized international society in the eighteenth and nineteenth centuries, and at the beginning of the twentieth century. It is well known that they were concluded at the instigation of certain great Powers which were considered by the law of the time to be sufficiently representative of the community of nations, or of its collective interests. Moreover, the same was the case in customary law: certain customs of wide scope became incorporated into positive law when in fact they were the work of five or six Powers.[5]

The preservation of this traditional position of the leading States underlay some concern which was expressed as to whether Article 9 of the Statute would ensure their membership of the proposed Court. That provision, as is well known, visualised that the membership of the Court should 'represent the main forms of civilisation and the principal legal systems of the world'. During the discussions in the Committee of Jurists concerning the provision, the president of the Committee was recorded as saying 'that the clause which he had proposed with reference to the representation of civilisations

---

[4] See *Continental Shelf (Tunisia/Libyan Arab Jamahiriya), Application for Permission to Intervene, ICJ Rep 1981*, pp. 29–30, Judge Oda, dissenting opinion; and *Continental Shelf (Libyan Arab Jamahiriya/Malta), Application for Permission to Intervene, ICJ Rep 1984*, at p. 62, separate opinion of Judge Jiménez de Aréchaga, and at pp. 94 and 103, dissenting opinion of Judge Oda. For a distant echo of the point, see Judge Schwebel's remark about the view of the law taken by 'leading States' not being likely to be influenced by a holding made by the Court in the absence of any pleading, in *Military and Paramilitary Activities in and against Nicaragua, ICJ Rep 1986*, p. 351, para. 181, dissenting opinion.

[5] *ICJ Rep 1970*, p. 308, separate opinion, footnote omitted.

and legal systems would ensure in so far as humanly possible the desired result; that is to say the representation of the Great Powers'.[6]

Thus, what probably gave Mr Balfour cause for concern was the possible erosion which the case law of the Court could bring about in the primacy which the major Powers had established for themselves within the mechanisms through which new rules of international law were generated. He was not so innocent of elementary principles as not to appreciate that a decision of the Court would only bind the parties to the case and could not *qua* decision bind non-parties. On the contrary, his presentation showed a deeper insight into the possibility that, although of course only the parties would be bound by the actual decision, the decision could lead to the creation of new law which, as part of the general law, would *ex hypothesi* be applicable to the international community as a whole. His thought, therefore, was that a non-party should have a right of intervention where this might happen. This proposed right of intervention was to be in addition to the specific right of intervention for the protection of a legal interest which might be affected by the decision, or in respect of the interpretation of a convention to which the intervening State was also a party, those cases being dealt with respectively in draft Articles 60 and 61 (now Articles 62 and 63).

As will be seen, Mr Balfour did not secure his additional right of intervention; but it does not appear that there was resistance to his basic assumption that decisions of the Court could 'have the effect of gradually moulding and modifying international law'. This is apparent from the Report presented by M. Bourgeois and adopted by the Council of the League of Nations at its meeting at Brussels on 27 October 1920. It included the following important passages:

The observations in the draft project of The Hague by one of our Colleagues draw attention to the following case: it might happen that a case appearing unimportant in itself might be submitted to the jurisdiction of the Court, and that the Court might take a decision on this case, laying down certain principles of international law which, if they were applied to other countries, would completely modify the principles of the tra-

---

[6] See *Procès-Verbaux*, 1920, p. 371; and Dr Karol Wolfke, 'The Privileged Position of the Great Powers in the International Court of Justice', in *Die Friedenswarte*, (1961/66), LXVI, p. 159. For the significance of the reference to 'the main forms of civilisation', in addition to the reference to 'the principal legal systems of the world', see Hudson, *The Permanent Court*, p. 157.

ditional law of this country, and which might therefore have serious consequences. The question has been raised whether, in view of such an alternative [*une telle hypothèse*], the States not involved in the dispute should not be given the right of intervening in the case in the interest of the harmonious development of the law, and otherwise after the closure of the case, to exercise, in the same interest, influence on the future development of law. Such action on the part of a non-litigant State would moreover have the advantage of drawing attention to the difficulty of making certain States accept such and such a new development of jurisprudence.

These considerations undoubtedly contain elements of great value. The Hague Jurists have not moreover disregarded the necessity of bearing in mind considerations which, if not exactly identical, are at least in the same order of ideas. They have, indeed, given to non-litigant States the right to intervene in a case where any interest of a judicial nature which may concern them is involved.

Moreover, Article 61 of the Draft lays down that: 'Whenever the construction of a convention in which States other than those concerned in the case, are parties, is in question, the Registrar shall notify all such States forthwith. Every State so notified has the right to intervene in the proceedings: but if it uses this right, the construction given by the judgment will be as binding upon it as upon the original Parties to the dispute.' This last stipulation establishes, in the contrary case, that if a State has not intervened in the case the interpretation cannot be enforced against it.

No possible disadvantage could ensue from stating directly what Article 61 indirectly admits. The addition of an Article drawn up as follows can thus be proposed to the Assembly:

The decision of the Court has no binding force except between the Parties and in respect of that particular case.[7]

M. Bourgeois spoke of the Court making a decision 'laying down certain principles of international law which, if they were applied to other countries, would completely modify the principles of the traditional law of this country'; he also spoke of 'the difficulty of making certain States accept such and such a new development of jurisprudence'. These remarks did not deny that decisions of the Court could affect the development of international law; they were relevant to the methodology of the development, a matter dealt with in the following chapter.

A difficulty which appears in the statement made by M. Bourgeois is the following. Mr Balfour had made it clear that the right of protest which he was proposing was directed '*not* against

---

[7] *Documents concerning the Action Taken by the Council of the League of Nations*, 1921, p. 50. And see *Procès-Verbaux*, 1920, pp. 592, 593, 745, 746, 754.

any particular decision arrived at by the Court, but against any ulterior conclusions to which that decision may seem to point', the latter being explained by his reference to the fact 'that the decision of the Permanent Court cannot but have the effect of gradually moulding and modifying international law'. And this, indeed, was how M. Bourgeois understood the point in the earlier part of his statement, in which he spoke of the question being 'raised whether ... the States not involved in the dispute should not be given the right of intervening in the case in the interest of the harmonious development of the law'. The second part of his statement seems however to be addressed to the force of a decision being confined to the parties to the case only. As observed above, one might credit Mr Balfour with knowing this, as indeed is suggested by the form taken by his statement; but it was not what was concerning him. The larger interest which he had in mind about decisions of the Court 'gradually moulding and modifying international law' and about the desirability of non-parties being given a right of protest wherever that might happen was not addressed by stating that the binding force of a decision is limited to the parties only. The fact that the binding force of a decision is confined to the parties to the case is distinct from the influence which the decision could have in gradually moulding and modifying the general law. M. Bourgeois recognised the problem raised by Mr Balfour, but he did not respond to it.[8]

The logic of Mr Balfour's statement should have led naturally to an extension of the intervention provisions of Articles 62 and 63 (then draft Articles 60 and 61) so as to permit of intervention on the mere ground of concern over the wider jurisprudential implications of a decision; alternatively, it should have led to the insertion of a provision excluding the possibility of these wider implications. It was not in fact followed by either of these two types of possible modifications. In fact, the amendments proposed by the British delegation did not include any suggestion for an additional right of intervention.[9] General as were its terms, the provision which was actually inserted merely emphasised that a non-party State was not bound by a decision in the sense in which a party

[8] Sørensen, *Les Sources*, p. 160.
[9] *Documents concerning the Action Taken by the Council of the League of Nations*, 1921, p. 70.

60

would be.[10] That was merely an articulation of a generally accepted principle as to the limits of the binding power of a judgment – a direct statement of a proposition that was already indirectly embodied in Article 63 (then draft Article 61).

The only sense in which the Statute gave a third State a right to influence the general jurisprudential effect of a decision was if it intervened where its legal interest would be affected or where the construction of a convention to which it was also a party was involved; there was no right of intervention in other cases. In *Continental Shelf (Tunisia/Libyan Arab Jamahiriya), Application for Permission to Intervene*,[11] in which Malta's request for permission to intervene failed on other grounds, Malta took care not to 'base its request for permission to intervene simply on an interest in the Court's pronouncements in the case regarding the applicable general principles and rules of international law'.[12]

Draft intervention schemes

It is useful to recall how the matter might have been understood in the Advisory Committee of Jurists. The background against which the intervention provisions of Article 63 (then draft Article 61) were drafted included the Swedish draft, Article 27 of which read, 'As to verdicts appertaining to the interpretation of international Conventions, rules are to be drawn up by special agreement, enabling those verdicts to acquire legal force in relation to other States besides those that were parties to the dispute in the first instance or were implicated in it as intervening parties.'[13] The mechanism proposed in the Swedish draft was different from that later adopted in the intervention provisions of Article 63,[14] in that it was designed to provide a way by which a judicial interpretation of a multilateral convention given in a case between some only of the parties to the convention (including intervening parties) might be made additionally binding on others; however, like Article 63, it

[10] See Sir Arnold Duncan McNair, *The Development of International Justice* (New York, 1954), p. 13.
[11] *ICJ Rep 1981*, p. 3.
[12] *Ibid.*, p. 17, para. 30.
[13] *Documents Presented*, 1920, p. 243. For the origins of Articles 62 and 63, see *Procès-Verbaux*, 1920, pp. 745–746, 754, and *Documents concerning the Action Taken by the Council of the League of Nations*, 1921, p. 60.
[14] For draft Article 61, now Article 63, see *Procès-Verbaux*, 1920, p. 746.

assumed that the normal position was that the binding effect of the decision would be confined to the parties to the case.

Article 49 of the draft scheme presented by The Netherlands to the Advisory Committee read:

1. The sentence shall be binding only upon the Parties to the dispute.
2. When the subject of the dispute is the interpretation of a convention in which Powers who have participated are not parties to the dispute, each signatory Power shall be given due notice by the Parties. Each of these Powers shall have the right to take part in the proceedings. If one or several Powers have availed themselves of this provision, the interpretation contained in the sentence shall be binding on them also.[15]

In substance, paragraph 1 of Article 49 of The Netherlands draft corresponded to Article 59 of the Statute, while paragraph 2 corresponded to Article 63. So the Advisory Committee of Jurists had before it the essence of both provisions.[16] In accepting the substance of paragraph 2, but not that of paragraph 1, it presumably considered that paragraph 1 was an unnecessary duplication of an accepted general principle that non-parties could not be bound by a decision rendered as between others. Further, Article 59 harked back to an element of Article 84 of the Hague Convention for the Peaceful Settlement of International Disputes of 1907, and the Advisory Committee of Jurists was aware of the latter.[17]

Thus, in treating of the subject of intervention in relation to the construction of a convention, the Committee proceeded on the basis that a decision would not bind non-parties. On the draft text which it produced, States which were not parties to the case or which had not intervened could not be bound by the resulting interpretation placed by the Court on the relevant convention. To secure this position, it was not necessary to insert a provision corresponding to Article 59. It is evident, however, that had the Committee thought it necessary to include such a provision, it would have done so for the purpose of limiting the

---

[15] *Documents Presented*, 1920, p. 291. And see, at p. 269, Article 46 of the Swiss draft.
[16] See Röben, 'Le précédent', pp. 386–387.
[17] *Procès-Verbaux*, 1920, p. 594.

force of the decision as *chose jugée*, and not for the purpose of limiting its possible precedential effect.

The object of Article 59 of the Statute

Article 59 has no bearing on the question of precedents. It is directed to emphasising that the juridical force of a judgment *en tant que jugement* is limited to defining the legal relations of the parties only.[18] But, as remarked by Sørensen, the fact that a judicial decision authoritatively defines the relations of the parties to the particular case has nothing to do with the fact that it can serve as a model in subsequent litigation.[19] The distinction is illustrated by the stand which the Court took in the *Temple of Preah Vihear, Preliminary Objections*,[20] in relation to *Israel* v. *Bulgaria*.[21] Speaking in the former of the latter, the Court said:

> The Court's decision in the *Israel* v. *Bulgaria* case was of course concerned with the particular question of Bulgaria's position in relation to the Court and was in any event, by reason of Article 59 of the Statute, only binding, *qua* decision, as between the parties to that case. It cannot therefore, as such, have had the effect of invalidating Thailand's 1950 Declaration. Considered however as a statement of what the Court regarded as the correct legal position, it appears that the sole question, relevant in the present context, with which the Court was concerned in the *Israel* v. *Bulgaria* case was the effect – or more accurately the scope – of Article 36, paragraph 5.[22]

Thus, Article 59 is concerned to ensure that a decision, *qua* decision, binds only the parties to the particular case; but this does not prevent the decision from being treated in a later case as 'a statement of what the Court regarded as the correct legal position'.

Further, Article 59 applies only to decisions given in contentious matters; it has no reference to advisory opinions.[23] It is

---

[18] Brierly, 'Règles générales du droit de la paix', p. 141.

[19] Sørensen, *Les Sources*, p. 157. See also Castberg, 'La Méthodologie', p. 366, and Edvard Hambro, 'The Relations between International Law and Conflict Law', *Hag R*, 105 (1962–I), p. 17.

[20] *ICJ Rep 1961*, p. 27.

[21] *ICJ Rep 1959*, p. 127.

[22] *ICJ Rep 1961*, p. 27.

[23] 'The Court's reply [to a request for an advisory opinion] is only of an advisory character: as such it has no binding force.' See *Peace Treaties, ICJ Rep 1950*, p. 71.

well settled that, though of course not binding as precedents, such opinions do have precedential force as authoritative statements of the legal position.[24] It is obvious that the position must be the same as regards the Court's decisions in contentious matters.

In the words of Jennings, 'Article 59 has strictly no relevance to judicial decisions considered as a "subsidiary means for the determination of rules of law". It is presumably inserted out of abundant caution.'[25] A fair interpretation is that the provision was indeed inserted by the League of Nations out of abundant caution.[26] Since draft Article 57*bis* (now Article 59) was merely stating directly what draft Article 61 (now Article 63) indirectly admitted, the former was really tautologous. However, the prudent draftsman sometimes includes a tautologous statement out of abundant caution, the object being not merely to provide for the solution of disputes, but also to prevent them from arising in the first instance. The point of interest is to know why he did so in any particular case. In this case, apart from being tautologous, draft Article 57*bis* did not really go all the way to meet the aim being advanced by Mr Balfour; but, this notwithstanding, it remains true that what led to the insertion of the provision was the point made by him to the effect that decisions of the Court would inevitably 'have the effect of gradually moulding and modifying international law'. The specific remedy sought by him on the basis of that view was not provided for by the League of Nations, but it did not follow that the view itself was rejected. Indeed, having refrained from providing for any wider right of intervention to permit a non-party State to intervene for the purpose of protesting against the way in which the principle of a possible decision could affect the development of international law, a plausible inference is that the League accepted as normal the capacity of decisions of the Court to affect the development of international law. Thus, Article 59 is not relevant to the Court's system of precedents. In the words of McNair, the provision has not 'hampered the operation of the natural process of looking to previous decisions for guidance in the solution of

---

[24] See p. 165 below.
[25] Jennings, 'General Course', p. 341.
[26] Lauterpacht, 'Schools of Thought in International Law', p. 58.

similar problems. It requires no doctrine of judicial precedent to explain that inevitable practice.'[27]

Looking at the matter from the point of view of Article 38, paragraph 1 *(d)*, of the Statute, a provision relating to precedents has no need to refer to a provision dealing only with *chose jugée*.[28] The reference in that provision to Article 59 is not an argument against the possibility of judicial creativity; nor is the phrasing of the former necessarily an impediment. It is helpful to bear in mind Brierly's observation to the following effect:

On a pu, en toute vérité, faire remarquer que les dispositions de l'article 38 étaient inspirées par de la méfiance vis-à-vis du juge international. Les rédacteurs de cet article ne désiraient pas, conformément à la thèse volontariste, limiter les ressources du juge international aux traités et à la coutume, mais ils ne voulaient pas non plus aller jusqu'à admettre la jurisprudence comme troisième source du droit. A la place, ils se sont contentés d'indiquer quelques ressources matérielles supplémentaires: les principes généraux de droit, les décisions judiciaires, la doctrine des publicistes, auxquelles le juge pourrait avoir recours quand ces deux sources formelles ne suffiraient pas à lui fournir une solution.

Mais les ressources matérielles, mentionnées spécifiquement ici, ne constituent pas en fait une énumération complète, mais sont seulement des exemples des ressources auxquelles un juge fait habituellement appel, sans avoir besoin d'y être spécialement autorisé. Le compte des sources du droit, international ou étatique, ne pourra jamais être complet s'il ne fait pas place à cette activité créatrice du juge. Une formule peut exprimer le mécanisme de l'acte de juger, mais un jugement est toujours plus qu'une action mécanique. Si nous ne voulons pas accepter franchement la jurisprudence comme source formelle du droit, il nous faudra au moins admettre que, derrière les sources formelles, il existe une réserve dont, au besoin, le juge peut tirer des principes nouveaux.[29]

Brierly's remark about mistrust of the international judge accounting for the particular formulation of Article 38, paragraph 1 *(d)*, assumes significance in the light of the fact that the Advisory Committee was labouring in a context in which the tolerance of the international community to the idea of a global court of justice still had to be tested; it recalls too the point made above about

---

[27] Sir Arnold Duncan McNair, *The Development of International Justice* (New York, 1954), pp. 13–14. And see *Lord McNair: Selected Papers and Bibliography* (Leiden/ Dobbs Ferry, 1974), pp. 213, 254–256, 355.

[28] Sørensen, *Les Sources*, p. 158.

[29] Brierly, 'Règles générales du droit de la paix', pp. 78–79.

apprehension on the part of the major Powers of erosion of their customary leading role in the fashioning of international law. Before the Committee, Mr Root found it necessary to observe that 'the world must be induced to accept the judgments of the Court upon questions of law'.[30] As Georges Scelle later remarked, 'Le paragraphe 4 de l'article 38 a été dicté non pas par des considérations tirées de la nature intrinsèque de la fonction juridictionnelle, mais par des scrupules d'opportunité politique. On s'est préoccupé beaucoup moins de la logique interne des institutions sociales interétatiques que de ce que les gouvernements étaient disposés à accepter.'[31]

The problem was apparent from the two conflicting streams of thought which were discernible in the work of the Advisory Committee of Jurists of 1920, namely, on the one hand, an affirmation that the judge only declares the law but does not create it, and, on the other hand, the presence of material before the Committee that evidenced an anticipation by several States which took an interest in the matter that the Court would inevitably create some law. In this respect, it may be recalled that when the matter went before the Sub-Committee of the Third Committee of the First Assembly of the League of Nations, the Sub-Committee significantly declined to adopt an Argentine proposal 'to limit the power of the Court to attribute the character of precedents to judicial decisions' and added: 'On the contrary, it considers that it would be one of the Court's important tasks to contribute, through its jurisprudence, to the development of international law.'[32]

The statement is usually made that, paradoxically, it was the representatives of the legal systems where judge-made law prevailed who most strenuously opposed its extension to the field of international relations.[33] So they did; but the effort fell short of the aim. It certainly did not go far enough to prevent acknowledgment that decisions of the Court could at least contribute to the development of the law. Whether that development could proceed without some law being created, if only marginally, is considered in the next chapter.

[30] *Procès-Verbaux*, 1920, p. 294.
[31] Scelle, 'Les Sources des diverses branches du droit', p. 426.
[32] *Documents concerning the Action Taken by the Council of the League of Nations*, 1921, p. 211.
[33] Scelle, 'Les Sources des diverses branches du droit', p. 428.

7

The possibility of judge-made international law

Introductory remarks

A problem, which has to be acknowledged and which will be returned to later, is this: The adjudicating machinery on the international plane consists of a number of tribunals, some instituted on a bilateral basis, others on a multilateral basis, but with nothing to hold them together in a coherent system. They all make decisions which can influence the development of international law. If that influence can amount to law-making in the case of all of them, the absence of hierarchical authority to impose order is a prescription for conflicting precepts. On the other hand, from the point of view of individual members of the international community, it may not be clear why that influence should amount to law-making in the case of one particular tribunal. It is submitted, however, that there is another point of view from which the matter may be seen, namely, that of the Court itself. The Court can only decide in accordance with international law. How then should the Court itself regard a new principle adopted in a previous case for the solution of a problem presented in that particular case? One cannot of course speak for the Court and can only speculate with hesitation.

The Statute of the Court left the hands of the League of Nations on the understanding that decisions of the Court could contribute to the development of international law; that developmental responsibility has been generally acknowledged. Can the contribution made by the Court through its decisions to the development of international law involve the production of judge-made international law? A representative view, as given in the ninth edition of *Oppenheim*, is this:

Decisions of courts and tribunals are a subsidiary and indirect source of international law. Article 38 of the Statute of the International Court of Justice provides that, subject to Article 59, the Court shall apply judicial decisions as a subsidiary means for the determination of rules of law. Since judges do not in principle make law but apply existing law, their role is inevitably secondary since the law they propound has some antecedent source. Nevertheless, judicial decision has become a most important factor in the development of international law, and the authority and persuasive power of judicial decisions may sometimes give them greater significance than they enjoy formally.

In the absence of anything approaching the common law doctrine of judicial precedent, decisions of international tribunals are not a direct source of law in international adjudications. In fact, however, they exercise considerable influence as an impartial and well-considered statement of the law by jurists of authority made in the light of actual problems which arise before them. They are often relied upon in argument and decision. The International Court of Justice, while prevented from treating its previous decisions as binding, has, in the interest of judicial consistency, referred to them with increasing frequency. It is probable that in view of the difficulties surrounding the codification of international law, international tribunals will in the future fulfil, inconspicuously but efficiently, a large part of the task of developing international law.[1]

The problem which these thoughtfully worded views are likely to present is this: if decisions of the Court cannot make law but can contribute to its development, presumably that development ultimately results in the creation of new law; and, however minute this might be in any one instance, incrementally it acquires mass. It does not accord with reality to suggest that the Court may develop the law only in the limited sense of bringing out the true meaning of existing law in relation to particular facts, as, to take the ordinary example, by determining whether a statutory reference to 'domestic animal' includes some particular animal. As Judge Alvarez remarked, 'in many cases it is quite impossible to say where the development of law ends and where its creation begins'.[2] The inquiring mind will encounter difficulty in accepting that the devel-

---

[1] *Oppenheim's International Law*, 9th edn (Longman, 1992), I, p. 41, para. 13, footnotes omitted.

[2] *Reparation for Injuries Suffered in the Service of the United Nations, ICJ Rep 1949*, p. 190.

opment spoken of in *Oppenheim* and other texts can fail to eventuate in the creation of new law at some point. Where is that point located, if not within the Court's own decision-making process?

Another way of putting it is to ask whether decisions of the Court can serve as sources of law. As has been seen, the view given in *Oppenheim* is that 'decisions of international tribunals are not a direct source of law'; but, as the text also acknowledges, they 'are a subsidiary and indirect source of international law'. Hence, though 'subsidiary and indirect', they are a 'source of international law'. The matter is complicated by a certain ambiguity in the term 'source'.[3] The question whether decisions of the Court are sources of law has been much discussed. It is possible that the preponderance of opinion is in favour of the view that they are not.[4] It is not proposed to explore these difficult matters. It would do for present purposes that, as stated in *Oppenheim*, decisions of the Court 'are a subsidiary and indirect source of law'. But with what result?

Whether precedents can serve only as inputs in the processes of creating customary law

There is a view that decisions of the Court may generate new law but that they can do so only through the processes through which customary international law is developed. The approach has a long history in municipal law. It is visible in the state of the law of Scotland as it stood before reception of the English doctrine of precedent. In the words of John Erskine:

Decisions, . . . though they bind the parties litigating, create no obligations on the judges to follow in the same tract, if it shall appear to them contrary to law. It is, however, certain that they are frequently the occasion of establishing usages, which, after they have gathered force by a sufficient

---

[3] Georg Schwarzenberger, *International Law as Applied by International Courts and Tribunals*, 3rd edn (London, 1957), I, p. 26; Sir Gerald Fitzmaurice, 'Some Problems Regarding the Formal Sources of International Law', in *Symbolae Verzijl* (The Hague, 1958), p. 153; R. S. Pathak, 'The General Theory of the Sources of Contemporary International Law', *Indian JIL*, 19 (1979), p. 483; and M. K. Nawab, 'Other Sources of International Law: Are Judicial Decisions of the International Court of Justice a Source of International Law?', *ibid.*, p. 526.

[4] See, for example, Brierly, 'Règles générales du droit de la paix', p. 78; and, more recently, G. J. H. van Hoof, *Rethinking the Sources of International Law* (Deventer, 1983), p. 169.

length of time, must, from the tacit consent of the state, make part of our unwritten law.[5]

Writing in 1925, Charles De Visscher put the international law position thus: 'Les sentences judiciaires constituent également un élément de formation et un mode d'expression de la coutume internationale: il en est ainsi des décisions rendues par les tribunaux internes; il en est ainsi surtout des sentences des tribunaux internationaux.'[6] He added:

Il ne faut donc pas voir dans la jurisprudence une source de droit international distincte de la coutume. Les règles techniques ou constructives qui se dégagent des sentences judiciaires ne s'imposent jamais en tant que décisions jurisprudentielles, elles s'imposent comme règles coutumières lorsqu'elles s'appuient sur une jurisprudence suffisamment constante pour que l'on puisse affirmer qu'elles ont reçu l'assentiment général des États. A ce titre on peut dire de la jurisprudence ce qui a été dit plus haut du droit conventionnel particulier: elle est un élément de formation et un mode d'expression de la coutume. Si l'on veut employer le mot 'source', elle est une source de coutume, elle n'est pas une source de droit distincte, indépendante de la coutume.

La jurisprudence est une source de coutume, parce que les tribunaux étant les organes de l'État, leurs décisions constituent un des éléments de la pratique internationale. Cette observation suffit à faire comprendre la distinction qui doit être faite et qui est trop souvent méconnue entre la jurisprudence et la *doctrine*.[7]

Similar views were expressed by Frede Castberg in 1933;[8] by Jules Basdevant in 1936;[9] by Lazare Kopelmanas in 1937;[10] and by Charles Rousseau in 1944.[11]

---

[5] John Erskine of Carnock, Esq., *An Institute of the Law of Scotland*, a new edition by J. B. Nicolson (Edinburgh, 1871), Vol. I, book I, title I, para. 47, p. 21.

[6] Charles De Visscher, 'La codification du droit international', *Hag R*, 6 (1925–I), p. 356.

[7] *Ibid.*, p. 357.

[8] Castberg, 'La Méthodologie', pp. 366–367.

[9] J. Basdevant, 'Règles générales du droit de la paix', *Hag R*, 58 (1936–IV), pp. 510–511.

[10] Lazare Kopelmanas, 'Custom as a means of the Creation of International Law', *BYBIL*, 18 (1937), pp. 141–142; and see, also by him, 'Quelques réflexions au sujet de l'Article 38, 3° du Statut de la Cour permanente de Justice internationale', *RGDIP*, 43 (1936), p. 307.

[11] Charles Rousseau, *Principes généraux du droit international public*, (1944), I, p. 857, para. 501, disagreeing with Georges Scelle, *Précis de droit des gens, Principes et systématique*, Part II (Paris, 1934), pp. 315–316.

The idea that precedents operate only as inputs in the evolution of customary international law enjoys respect.[12] In support of that view, reference is sometimes made to a suggested discrepancy between the treatment of decisions of the Court under Article 38, paragraph 1 (d), of the Statute, and the treatment of its decisions under Article 24 of the Statute of the International Law Commission. The latter reads:

The Commission shall consider ways and means for making the evidence of customary international law more readily available, such as the collection and publication of documents concerning State practice and of the decisions of national and international courts on questions of international law, and shall make a report to the General Assembly on this matter.

The Report of the International Law Commission covering its second session, 5 January to 25 July 1950, commented as follows:

Article 24 of the Statute of the Commission seems to depart from the classification in Article 38 of the Statute of the Court, by including judicial decisions on questions of international law among the evidences of customary international law. The departure may be defended logically, however, for such decisions, particularly those by international courts, may formulate and apply principles and rules of customary international law. Moreover, the practice of a State may be indicated by the decisions of its national courts.[13]

The Statute of the Court is part of the Charter. The Statute of the International Law Commission is not; it was established by the General Assembly, a body coordinate in legal status with the Court. Thus, the provisions of the Statute of the Commission cannot amend those of the Statute of the Court. The Report of the Commission proceeds on the basis that there is a difference in meaning as between the two provisions. If there is a difference, the meaning of Article 38, paragraph 1 (d), of the Statute of the Court remains unaffected by the different meaning of Article 24 of the Statute of the Commission.

The development of customary international law depends on State practice. It is difficult to regard a decision of the Court as being in itself an expression of State practice. A case, it is true, is

---

[12] See, for example, in more recent times, Paul Guggenheim, *Traité de Droit international public* (Geneva, 1967), I, p. 112, para. 4; and Barberis, 'La Jurisprudencia', p. 652.

[13] *YBILC* 1950, II, p. 368, para. 30.

submitted to the Court with the consent of the parties. But the Court itself has not been set up by them alone; it has been set up as a permanent international judicial body under a multilateral instrument of a constitutional character to which practically all States are parties. It is difficult to see how it can be regarded as an organ of the particular litigating States, whatever may be the position of other international tribunals.[14] A decision made by it is an expression not of the practice of the litigating States, but of the judicial view taken of the relations between them on the basis of legal principles which must necessarily exclude any customary law which has not yet crystallised. The decision may recognise the existence of a new customary law[15] and in that limited sense it may no doubt be regarded as the final stage of development, but, by itself, it cannot create one. It lacks the element of repetitiveness so prominent a feature of the evolution of customary international law.[16] Objections to the customary international law approach have been persuasively made by Sørensen.[17] Lauterpacht seemed to be expressing a similar view when stating that '[d]ecisions of international courts are . . . not direct evidence of the practice of States or of what States conceive to be the law'.[18]

As regards procedural law governing the activity of the Court and of the parties in relation to the conduct of a case, this, like basic international law, is in important respects customary in origin; but it seems that a new procedural principle may come into being as a result of the precedential authority of the Court's decisions. In some cases, the Court, as in the case of the substantive law, refers *en bloc* to its previous decisions or jurisprudence; but, it is submitted, the possibility is not excluded of a single decision being relied on.[19]

---

[14] Cf. Charles De Visscher, 'La codification du droit international', *Hag R*, 6 (1925–I), p. 357; and J. Kosters, *Les fondements du droit des gens* (Leiden, 1925), p. 239.

[15] See Hubert Thierry, 'L'Evolution du droit international', *Hag R*, 222 (1990–III), p. 41.

[16] As to the issue relating to the element of repetitiveness, see and compare Sørensen, *Les Sources*, p. 155, and Barberis, 'La Jurisprudencia', p. 655. As to the creation of customary law, see in general the *North Sea Continental Shelf Cases*, *ICJ Rep 1969*, pp. 41 ff.

[17] Sørensen, *Les Sources*, pp. 153–155.

[18] Lauterpacht, *Development*, pp. 20–22.

[19] See chapter 2, p. 18, *supra*, and the discussion in Sørensen, *Les Sources*, pp. 169–172.

The Court's 'function is to decide in accordance with international law'

If a new 'rule' adopted by the Court for the disposal of a case can only become law if it subsequently emerges as a rule of customary international law, what exactly is the juridical status of the new 'rule' before it becomes a part of customary international law? Unless and until the new rule becomes a part of customary international law, it is not law; the Court would, therefore, have acted on a 'rule' which was not a rule of international law. In some systems a judicial decision may create 'une règle de droit' limited to the litigating parties;[20] it seems improbable that the Court could do that.

Referring to considerations of stability, Castberg says:

Ce sont des considérations de cet ordre qui peuvent conduire à attribuer une importance décisive au fait qu'une règle de droit a été exprimée dans une décision judiciaire internationale, même s'il ne s'est pas formé un droit coutumier. Le fait qu'il y a un précédent judiciaire pour un certain principe peut, en d'autres termes, dans le droit international comme dans le droit interne, être un élément décisif, pourvu que la sentence ne soit pas manifestement contraire aux dispositions positives du droit ou aux intérêts bien compris de la communauté internationale.[21]

In the case of a municipal system, Kopelmanas puts the problem which would arise this way:

Supposons qu'une Cour Suprême ait rendu une décision sur la base d'une règle non encore consacrée par son ordre juridique. Si cette Cour ne possède pas de compétence législative spéciale, elle ne pourra imposer sa décision qu'en ce qui concerne le cas d'espèce. La règle générale qui conditionne la solution d'espèce ne deviendra norme juridique que si la Cour Suprême l'adopte encore dans d'autres cas ou si les tribunaux inférieurs s'inclinent d'eux-mêmes devant la règle. Dans les deux cas, le caractère positif de la nouvelle règle ne deviendra évident qu'à la suite de plusieurs décisions jurisprudentielles qui la suivent, la règle de droit tirera sa force de la répétition des actes des tribunaux, son origine sera coutumière.

Contrairement à l'apparence, le premier arrêt de justice n'aura pas créé de nouvelle règle de droit, il ne l'aura introduite dans l'ordre juridique

[20] Paul Guggenheim, 'La sentence arbitrale et la décision judiciaire ne créent une règle de droit qu'entre les parties en litige', *Traité de Droit international public* (Geneva, 1967), I, p. 112, para. 4.

[21] Castberg, 'La Méthodologie', p. 367.

qu'en vue du cas d'espèce. Le caractère de généralité qui est un des éléments essentiels de la règle de droit manquera à la règle consacrée par une seule décision. Le juge enrichira l'ordre juridique en recourant à une règle extra-juridique; seulement, cet enrichissement consistera non pas dans la création d'une nouvelle procédure d'élaboration des normes juridiques, mais dans l'application directe des règles extra-juridiques aux cas d'espèce.[22]

Implicit in these statements (particularly when the first is read in the light of the second) is the assumption that, at the time of a decision, a principle adopted may not yet have become a part of the law.[23] But, as Kopelmanas points out, whether a judge can apply an extra-legal rule of conduct depends on the particular legal order; the judge may be able to do so in some systems but not in others.[24] He seems to think that the international judge is not competent to do so, stating, 'Les règles étrangères à l'ordre international sont-elles applicables *de plano* aux relations internationales? Le juge international peut-il se baser sur des principes qui n'ont pas encore reçu de consécration expresse dans son ordre juridique? Il semble que dans l'état actuel des choses, la réponse doive être négative.'[25]

It is not necessary to consider the question whether and, if so, how far the Court may, by agreement of the parties, deal with disputes not requiring the application of international law.[26] The concern here is with the normal situation in which the Court is acting under paragraph 1 of Article 38 of the Statute. Under that provision, the Court has to decide disputes 'in accordance with international law'. Judge Basdevant, dissenting, laid stress on those words in holding that, for the purpose of determining whether it

---

[22] Lazare Kopelmanas, 'Essai d'une théorie des sources formelles du Droit international', *Revue de Droit international*, 21 (1938–I), p. 127.

[23] See Paul Guggenheim, *Traité de Droit international public*, (Geneva, 1967), I, p. 112, para. 4; and Alf Ross, *A Textbook of International Law* (London, 1947), pp. 81–82.

[24] Lazare Kopelmanas, 'Essai d'une théorie des sources formelles du Droit international', *Revue de Droit international*, 21 (1938–I), p. 129.

[25] *Ibid.*, p. 130.

[26] See *Rights of Minorities in Upper Silesia (Minority Schools), 1928, PCIJ, Series A, No. 15*, p. 22; *Serbian Loans, 1929, PCIJ Series A, No. 20*; and *South West Africa, Preliminary Objections, ICJ Rep 1962*, p. 423, Judge Jessup, separate opinion, observing that the 'new words inserted in Article 38 of the Statute of this Court [in 1945] do not affect the validity of the Permanent Court's observation' in the *Serbian Loans* case as to the possibility of the Court's dealing with disputes which do not require the application of international law. But see the qualification in De Visscher, *Theory and Reality*, p. 366.

has jurisdiction, 'the Court must, of itself, seek with all the means at its disposal to ascertain what is the law'.[27] Hence also Fitzmaurice's reference to 'the fundamental principle that the tribunal must decide in accordance with international law'.[28] Thus, the International Court of Justice cannot adjudicate on the strength of a proposition before it becomes law. In the *Fisheries Jurisdiction* case it said:

> The Court is of the view that there is no incompatibility with its judicial function in making a pronouncement on the rights and duties of the Parties under existing international law which would clearly be capable of having a forward reach; this does not mean that the Court should declare the law between the Parties as it might be at the date of expiration of the interim agreement, a task beyond the powers of any tribunal. The possibility of the law changing is ever present: but that cannot relieve the Court from its obligation to render a judgment on the basis of the law as it exists at the time of its decision.[29]

And, as it added, 'the Court, as a court of law, cannot render judgment *sub specie legis ferendae*, or anticipate the law before the legislator has laid it down'.[30] The fact that he was dissenting did not impair the validity of the somewhat similar statement made earlier by Judge Badawi Pasha to the effect that the 'Court's duty is to declare the law in the state of evolution that it has reached'.[31]

It is true that parties may by agreement authorise the Court to decide on bases which may not necessarily correspond to existing international law. Thus, in *Continental Shelf (Tunisia/Libyan Arab Jamahiriya)*, by their Special Agreement the parties requested the Court 'to take account of . . . the recent trends admitted at the Third Conference on the Law of the Sea'.[32] However, the exception is more apparent than real, for it is international law which enables the Court to act on the particular basis consensually proposed, considered as *lex specialis*. Excluding situations of that kind, the Court cannot decide a dispute in accordance with a proposition on the

---

[27] *Certain Norwegian Loans, ICJ Rep 1957*, p. 74. The words were also stressed in the joint dissenting opinion in the *Nuclear Tests (Australia v. France), ICJ Rep 1974*, p. 322, para. 22.

[28] Fitzmaurice, *Law and Procedure*, II, p. 531.

[29] *ICJ Rep 1974*, p. 19, para. 40.

[30] *Ibid.*, pp. 23–24, para. 53.

[31] *Reparation* case, *ICJ Rep 1949*, p. 216.

[32] *ICJ Rep 1982*, p. 21, para. 2, and pp. 37–38, paras. 23–24.

off-chance that it may become part of customary international law; it may never become part of customary international law, and, even if it does, it is hard to see how this would relate backwards so as to convert a non-law proposition into a rule of international law as at the time when it was in fact acted on.

The logical impulsion is in the direction of holding that the only basis on which the Court can act on a new principle is that, in adopting the principle, it becomes part of international law, at any rate from the point of view of the Court itself. But, if new law is indeed created by the Court, can this be reconciled with the language of Article 38, paragraph 1 *(d)*, of the Statute?

Judicial decisions may operate in two ways

Article 38, paragraph 1 *(d)*, of the Statute of the Court requires the Court to apply, 'subject to the provisions of Article 59, judicial decisions and the teachings of the most highly qualified publicists of the various nations, as subsidiary means for the determination of rules of law'. It is possible that this provision visualises that decisions of the Court may operate in two ways.

First, they may serve as material for the determination of a rule of law by a later decision. Judicial decisions (including those of the World Court and of other courts) which serve in that way constitute 'subsidiary means for the determination of rules of law'. The second way in which judicial decisions (now restricted to decisions of the Court itself) may serve is by effecting the determination of rules of law on the basis of earlier judicial decisions. The new decision by which a rule of law has been determined on the basis of earlier decisions is not a subsidiary means; it is the source of a new rule of international law; it is made by the Court alone. Once the determination has been made in a new decision, the Court would in later cases be applying the rule of law as determined in that decision; outside of that decision, it may not be obvious that the rule of law exists.

Objection may be made that the foregoing assumes that the reference to 'the determination of rules of law' in Article 38, paragraph 1 *(d)*, of the Statute includes a decision which determines a rule of law in the sense of creating it, whereas the word 'determination' is arguably limited to a determination in the sense of finding out what is the existing law. In support of the objection, it may be urged that the *travaux préparatoires* of the Advisory Committee of Jurists which prepared the draft Statute show that the Committee considered that the Court's decisions would operate in a law-finding and not in a law-creating way. The debates between President Descamps, Lord Phillimore, Mr Root, Judge Loder, Mr Hagerup, Professor de Lapradelle and Mr Ricci-Busatti run in that direction.[33] The argument is strong therefore that the reference to 'the determination of rules of law' visualised a decision which would merely elucidate the existing law,[34] and not bring new law into being.

Is a different view possible? No doubt 'to determine' is to 'ascertain definitely by observation, examination, calculation, etc.'; but it can also mean to 'lay down decisively or authoritatively, to pronounce, declare, state', or to 'settle or fix beforehand; to ordain, decree ...'.[35] In a legal context, the meaning is not limited to a finding or discovering of what already exists; it may include the bringing into being of a new legal phenomenon. This is the way the word is often used in legal documents; but for the 'determination', the matter determined may not have any existence in law. As remarked by Jennings, 'the difference between making and determining law is one of degree rather than one of kind'.[36] The threshold point at which change occurs in the effect produced by a process may be difficult to identify; but the change can nevertheless occur.

Again, while the debates may throw light on the intended nature of the proposed organ, they cannot operate to cut down the objective character of the organ as it in fact emerged. From what has been set out in chapter 6, it seems reasonably clear that the Council and the Assembly of the League of Nations did not dissent from the view expressed by Mr Balfour almost immediately after receiving the draft Statute prepared by the Advisory Committee of Jurists

---

[33] See, *inter alia*, *Procès-Verbaux*, 1920, pp. 332, 336, 584; Maarten Bos, 'The Recognised Manifestations of International Law: A New Theory of "Sources" ', *Germ YBIL*, 20 (1977), pp. 35, 56 and 57; G. H. van Hoof, *Rethinking the Sources of International Law* (Deventer, 1983), p. 169; and Röben, 'Le précédent', pp. 385, 387.

[34] *Ibid.*, and see Hudson, *The Permanent Court*, p. 612; Charles Rousseau, *Principes généraux de droit international public*, (Paris, 1944), I, p. 857, para. 501; and Waldock, 'General Course', pp. 88, 92.

[35] *Oxford English Dictionary* (2nd edn, 1989), IV, p. 550.

[36] Jennings, 'General Course', p. 341.

that 'the decision of the Permanent Court cannot but have the effect of gradually moulding and modifying international law'.[37] It is not a credible proposition that such 'moulding and modifying' of international law has to exclude law-creation, however limited this might be.

For these reasons, it seems arguable that the reference in Article 38, paragraph 1 (d), of the Statute to 'the determination of rules of law' may be read as including a determination of new rules of law by a decision of the Court itself which is based on earlier judicial decisions or the writings of publicists.[38]

Three problems are resolved if one bears in mind the proposed distinction between judicial decisions used as subsidiary means for the determination of rules of law and a later decision of the Court effecting a determination of a rule of law on the basis of earlier decisions so used.

The first problem is one which arises from argument to the effect that to hold that the Court's decisions can create law is to exceed the limits of the role assigned by Article 38, paragraph 1 (d), of the Statute to judicial decisions 'as subsidiary means for the determination of rules of law'. Most observers agree that decisions of the Court are more than that.[39] Even writers who deny that a decision of the Court makes law hasten to add that it is an illusion to suppose that in practice its decisions are merely subsidiary means for the determination of rules of law.[40] Another way of putting it is to say that Article 38, paragraph 1 (d), of the Statute does not accurately describe the value, as a source of law, which, in practice, the Court attributes to its own precedents.[41] One author notes that '[o]n a souvent l'impression que c'est bien le précédent et non pas une norme de droit international qui est au coeur du débat'.[42] Recognising that in practice decisions of the Court are treated as creative of law, but arguing that there is need for theoretical justification, he says, 'La constatation, en forme de résignation, que ce

---

[37] *Documents concerning the Action Taken by the Council of the League of Nations*, 1921, p. 38.

[38] See discussion in Sørensen, *Les Sources*, p. 161.

[39] See W. E. Beckett, 'Les Questions d'Intérêt général au point de vue juridique dans la Jurisprudence de la Cour permanente de Justice internationale', *Hag R*, 39 (1932–I), p. 139.

[40] See Alf Ross, *A Textbook of International Law* (London, 1947), p. 87.

[41] Barberis, 'La Jurisprudencia', p. 670.

[42] Röben, 'Le précédent', p. 398.

phénomène est inhérent à la fonction judiciaire permanente et doit donc être accepté comme tel, ne saurait remplacer une base normative sur laquelle la Cour peut fonder sa pratique en matière de précédent. Ces auteurs peuvent donc expliquer la pratique de la Cour, mais ils ne parviennent pas à la légitimer.'[43]

The difficulty raised is resolved by the distinction suggested above between judicial decisions used in a later decision of the Court as subsidiary means for the determination of rules of law, and the rules of law determined in the later decision on the basis of the earlier decisions used as such subsidiary means. If the distinction is granted, the earlier decisions (which could include but are not limited to decisions of the Court) are not used otherwise than as subsidiary means for the determination of rules of law; but the provision also visualises, if elliptically, the making of a later decision determining a rule of law. This later decision, which is limited to a decision by the Court itself, is not subject to the limitation that it may be used only as a subsidiary means.

The second problem concerns a possible contradiction in the text of Article 38, paragraph 1, of the Statute.[44] Subparagraphs *(a)*, *(b)* and *(c)* of paragraph 1 require the Court to 'apply' conventional law, customary law and the general principles of law recognised by civilised nations, respectively, in deciding a dispute submitted to it. Subject to some argument in the case of subparagraph *(c)*,[45] these are capable of direct application in deciding the dispute submitted to the Court. Not so in respect of subparagraph *(d)*; in deciding a dispute, the Court cannot directly 'apply' judicial decisions and the teachings of publicists, since these are intended to serve only 'as subsidiary means for the determination of rules of law'. It is in application of rules of law, and not of 'subsidiary means for the determination of rules of law', that the dispute has to be decided. It has been put this way:

Cependant, d'aucuns font remarquer, dans la formule de l'art. 38, para. 1, lit. d), qu'il y a une contradiction entre le mandat de la Cour qui est d'appliquer les décisions judiciaires et l'affirmation que celles-ci étaient seulement des moyens de détermination. En effet on n'applique pas de

---

[43] *Ibid.*, p. 401. And see pp. 384, 385, 389, 398, 401, 402, 403.

[44] See R. Quadri, 'Cours général de droit international public', *Hag R*, 113 (1964–III), p. 355.

[45] The exact meaning of subparagraph *(c)* has been the subject of an extensive literature. See the references gathered up in *Oppenheim* (9th edn), I, pp. 36 ff.

tels moyens, on peut seulement les utiliser. Ce sont des règles émanant de sources de droit que l'on applique.[46]

What is the answer? The drafting of Article 38, paragraph 1, has not met with universal approval,[47] but it is probably putting it too high to say that 'rien ou presque ne peut être déduit de l'art. 38'.[48] Unsatisfactory as the formulation may be thought, the meaning is tolerably clear. Reading the provision as a whole, and starting from the top, it requires the Court in all cases 'to decide disputes in accordance with international law'; consequently, in the case of sub-paragraph (d), it requires the Court to decide in accordance with 'rules of law' determined by it on the basis of 'judicial decisions . . . [used] as subsidiary means for the determination of' those rules.

A third problem is that it can be said that parity of reasoning would require other judicial decisions to be equally treated as capable of creating law if this capability is attributed to decisions of the Court, and indeed that the teachings of publicists would also have to be similarly treated, for they are all referred to in the same breath in Article 38, paragraph 1 (d), of the Statute. That problem is not, however, raised if the 'rules of law' contemplated by that provision are determined not by such non-World Court material, but by a later decision of the Court itself made on the basis of judicial decisions (including World Court decisions) and the teachings of publicists.

One question remains. If a later decision of the Court can create a rule of law on the basis of earlier judicial decisions and the teachings of publicists, how is the rule of law created by the later decision to be accommodated within the scheme of Article 38, paragraph 1, of the Statute? One answer, given above, is that paragraph 1 (d) may itself be construed as furnishing the necessary authority for the application of such a newly created rule. An alternative possibility is this. If a decision creates a new rule of law, the new rule of law so created forms part of 'international law' within the meaning of the opening words of paragraph 1, under which it is the duty of the Court 'to decide in accordance with international law . . .'. A view

---

[46] Röben, 'Le précédent', p. 385. And see Moustapha Sourang, 'La Jurisprudence et la doctrine', in Mohammed Bedjaoui (ed.), Droit international, Bilan et perspectives (Paris, 1991), I, p. 295.

[47] Fisheries Jurisdiction, ICJ Rep 1974, p. 100, Judge de Castro, separate opinion.

[48] R. Quadri, 'Cours général de droit international public', Hag R, 113 (1964–III), p. 355.

is discernible that subparagraphs *(a)* to *(d)* of Article 38, paragraph 1, are not exhaustive of 'international law' as more generally referred to in Article 36, paragraph 2 *(b)*.[49] Since the Court's function is 'to decide in accordance with international law', if a principle can be shown to form part of international law the Court must decide in accordance with that principle where relevant, whether or not it falls under subparagraphs *(a)* to *(d)* of Article 38, paragraph 1. The structure of the provision encourages the view that these subparagraphs may be construed as a standing directive to the Court to apply certain elements in order to assist it in finding what is the 'international law' in accordance with which it must decide the dispute.[50] On that view, it is at least arguable that the Court is not prevented from discovering international law by other means if it can.

To the extent that this argument is dependent on the words 'whose function is to decide in accordance with international law such disputes as are submitted to it', which appear in the *chapeau* of Article 38, paragraph 1, of the Statute, it may be objected that those words were introduced as part of the provision only in 1945; that being so, it may be said that the argument does not explain the position as it stood before the amendment was made. However, an explanation might well be that the words, though inserted only in 1945, were declaratory of the position as it always had been. The Report on the Draft Statute of an International Court of Justice referred to in Chapter VII of the Dumbarton Oaks Proposals (Professor Jules Basdevant, Rapporteur) of 25 April 1945, had noted:

Article 38, which determines, according to its terms, what the Court 'shall apply' has given rise to more controversies in doctrine than difficulties in practice. The Committee thought that it was not the opportune time to

---

[49] See *South West Africa, ICJ Rep 1966*, p. 464, Judge Padilla Nervo, dissenting opinion; Brierly, 'Règles générales du droit de la paix', pp. 78–79; Hudson, *The Permanent Court*, pp. 523–524; Jennings, 'General Course', p. 343; Wang Tieya, 'The Third World and International Law', in *Selected Articles from the Chinese Year Book of International Law* (Beijing, 1983), p. 22; and Wang Tieya, 'The Third World and International Law', in R. St J. Macdonald and D. M. Johnston (eds.), *The Structure and Process of International Law* (Dordrecht, 1986), p. 963. Cf. Alfred P. Rubin, 'The International Legal Effects of Unilateral Declarations', *AJIL*, 71 (1977), p. 29.

[50] See and consider Sir Gerald Fitzmaurice, 'Some Problems Regarding the Formal Sources of International Law', in *Symbolae Verzijl*, (The Hague, 1958), pp. 173 ff.

undertake the revision of this article. It has trusted to the Court to put it into operation, and has left it without change other than that which appears in the numbering of the provisions of the article.[51]

The words in question resulted from a modified Chilean proposal, which was later adopted at San Francisco by Committee I of Commission IV. The records of the meeting read:

> The First Committee has adopted an addition to be inserted in the introductory phrase of this article referring to the function of the Court to decide disputes submitted to it in accordance with international law. The lacuna in the old Statute with reference to this point did not prevent the Permanent Court of International Justice from regarding itself as an organ of international law; but the addition will accentuate that character of the new Court.[52]

Commenting on the change, in 1946 Hudson remarked that no 'doubt had ever been expressed on this point; indeed, the Permanent Court had without challenge often referred to itself as an "organ of international law" or as possessing a mandate to apply international law'.[53] In his major work on the Permanent Court he observed that the 'Statute of the Court fails to confer upon it an expressed mandate with reference to the application of international law',[54] and he added: 'This lacuna in the Statute does not obscure its general purpose that the Court should be an organ of international law.'[55] The decided cases which he proceeded to cite supported the point.[56] In *Certain German Interests in Polish Upper Silesia, Merits*, the Permanent Court spoke of 'the standpoint of Inter-

---

[51] 14 *UNCIO*, p. 843.
[52] Report of the Rapporteur (Nasrat Al-Farsy, Iraq) of Committee IV/I, 13 *UNCIO*, p. 392.
[53] M. O. Hudson 'The Twenty-Fourth Year of the World Court', *AJIL*, 40 (1946), p. 35.
[54] Hudson, *The Permanent Court*, p. 603, para. 545.
[55] *Ibid.*, p. 604.
[56] *Certain German Interests in Polish Upper Silesia, Merits, PCIJ, Series A, No. 7*, p. 19; the *Brazilian Loans* case, *PCIJ, Series A, No. 21*, p. 124; the *Free Zones* case, *PCIJ, Series A, No. 24*, p. 15, and *Series A/B, No. 46*, p. 138 (cf. *ibid*, p. 162); the *Serbian Loans* case, *PCIJ, Series A, No. 20*, pp. 19–20; the *Exchange of Populations* case, *PCIJ, Series B, No. 10*, p. 17; *Consistency of Certain Danzig Legislative Decrees with the Constitution of the Free City, PCIJ, Series A/B, No. 65*, p. 61 (Judge Anzilotti, 'la Cour a été créée pour être l'organe du droit international'); and the *'Lotus'* case, *PCIJ, Series A, No. 10*, pp. 16–18. And see *Oscar Chinn, PCIJ, Series A/B, No. 63*, p. 149 (Judge Schücking, dissenting, 'Our Court has been set up by the Covenant as the custodian of international law').

national Law and of the Court which is its organ'.[57] In the *Brazilian Loans* case it described itself as 'a tribunal of international law';[58] this description was noted by Judge Hudson in *Diversion of Water from the Meuse*.[59] The idea of the Permanent Court being an organ of international law was being floated by interested States before the Court was established. Thus, a Norwegian paper, placed before the 1920 Advisory Committee of Jurists, stated that the proposed Tribunal was 'intended to be one of the chief organs of international law in the future, an indispensable link in the framework of institutions established by the Covenant for the safeguarding of peace and for the development of international law'.[60] So far as the present Court is concerned, it is noteworthy that in the *Corfu Channel, Merits*, it considered itself as having a duty 'to ensure respect for international law, of which it is the organ'.[61]

One can see an argument as to whether subparagraphs *(a)* to *(d)* of Article 38, paragraph 1, of the Statute embrace the entirety of international law; it is difficult to see how it can be argued that, assuming that they do not, a principle which is part of international law may not be applied by the Court simply because it is not comprehended by those subparagraphs. The Court may not be the exclusive organ of international law, but, if it is an organ – and, at that, an important one – it is obliged to apply a rule which forms part of international law, even if it may be possible to argue that the rule is not comprehended by subparagraphs *(a)*, *(b)*, *(c)* and *(d)* of Article 38, paragraph 1, of the Statute.

Judicial *dicta* on the point

In his dissenting opinion in the *'Lotus'*, Judge Weiss put the case against judge-made international law thus:

International law is not created by an accumulation of opinions and systems; neither is its source a sum total of judgments, even if they agree with each other. Those are only methods of discovering some of its aspects, of finding some of its principles and of formulating these principles satisfactorily.

[57] *1926, PCIJ, Series A, No. 7*, p. 19.
[58] *1929, PCIJ, Series A, No. 21*, p. 124.
[59] *1937, PCIJ, Series A/B, No. 70*, p. 76.
[60] *Documents Presented*, 1920, p. 211.
[61] *ICJ Rep 1949*, p. 35.

In reality the only source of international law is the *consensus omnium*. Whenever it appears that all nations constituting the international community are in agreement as regards the acceptance or the application in their mutual relations of a specific rule of conduct, this rule becomes part of international law.[62]

Following in this line, in 1950 Judge Read declared that the Court 'is not a law-making organ'.[63] In the *Barcelona Traction* case, stating the opposite view just as flatly, Judge Armand-Ugon said: 'The Permanent Court and the International Court, which were created by States, have the capacity to lay down mandatory rules of law in the same way as any national legislature.'[64]

For what may be thought of as an interesting attempt to reconcile competing views, one may consider Judge Ammoun's statement reading:

The Court is not a law-making body. It declares the law. But it is a law discernible from the progress of humanity, not an obsolete law, a vestige of the inequalities between men, the domination and colonialism which were rife in international relationships up to the beginning of this century but are now disappearing, thanks to the struggle being waged by the peoples and to the extension to the ends of the world of the universal community of mankind.[65]

In Judge Krylov's view, 'The Court can only interpret and develop the international law in force; it can only adjudicate in conformity with international law.'[66] The problem remains of deciding whether the interpretation and development of 'the international law in force' can result in the creation of new law, and, if so, whether this is at variance with the duty of the Court 'to adjudicate in conformity with international law'.

It is, of course, not right to equate the Court with a legislature; but that does not end the argument. Judge Tanaka stated the position thus:

Undoubtedly, a court of law declares what is the law, but does not legislate. In reality, however, where the borderline can be drawn is a very delicate and difficult matter. Of course, judges declare the law, but they

---

[62] *PCIJ, Series A, No. 10*, pp. 43–44.
[63] *Peace Treaties, Second Phase, ICJ Rep 1950*, p. 244, dissenting opinion.
[64] *Barcelona Traction, Light and Power Company Limited, Preliminary Objections, ICJ Rep 1964*, p. 116, dissenting opinion.
[65] *Namibia, ICJ Rep 1971*, p. 72.
[66] *Reparation for Injuries Suffered in the Service of the United Nations, ICJ Rep 1949*, p. 219.

do not function automatically. We cannot deny the possibility of some degree of creative element in their judicial activities. What is not permitted to judges, is to establish law independently of an existing legal system, institution or norm. What is permitted to them is to declare what can be logically inferred from the *raison d'être* of a legal system, legal institution or norm. In the latter case the lacuna in the intent of legislation or parties can be filled.[67]

Somewhat similarly, President Winiarski remarked:

The function of the Court is to state the law as it is; it contributes to its development, but in the manner of a judicial body, for instance when it analyses out a rule contained by implication in another, or when, having to apply a rule to a specific instance, which is always individualized and with its own clear-cut features, it gives precision to the meaning of that rule, which is sometimes surrounded by what the great jurist, Vittorio Scialoja, called, without intending the expression critically, the *chiaroscuro* of international law.[68]

Though sparingly worded (and rightly so), these passages do not necessarily exclude the view that the Court has a limited power of creativity; their real force is directed to the scope within which the power is exercisable, a point taken up more fully later. A legislature, possibly after appropriate studies have been made, may enact legislation where no relevant law existed, or deliberately change the accepted law in radical ways. The Court cannot do that; it must proceed on the basis that the law which it lays down is somehow implicit in the existing legal system. However, when it has done so, it may well appear that, contrary to the asserted mode of operation, new law has in fact been made. And some of it could be significant; just as cases of great political or other consequences seldom result in much jurisprudence, it is often the position that important legal holdings can emerge from cases of modest proportions: 'cases need not have monumental outcomes to make monumental law'.[69] See, for example, the comparison made by Beckett[70] between the *Austro-German Customs Union* case[71] and the *Mavrommatis* case.[72]

---

[67] *South West Africa, Second Phase, ICJ Rep 1966*, p. 277, dissenting opinion.
[68] *ICJ Pleadings, the Temple of Preah Vihear*, II, p. 122.
[69] See Thomas M. Franck, 'World Made Law: The Decision of the ICJ in the Nuclear Test cases', *AJIL*, 69 (1975), p. 612.
[70] Fitzmaurice, *Law and Procedure*, I, p. xxviii.
[71] *1931, PCIJ, Series A/B, No. 41*.
[72] *1924, PCIJ, Series A, No. 2*, and *1925, PCIJ, Series A, No. 5*.

The Court itself has, of course, been careful never to assert a power to make law. But it has not always managed to avoid the use of language susceptible of the interpretation that it has such a power. In 1987, referring to previous advisory opinions given by it in 1973 and 1982 in administrative review proceedings, it said:

In those opinions the Court *established a principle* as to the scope of its action in response to such requests, and a limited exception to the principle in the case of one of the two grounds considered. In the case of the *Application for Review of Judgement No. 158 of the United Nations Administrative Tribunal*, the Court *established the principle* that the role of the Court in review proceedings is not to retry the case, . . .[73]

Thus, not only does the Court treat its decisions in the bulk as case law, but it may well regard a single opinion as *establishing* a legal *principle*, however modest this may be. It is possible to speak of the Court establishing a principle of law as opposed to the Court creating a principle;[74] but that opposition cannot apply here without much straining. If this is correct, then it is submitted that what the passage cited above suggests is that it is not right to suppose that the Court could develop the law (as no one doubts it could) without inevitably also creating some new law in the course of the developmental process. In *International Status of South West Africa* Judge McNair saw through the illusion when characterising part of the Court's holding as 'a piece of judicial legislation'.[75] Judge Alvarez had no doubt that *Reparation* was an act of judicial law-creation.[76] It is of course an exaggeration to suggest that the Court is a legislator; it is also an exaggeration to assert that it cannot create any law at all.

Scholarly opinion

Scholarly opinion is divided on the subject. Presenting a point of view which was probably reflective of the Continental approach, in 1924 Politis said, 'La nouvelle Cour doit se borner à 'dire' le droit. Elle n'a pas reçu le pouvoir d'aller au-delà, en 'faisant' le droit là

---

[73] *Application for Review of Judgment No. 333 of the United Nations Administrative Tribunal, ICJ Rep 1987*, p. 33, para. 27, emphasis added.
[74] See *Western Sahara, ICJ Rep 1975*, p. 77, para. 17, Judge Gros, declaration.
[75] *ICJ Rep 1950*, p. 162, separate opinion.
[76] *Asylum, ICJ Rep 1950*, p. 300.

où il n'existe pas.'[77] Striking a note of flexibility, he added, 'Mais dans l'application du droit en vigueur, elle peut pousser son examen jusqu'aux dernières limites.' But for him those limits were real enough to mean that the Court 'peut et même doit refuser de statuer en cas d'obscurité ou d'insuffisance du droit international'.[78] In his view, it was for this reason that Article 38 of the Statute gave the Court the faculty, if the parties agreed, to decide *ex aequo et bono*.[79] Putting it more picturesquely, five years later the Italian jurist Scialoja declared that he 'did not think that it had been the intention of those who created the Court that it should act as a factory of international law or that its judgments should build up a system of international law'.[80] The limits which he and Politis saw did not exist for Hersch Lauterpacht for the reason that in the view of the latter the Court was under a duty to avoid a *non liquet* – a concept the very existence of which he denied.[81]

Sørensen's view runs in the direction of holding that decisions of the Court can create law.[82] So does Lauterpacht's.[83] Fitzmaurice links the question whether a decision of the Court is a formal source of law to the question whether it 'is authoritative and binding'.[84] He states:

It is usually held that the decisions of international tribunals do not operate to create law in the same way that the judicial precedent does under certain systems of domestic law. That they are not in the strict sense formal sources of law can indeed hardly be contested: they are only binding on the parties to the dispute, and binding on them only for the purposes of the particular case; they need not be followed by other international tribunals, or even by the same tribunal in another case. These propositions are true equally of the International Court of Justice. Yet further reflexion seems to indicate that if such decisions cannot be classed as direct formal sources of law, it is also not

---

[77] Nicolas Politis, *La Justice internationale* (Paris, 1924), p. 169.
[78] *Ibid.*, p. 170.
[79] *Ibid.*
[80] Committee of Jurists on the Statute of the Permanent Court of International Justice, *Minutes of the Session held at Geneva, March 11th–19th, 1929* (Geneva, 1 May 1929), p. 33.
[81] See Fitzmaurice, *Law and Procedure*, II, p. 649; and Rosenne, *Law and Practice* (1985), pp. 98 and 605.
[82] Sørensen, *Les Sources*, pp. 174–175.
[83] Lauterpacht, *Development*, pp. 20–22.
[84] See Sir Gerald Fitzmaurice, 'Some Problems Regarding the Formal Sources of International Law', in *Symbolae Verzijl* (The Hague, 1958), p. 169.

satisfactory to regard them as being simply one amongst various material sources of law.[85]

He adds:

[I]t is suggested that the decisions of international tribunals, while no doubt of varying weight and authority, cannot be regarded simply as no more than one among various material sources of law. It is not so much that they necessarily possess a higher intrinsic value than, for instance, eminent juridical opinion, but that they have a more direct and immediate impact on the realities of international life, the attitude of States, and the mind of judges and arbitrators in later cases. A decision is a *fact*: an opinion, however cogent, remains an opinion. For these reasons it would seem that, if the judicial or arbitral decision is not, in the international field, technically a formal source of law, it must be regarded as having a special status that differentiates it from other material sources, and causes it to be at least a quasi-formal source. Alternatively decisions might, *qua* material sources, be characterized as 'formally material' – i.e., as sources which tribunals are bound to take into account, even if they are not bound to follow them; so that, if the tribunal concerned does not follow a given decision, it must at least be in a position to distinguish or refute it on specific grounds.[86]

These views have been characterised as evidencing some degree of theoretical hesitation;[87] but he does also say that 'even controversial [decisions] tend in the course of the years to be generally regarded as law'.[88] Parry trenches on the general subject but adopts no distinct position.[89]

Somewhat clearer is Waldock's view that, 'once the judicial function is admitted in any legal system, it operates, even if within narrow limits, as a creative source of law'.[90] Why must this be so? Because, in the words of Lord Wright, 'Judging is a practical matter, and an act of will. Notwithstanding all the

---

[85] Fitzmaurice, 'Some Problems', p. 170.

[86] *Ibid.*, pp. 172–173. And see, *ibid.*, pp. 154, 168, and, also by him, *Law and Procedure*, II, pp. 583–584.

[87] Maarten Bos, 'The Recognised Manifestations of International Law: A New Theory of "Sources" ', *Germ YBIL*, 20 (1977), p. 57.

[88] Fitzmaurice, *Law and Procedure*, I, p. xxxii.

[89] Clive Parry, *The Sources and Evidences of International Law* (Manchester/New York, 1965), pp. 91 ff.

[90] Waldock, 'General Course', p. 95.

apparatus of authority, the judge has nearly always some degree of choice.'[91] In exercising that choice he is inevitably selecting a rule to govern the case; if no suitable rule exists, he makes one, assuming, safely it is believed, that he cannot simply decline to decide on the ground of alleged absence of law. Either the new rule is law or it is not. If it is not, he has acted illegally, for he can only decide in accordance with law. But, this being so, the view enforces itself, notwithstanding some appearance of circularity, that the new rule, on being adopted by him, itself becomes part of the law. And why? Because, as it was put by Bishop Hoadly, 'whoever hath an *absolute authority* to *interpret* any written or spoken laws it is *he* who is the *Law-giver* to all intents and purposes and not the person who first wrote or spoke them'.[92] Some exaggeration does not diminish a certain core truth.

Writing in the early years of the life of the present Court, Alf Ross foreshadowed developments this way:

In Art. 38, No. 4, too, the judicial decision is not mentioned as an actual source but only as 'subsidiary means' to deciding what is law. Nevertheless it necessarily follows from the tendency of the law to regularity that precedents must exercise a decisive influence on later decisions. The reluctance to admit this is connected with the reluctance to concede that courts are law-creating. Hence the illusion that practice is merely 'subsidiary means', and not an actual source. And as a matter of fact courts as well as the authors constantly quote precedents in support of their results. In the face of this everything else is merely futile speculation. That this fact has not so far been recognised is connected with the circumstance that until quite recently there did not exist any permanent, organised court. It is understandable that arbitration tribunals instituted ad hoc have not the same authoritative binding force on each other as the decisions of a permanent court. There is reason to believe that gradually, as the number of precedents of the Permanent Court increases, an international judge-made law will be established by practice, a law which will be of the greatest importance by giving to International Law that stability in which it is now so wanting. Whether or not the court formally believes in the binding force of precedents is actually of no great consequence.[93]

---

[91] Lord Wright, *Legal Essays and Addresses* (1939), p. 25, cited in Dennis Lloyd, 'Reason and Logic in the Common Law', *LQR*, 64 (1948), p. 483.

[92] John Chipman Gray, *The Nature and Sources of Law* (New York, 1931), pp. 125, 172.

[93] Alf Ross, *A Textbook of International Law* (London, 1947), pp. 86–87.

However hesitant might have been the course of general recognition,[94] it is not much in doubt today that decisions of the Court can create law.[95] Chapter 12 of Lauterpacht's well-known work on *The Development of International Law by the International Court* is entitled, significantly, 'Judicial Legislation and the Jurisdiction of the Court'. There seems to be no convincing way of separating the Court from Brierly's general remark that the 'act of the court is a creative act, in spite of our conspiracy to represent it as something less'.[96]

Possible instances of judicial law-making

Identification of instances of judicial law-making is complicated by the fact that the Court itself, like all courts but perhaps more so in view of the fact that it is adjudicating between sovereign States, takes care to avoid expressions suggestive of judicial law-making; it prefers the use of terms indicating that all that is involved is a working out of the true meaning of existing legal principles, as, indeed, is broadly true. Thus, in the words of Lauterpacht, 'many an act of judicial legislation may in fact be accomplished under the guise of the ascertainment of customary international law'.[97] These considerations may lend special interest to an examination of particular instances of judicial law-making. However, such an examination would seem more appro-

---

[94] See Clive Parry, *The Sources and Evidences of International Law* (Manchester/New York, 1965), pp. 93–94.

[95] Beckett, 'Jurisprudence', pp. 139–140; Brierly, 'Règles générales du droit de la paix', pp. 78–79; Alf Ross, *A Textbook of International Law* (London, 1947), pp. 79–80, 86–87; Edvard Hambro, 'The Reasons behind the Decisions of the International Court of Justice', *Current Legal Problems*, 7 (1954), p. 218; Edvard Hambro, 'Function of the International Court of Justice in the Framework of the International Legal Order', in G. H. J. van der Molen et al. (eds.), *The United Nations Ten Years' Legal Progress* (London, 1956), pp. 105–106; E. Lauterpacht, 'The Development of the Law of International Organization by the Decisions of International Tribunals', *Hag R*, 152 (1976–IV), p. 387; Maarten Bos, 'The Recognised Manifestations of International Law: A New Theory of "Sources" ', *Germ YBIL*, 20 (1977), p. 60; Oscar Schachter, 'The Nature and Process of Legal Development in International Society', in R. St J. Macdonald and D. M. Johnston (eds.), *The Structure and Process of International Law* (Dordrecht, 1986), p. 767; and Pierre-Marie Dupuy, 'Le juge et la règle générale', *RGDIP*, 1989, p. 566.

[96] Sir Hersch Lauterpacht and C. H. M. Waldock, *The Basis of Obligation in International Law and other Papers of the late James Leslie Brierly* (Oxford, 1958), p. 98.

[97] Lauterpacht, *Development*, p. 368.

priate to a work dealing with the case law of the Court; the present effort is limited to the system of precedents governing the use of that case law. There are places in which the question of law-making by the Court may be pursued. Possible areas include reservations to multilateral treaties, the functioning of the United Nations, its capacity to claim reparation against a State for injuries sustained by one of its agents in the course of performing his duties, *forum prorogatum*, the *erga omnes* principle, maritime delimitation and other fields.[98]

Conclusion and caveat

There is general agreement that the Court has power, and indeed a responsibility, to develop the law. Some authors, who freely acknowledge this, tend delicately to terminate the discussion at that point without stating clearly whether or not the power to develop includes a power to create. Others, who accept that development includes creation, stress, rightly, the limited nature of the latter or the particular sense in which it occurs. Thus, in the words of Judge Jennings, 'Even where a court creates law in the sense of developing, adapting, modifying, filling gaps, interpreting, or even branching out in a new direction, the decision must be seen to emanate reasonably and logically from existing and previously ascertainable law. A court has no purely legislative competence.'[99] That is of course correct; but the molecular nature of the activity does not obscure its creative character. As has been earlier argued, it is difficult to visualise a process of development which does not at some point eventuate in creation. That point, it is submitted, is located within the judicial process itself and is represented by some particular decision or decisions of the Court.

[98] See, generally, *Asylum, ICJ Rep 1950*, pp. 300–301, Judge Alvarez; *Fisheries (United Kingdom v. Norway), ICJ Rep 1951*, p. 146, Judge Alvarez; R. P. Anand, *Studies in International Adjudication* (Delhi, 1969), pp. 173 ff; Lauterpacht, *Development*, p. 179, and chapter 12; Alejandro Alvarez, *Le Droit international nouveau, son acceptation – son étude* (Paris, 1960), pp. 87–89; Manfred Lachs, 'Some Reflections on the Contribution of the International Court of Justice to the Development of International Law', *Syracuse Journal of International Law and Commerce*, 10 (1983), p. 239; and, also by him, 'Thoughts on the Recent Jurisprudence of the International Court of Justice', *Emory International Law Review*, 4 (1990), p. 92.

[99] Sir Robert Jennings, 'The Judicial Function and The Rule of Law', in *International Law at the Time of its Codification, Essays in Honour of Roberto Ago*, 4 Vols. (Milan, 1987), III, p. 145.

It is necessary, however, to return to the problem mentioned at the beginning of this chapter and to give thought to the remark of Judge Gros that 'the Court's Statute and mission make of it neither a universal judge nor a universal provider of advisory opinions'.[100] Several tribunals being at work in a non-hierarchical situation, there is force in the argument that a new rule adopted in a particular decision by a particular tribunal does not immediately become part of international law. Different tribunals could adopt different rules; two different rules on the same point cannot both form part of international law at the same time.[101] Some other process will have to determine which, if either, eventually acquires the status of a rule of international law. The problem would be particularly noticeable where different holdings are made by major international tribunals exercising coordinate jurisdiction in the same field; and there are more of these today than yesterday.[102] To say that a holding made by one such tribunal creates law even if it is at variance with a holding by another is a matter of difficulty. The difficulty is obvious to the observer viewing the international legal system as a whole; it is however less apparent to a permanent judicial body considering the law as enunciated in its own previous decisions. It is accordingly stressed that all that is sought to be done here is to view the matter as it might be seen from the standpoint of a particular court, without of course presuming to speak for it.

On this approach, it has to be recognised that the conclusion that a new rule adopted by the World Court may only be acted on (consistently with the Court's Statute) on the basis that it forms part of international law is valid only from the point of view of the

[100] *Application for Review of Judgment No. 158 of the United Nations Administrative Tribunal, ICJ Rep 1973*, p. 257, para. 15. And see, André Gros, 'La Cour internationale de Justice 1946–1986: Les réflexions d'un juge', in Y. Dinstein (ed.), *International Law at a Time of Perplexity* (Dordrecht, 1989), p. 305.

[101] *Electricity Company of Sofia and Bulgaria, 1939, PCIJ, Series A/B, No. 77*, p. 90, Judge Anzilotti. As to the different question of conflicts between treaty norms, see Charles Rousseau, 'De la compatibilité des normes juridiques contradictoires dans l'ordre international', *RGDIP*, 39 (1932), p. 133, and Emmanuel Roucounas, 'Engagements parallèles et contradictoires', *Hag R*, 206 (1987–VI), p. 21.

[102] See, generally, Gilbert Guillaume, *The Future of International Judicial Institutions*, The Wilberforce Lecture, 11 May 1995, in which he called attention to 'the danger of divergences resulting from the proliferation of tribunals, courts, and quasi-judicial bodies'. See *ICLQ*, 44 (1995), p. 862.

Court itself. Thus, the status of the new rule as a fully established part of international law may well be challenged; however, before the Court the challenge is not likely to get far.

There is force in an argument which would differentiate the municipal position on the ground that a domestic court derives power ultimately from the sovereignty of the State and is, by implication, clothed by the State with power to make law where necessary for the disposal of a case; there is no comparable sovereign source from which the World Court can derive similar power. It may, however, be answered that States constituting the international community (as parties to the Statute now effectively do) have, by establishing and maintaining the Court as a permanent and global court of justice, likewise impliedly empowered it to make law where necessary for the disposal of a case, as courts of justice generally can. This, possibly, was the reasoning behind Judge Armand-Ugon's somewhat bold statement, cited above, that the 'Permanent Court and the International Court, *which were created by States*, have the capacity to lay down mandatory rules of law in the same way as any national legislature'[103] – not of course to the same extent, but only 'in the same way' so far as the making of a mandatory rule is concerned, the permissible extent being determined by the necessities of the particular case.

The World Court is permanent; its judges are globally drawn; its litigating constituency is also global, practically all States being parties to its Statute. Under special procedures, States which are not members of the United Nations are in a position to submit their disputes to it.[104] It was always regarded as an organ of international law; as has been shown, the point was intended to be emphasised by a 1945 revision of the introductory part of Article 38, paragraph 1, of the Statute. Five years later President Basdevant remarked that the Court was 'the world's leading judicial organisation'.[105] Huber described it as 'la suprême magistrature internationale'.[106] Counsel at the bar of the Court not infrequently treat it

---

[103] *Barcelona Traction, Light and Power Company, Limited, Preliminary Objections, ICJ Rep 1964*, p. 116, dissenting opinion, emphasis added.
[104] Hermann Mosler, 'The International Court of Justice at its Present Stage of Development', *Dalhousie Law Journal*, 5 (1979), pp. 545–546.
[105] *ICJYB, 1950–1951*, p. 17.
[106] *Annuaire de l'Institut de Droit international*, 45 (1954–II), p. 62.

that way. In the words of Mr Fitzmaurice, 'the Court is a World Court';[107] in those of Professor Quentin-Baxter, it is 'the principal judicial organ of the international community';[108] and in those of Professor R.-J. Dupuy, 'vous êtes de toutes les juridictions celle qui se situe à l'échelon suprême'.[109] It was not without reason that Verzijl referred to it as 'the World Court, the supreme Court of the international community against whose judgments no higher recourse is conceivable'.[110] In the view of Judge Mosler, it is 'the general court of the community of nations' and is 'in a better position to contribute to developing international law than any other court or arbitrator in the world'.[111] Its competence in this respect is of course limited, for the reason that

[t]he Court's outstanding task is the preservation of the unity of international law. Since the Court is the only judicial institution of general international law without any limitation with regard to groups of States or to special treaty law, it has to apply international law as a single coherent body of norms applicable to any legal relations between the States constituting the international society.[112]

That consideration rightly operates as a restraint; but it also means that, so far as the Court is concerned, a statement by it as to what is the law is of universal applicability.

Nor should this be strange. Jules Basdevant recalls: 'Lorsqu'en 1907, James Brown Scott, dans son rapport sur le projet d'une Cour de Justice internationale, disait de celle-ci: "Une telle Cour prononcera ses arrêts de par l'autorité des Nations Unies"; il employait des termes que reprend à peu près l'article 92 de la Charte de San Francisco lorsqu'il dit: "La Cour internationale de Justice constitue l'organe judiciaire principal des Nations Unies".'[113] The intent of

---

[107] *ICJ Pleadings, Interpretation of Peace Treaties with Bulgaria, Hungary and Romania*, p. 296.

[108] *ICJ Pleadings, Nuclear Tests*, II, p. 132.

[109] *ICJ Pleadings, Application for Revision and Interpretation of the Judgment of 24 February 1982 in the case concerning the* Continental Shelf (Tunisia/Libyan Arab Jamahiriya), p. 187.

[110] J. H. W. Verzijl, *International Law in Historical Perspective* (Leiden, 1976), VIII, p. 576.

[111] Hermann Mosler, 'The International Court of Justice at its Present Stage of Development', *Dalhousie Law Journal*, 5 (1979), p. 546.

[112] *Ibid.*, p. 550.

[113] 'Cinquantième anniversaire de la Première Conférence de la Paix: La Haye 18 mai 1899, Discours commémoratif prononcé le 18 mai 1949 par M. J. Basdevant', *RGDIP*, 1949, p. 280.

that provision may in turn be grasped in the light of the statement in Article 36, paragraph 2, of the Charter 'that legal disputes should as a general rule be referred by the parties to the International Court of Justice in accordance with the provisions of the Statute of the Court'. Not surprisingly, Judge Lachs remarked that the 'Court can be said to be not only the judicial organ of the United Nations but of the whole international community'.[114] Speaking of Waldock, Brownlie remarks that 'when in the *Anglo-French Continental Shelf* case the United Kingdom presented arguments very similar to those he had made as Counsel in 1969, Waldock, as arbitrator, rejected them'.[115] The observation testifies to Waldock's professionalism; it also calls attention to the extent to which other tribunals defer to the jurisprudence of the Court.

Thus, even though it may be open to a State to take the position that a new holding by the Court is not part of international law, the practical enjoyment of that right is not likely to mean much before the Court. It is believed that traces of a corresponding idea are to be found in the following passage from *Oppenheim*:

Article 2(6) of the Charter of the United Nations lays down that the Organisation shall ensure that states which are not members of the United Nations act in accordance with the principles of the Organisation so far as may be necessary for the maintenance of international peace and security. This is a mandatory provision which, upon analysis, constitutes a claim to regulate the conduct of non-members to the extent required for the fulfilment of the object of that Article. It cannot be admitted that the International Court of Justice or any other organ of the United Nations established under the Charter would be at liberty to hold that action taken in pursuance of Article 2 is contrary to international law.[116]

As Cardozo remarked, 'We may try to see things as objectively as we please. None the less, we can never see them with any eyes except our own.'[117] The Court can only see international law within the perspective in which it is functioning. It is always free to review

---

[114] Manfred Lachs, 'Jurisdictional Organs (Organization and Procedure)', in René-Jean Dupuy (ed.), *A Handbook on International Organizations* (Dordrecht, 1988), p. 147.
[115] Ian Brownlie, 'The Calling of the International Lawyer: Sir Humphrey Waldock and his Work', *BYBIL*, 54 (1983), p. 34.
[116] *Oppenheim* (9th edn), I, Pt 2, p. 1264, para. 627, footnote omitted.
[117] Benjamin Cardozo, *The Nature of the Judicial Process* (New Haven, 1921), p. 13, cited in *South West Africa, ICJ Rep 1966*, p. 434, footnote 2, Judge Jessup, dissenting opinion.

a previous decision and to depart from it for good reason; but, until changed, so far as it is concerned, the law in a decided case is the law of the Court. For all purposes of the Court, it is international law.

8

Stare decisis

Stare decisis does not apply

A leading English work says that the 'general orthodox interpretation of *stare decisis* ... is *stare rationibus decisis* ("keep to the *rationes decidendi* of past cases")'.[1] It is not in dispute that the doctrine does not apply in relation to the Court.[2] There is a broad reason of principle why it should not. Grisel put it thus: '[Q]uelque souhaitable que paraisse la stabilité dans n'importe quel ordre juridique, celui des Nations a aussi besoin d'une certaine souplesse, qui permette de prendre en compte la diversité des circonstances et qui est d'ailleurs en harmonie avec l'extrême décentralisation du pouvoir dans la société internationale.'[3] Whatever might have been the *ratio decidendi* of the *Status of Eastern Carelia*, the literature makes it clear that the contemporary understanding was that the holding could later be departed from precisely because *stare decisis* did not apply; this lack of assurance as to the precise status of the holding was one of the reasons for United States reservations on the question of acceding to the Protocol of Signature of the Statute of the Court.[4]

In chapter 2 reference was made to remarks in the jurisprudence about the importance of maintaining consistency in holdings. Some

[1] Cross and Harris, *Precedent*, p. 100.
[2] Maarten Bos, 'The Interpretation of International Judicial Decisions', *Revista Española de Derecho Internacional*, 33 (1981) p. 46.
[3] Etienne Grisel, '*Res judicata*: l'autorité de la chose jugée en droit international', in Bernard Dutoit (ed.), *Mélanges Georges Perrin* (Lausanne, 1984), p. 141.
[4] See Michael Dunne, *The United States and the World Court, 1920–1935* (London, 1988), p. 111, citing Judge Moore's view. As to the relevant reservation, see footnote 2, chapter 2, at p. 13 *supra*.

of the observations are strong; but they do not amount to an endorsement of the strict doctrine of binding precedent. Take the case of Judge Read. In 1952 he said:

Article 38 of the Statute is mandatory, and not discretionary. It requires the Court to apply judicial decisions as a subsidiary means for the determination of rules of law. The expression 'judicial decisions' certainly includes the jurisprudence of this Court and of the Permanent Court. I have no doubt that it includes the principles applied by the Court as the basis of its decisions. It is, however, equally clear that it cannot possibly be construed as requiring this Court to apply *obiter dicta*.[5]

Although observing that Judge Read 'in more than one case has used the language of being actually bound by former decisions',[6] Fitzmaurice correctly accepted that, in the passage cited above, Judge Read did not intend 'to go so far as to suggest that the Court was bound by precedent in the sense that it must actually *decide* the pending case in accordance with any applicable precedent not distinguishable on valid grounds'.[7] Judge Read noted that Article 38, paragraph 1 *(d)*, was mandatory in requiring the Court to 'apply ... judicial decisions', including those of the Court itself; but nothing in the requirement, or in what he said, suggests that such decisions are to apply with the force of binding precedent. In 1950 he had already made it clear that his view was that decisions of the Permanent Court of International Justice were not binding 'in the sense in which decisions may be binding in common-law countries'.[8] Speaking of the principle that a State is not allowed to profit from its own wrong, he said:

There can be no doubt as to the law on this point. It was settled by the Permanent Court in Judgment No. 8: Series A, No. 9. The Factory at Chorzów (Claim for Indemnity) (Jurisdiction), at page 31. No reasons have been submitted, in the Written Statements or Observations or during the oral argument, on which any distinction in principle between the two cases could be based or which would justify the rejection of the legal principles adopted and applied in that case.[9]

Thus, Judge Read was prepared to decline to apply a precedent not only if it could be distinguished, but also if there were any reasons

[5] *Anglo-Iranian Oil Co., ICJ Rep 1952*, p. 143, dissenting opinion.
[6] Fitzmaurice, *Law and Procedure*, II, p. 583.
[7] *Ibid.*, p. 584.
[8] *Peace Treaties, ICJ Rep 1950*, p. 233.
[9] *Ibid.*, p. 244, dissenting opinion.

'which would justify the rejection of the legal principles adopted and applied in that case', words which would *prima facie* comprehend a right to review the correctness of those principles. The existence of that right means that *stare decisis* does not apply.

Stare decisis and the Statute

However, while it is universally accepted that *stare decisis* does not apply in relation to the Court, there has been some controversy over the question whether its exclusion is the result of Article 59 of the Statute. Conceding that this provision does not operate to bar the precedential effect of decisions of the Court, some arguments nevertheless hold that it prevents decisions from exerting precedential effect with binding force. If correct, this would mean that, in the absence of that provision, the doctrine of binding precedent would have applied. It would in turn follow that the draft Statute as presented by the Advisory Committee of Jurists incorporated the doctrine, the latter being eventually shut out only by the action of the Council and the Assembly of the League of Nations in inserting Article 57*bis* (now Article 59) as well as the prefatory words 'Subject to the provisions of Article 57*bis*', which were introduced in Article 38, paragraph 4.

If Article 57*bis* was directed only to the 'binding force' of a decision in the sense of *chose jugée*, and not to the 'binding force' of decisions as precedents, then, since Article 38, paragraph 4, was concerned only with the use of decisions as precedents, the two provisions would be operating in different fields and there should have been no need for the saving reference in Article 38, paragraph 4, to Article 57*bis*. The fact that it was considered necessary to introduce the saving reference suggests that the League of Nations, as the final architects of the Statute, thought that, but for the saving reference, the two provisions would have collided over common ground. This is some argument for saying that Article 57*bis* (now Article 59) was directed to excluding *stare decisis*. Was this the object?

As has been argued above, Article 59 is not concerned one way or another with the precedential effect of decisions; *a fortiori*, it has no bearing on the question whether decisions exert precedential effect with binding force. The language of the Article is not apt to encompass the use or non-use of judicial decisions as binding precedents. One may speak of a judicial decision, *qua* judicial decision, being binding on the parties. It is not usual to speak of a judicial decision, *qua* precedent, being binding on the parties. The effect of a judicial decision, *qua* judicial decision, is exerted directly on the parties; the effect of a judicial decision, *qua* precedent, is exerted not directly on the parties, but on the shape of general international law. A judicial decision binds the parties in the sense that it constitutes an authoritative definition of their legal relations on the particular matter in dispute by the application of the law to the facts of the specific case; general international law, on which the precedential force of judicial decisions is exerted, applies to all States, but it does not, by itself, operate to impose on them a judicial definition of their relations on any particular matter. Thus, Article 59 could not have been contemplating the force with which decisions of the Court would exert precedential effect when it said that the 'decision of the Court has no binding force except between the parties and in respect of that particular case'. The distinction is between the juridical force of a decision, which is confined to the parties to the case, and its general jurisprudential effect on international law, which is of wider import. As was pointed out by Judge *ad hoc* Guggenheim, 'The scope of the judicial decision extends beyond the effects provided for in Article 59 of the Statute.'[10] Or, in the words of Judge Jessup, 'the influence of the Court's decisions is wider than their binding force'.[11]

It has to be remembered that the reference to 'judicial decisions' in Article 38, paragraph 1 (*d*), includes decisions of tribunals other than the International Court of Justice.[12] It is equally clear that the reference in that provision to Article 59 relates only to decisions of the Court. Assuming that this reference operates to prevent decisions of the Court from exerting precedential effect with binding force, the decisions of other courts and tribunals presumably

---

[10] *Nottebohm, ICJ Rep 1955*, p. 61, dissenting opinion.

[11] *Barcelona Traction, Light and Power Company, Limited, ICJ Rep 1970*, p. 163, para. 9. See also, by him, *ibid.*, p. 220, para. 106; separate opinion of Judge Nagendra Singh in *Aegean Sea Continental Shelf, ICJ Rep 1978*, pp. 46–47; *ICJ Pleadings, Delimitation of the Maritime Boundary in the Gulf of Maine Area*, IV, p. 100, para. 234, Counter-Memorial of the United States; and *Continental Shelf (Libyan Arab Jamahiriya/Malta), ICJ Rep 1984*, pp. 157–158, Judge Jennings, dissenting.

[12] See, *inter alia*, Lauterpacht, 'Schools of Thought in International Law', p. 57; Clive Parry, *The Sources and Evidences of International Law* (Manchester/New York, 1965), p. 94; and *Anglo-Iranian Oil Co., ICJ Rep 1952*, p. 143, Judge Read, dissenting.

stand on higher ground, not being caught by the Article 59 limitation. The consequence is so improbable as to suggest that the interpretation on which it rests cannot be correct.[13]

Conceivably, the drafting of the provisions under consideration was not as clear as hindsight would have liked. A solvent of the problem which they present may well be found in the fact that, as remarked above, the draftsman occasionally puts in words out of abundant caution even if regrettably they sometimes open up another aspect of the controversy they were intended to shut out. Just as it appears that Article 59 was itself inserted out of abundant caution, there seems to be a case for holding that the reference to Article 59 in Article 38, paragraph 1 *(d)*, was also an *ex abundanti cautela* provision[14] intended to affirm what in any event would have been the position, namely, that the general precedential effect of a judicial decision was to be distinguished from its binding juridical effect on the relations between the particular parties to the case. Neither of the two provisions was directed to the question of *stare decisis*.

The rules of interpretation discountenance a construction which gives no effect to the provision being interpreted; but the rules are not always violated when a provision is interpreted as directed to achieving an object for which it was not strictly necessary. The argument of surplusage is not always decisive.[15] The law is familiar with the concept of provisions enacted out of abundant caution. A provision so enacted is neither meaningless nor without effect; all that happens is that the effect which it produces is the same as that produced by some existing element of the legal system.

It cannot be said that the saving reference in Article 38, paragraph 1 *(d)*, to Article 59 is altogether without difficulty. It seems, however, to be a reasonable way of explaining the relationship between the two provisions to say, as one writer puts it, that 'la référence qui est faite au deuxième par le premier indique que l'article 38 concerne l'effet des décisions judiciaires au-delà de la

---

[13] See Edvard Hambro, 'The Reasons behind the Decisions of the International Court of Justice', *Current Legal Problems*, 7 (1954), p. 218.

[14] See, generally, Jennings, 'General Course', pp. 338–341.

[15] See, in English law, *Re Samuel*: 'It is not a conclusive argument as to the construction of an earlier Act to say that unless it be construed in a particular way a later Act would be surplusage. The later Act may have been designed, *ex abundanti cautela*, to remove possible doubts'; [1913] AC 514, 526, PC, cited in *Craies on Statute Law*, 7th edn. (London, 1971), p. 148.

sphère précisée par l'article 59, et que cet effet 'exorbitant' ne saurait être confondu avec celui, obligatoire *inter partes*, de la chose jugée internationale, basé sur la volonté commune des parties en différend'.[16]

Judicial *dicta* on the point

In 1926, while making it clear that Article 59 did 'not exclude purely declaratory judgments', the Permanent Court of International Justice added that the 'object of the article is simply to prevent legal principles accepted by the Court in a particular case from being binding upon other States or in other disputes'.[17] This, accepted literally, might seem to suggest that the object of Article 59 was to exclude the system of binding precedents. The passage was referred to in later cases.[18] In 1984 Judge Jennings considered it in the following way:

The Court begins its discussion of Article 59 by citing the observation of the Permanent Court of International Justice (*Series A, No. 13*, p. 21) that 'the object of Article 59 is simply to prevent legal principles accepted by the Court in a particular case from being binding also upon other States or in other disputes' (see paragraph 42 of the Judgment). This is no more than to say that the principles of decision of a judgment are not binding in the sense that they might be in some common law systems through a more or less rigid system of binding precedents. But the slightest acquaintance with the jurisprudence of this Court shows that Article 59 does by no manner of means exclude the force of persuasive precedent. So the idea that Article 59 is protective of third States' interests in this sense at least is illusory.

Alternatively, Article 59 may be considered as applying, as it clearly does also, more particularly to the *dispositif* of a judgment; and it is true that the particular rights and obligations created by the *dispositif* are addressed, and only addressed, to the parties to the case, and in respect only of that case. And in that quite particular and technical sense, Italy will certainly be protected. This is an important protection, and it would be quite wrong to suggest otherwise.[19]

---

[16] Condorelli, 'L'Autorité', p. 309.

[17] *Certain German Interests in Polish Upper Silesia, Merits, 1926, PCIJ, Series A, No. 7*, p. 19.

[18] *Interpretation of Judgments Nos. 7 and 8 (Factory at Chorzów), 1927, PCIJ, Series A, No. 13*, pp. 20–21; and the *Continental Shelf (Libyan Arab Jamahiriya/Malta), ICJ Rep 1984*, p. 26.

[19] *Continental Shelf (Libyan Arab Jamahiriya/Malta), ICJ Rep 1984*, p. 157, para. 27.

So, in the first paragraph, Judge Jennings considered that Article 59 was saying 'that the principles of decision of a judgment are not binding in the sense that they might be in some common law systems through a more or less rigid system of binding precedents'. Preference may be given to the alternative view stated in the second paragraph, to the effect that Article 59 applies to the *dispositif* of a judgment; it was not addressed to the question of *stare decisis*.

It is difficult to deny that judicial *dicta* are not free from difficulty; but they do not as a whole support the view that the object of Article 59 of the Statute was the exclusion of *stare decisis*.

Scholarly opinion

The matter was put this way by Beckett:

On a quelquefois pensé que l'article 59 était en complète contradiction avec la thèse que je viens d'exposer, à savoir que les déclarations de la Cour sur les points de droit pouvaient être considérées comme des sources de droit international d'une très grande autorité. Une telle opinion, cependant, est, à mon avis, basée sur une incompréhension du sens de l'article 59. L'article 59 se réfère à la *'décision'* de la Cour, – et ces mots signifient, il me semble, le dispositif de l'arrêt, – par exemple une décision que le sens d'une certaine stipulation d'un traité déterminé est tel ou tel, ou une décision que, dans des circonstances données, un Etat A a traité les nationaux de l'Etat B d'une manière contraire au droit international, et doit, par conséquent, payer de ce chef des dommages-intérêts, etc. L'article 59 stipule que la 'décision' dans ce sens-là n'a force obligatoire qu'entre les parties en litige et que dans le cas qui a été décidé. Par les mots 'force obligatoire', j'entends 'force de chose jugée'. Telle est la règle générale dans tous les systèmes de droit interne. C'est même une règle de simple bon sens. Elle prévaut également dans tous les pays où la force obligatoire des précédents comme source du droit est amplement reconnue, tels que l'Angleterre. L'article 59 traite de la force obligatoire de la 'décision' en tant que *jugement*. Il n'envisage pas les énoncés de points de droit que la Cour peut faire en indiquant les bases (ou les motifs) de ses décisions, parties des arrêts de la Cour qui peuvent seules être considérées comme sources de droit d'après l'article 38.

Il est vrai que la Cour dit, dans un passage de l'un de ses arrêts concernant l'article 59, que *'son but est seulement d'éviter que des principes juridiques admis par la Cour dans une affaire déterminée soient obligatoires pour d'autres Etats ou d'autres litiges'*.[20] Mais toute la pratique de la Cour à laquelle je me suis

---

[20] *PCIJ, Series A, No. 7*, p. 19.

référé plus haut est en contradiction avec l'opinion que la Cour ait voulu qu'une de ses décisions ne soit pas une source de droit d'après l'article 38 – bien que cette déclaration puisse signifier que l'article 59 s'oppose à ce que la Cour soit légalement liée par ses propres arrêts, en tant que précédents, comme c'est le cas pour un tribunal anglais. Mais je pense que les 'principes juridiques admis par la Cour' dans ce passage se rapportent réellement à la décision (le dispositif) elle-même en opposition avec le raisonnement sur lequel elle est fondée, et que les mots 'soient obligatoires' signifient avoir force de 'chose jugée' (res judicata). L'arrêt relatif à l'interprétation des arrêts nos. 7 et 8[21] me semble démontrer que la Cour ne considère pas elle-même que les motifs sur lesquels l'arrêt est fondé sont comme tels obligatoires, même entre les parties comme res judicata, bien qu'ils indiquent, s'il y a lieu, l'étendue et le vrai sens du dispositif.[22]

Thus, in speaking of the binding force of a decision, Article 59 contemplated the *dispositif*, and not the *motifs* of a decision. It is possible, notwithstanding the last sentences from Beckett, that there is a limited, but distinguishable, sense in which it may be said that the provision operates to exclude the *motifs* from exerting binding force on non-parties. The *motifs* of a judgment may explain the *dispositif*; to the extent that they do, they exert an effect which attracts the binding force of the judgment as *chose jugée*.[23] Article 59 then restricts to the parties the binding force of the *motifs* in so far as they thus explain the *dispositif* and form part of it.[24] But the provision is not concerned, one way or another, with the larger question whether a decision exerts precedential effect with binding force.

In considering that decisions of the Court do not apply as binding precedents, Fitzmaurice says:

Article 38, paragraph 1 *(d)*, of the Statute would itself preclude that, not so much because it states judicial decisions to be a 'subsidiary means for the determination of rules of law', but because it is prefaced with the words 'Subject to the provisions of Article 59' – the effect of which is that the decisions of the Court are binding only for the parties and for the particular case.[25]

---

[21] *PCIJ, Series A, No. 13*, pp. 10–12.

[22] Beckett, 'Jurisprudence', pp. 140–142.

[23] See below, at p. 163; and Judge Koretsky, dissenting, in *South West Africa, ICJ Rep 1966*, p. 241.

[24] Cf. Libya's argument 'that for the purposes of Article 62 [of the Statute], the 'decision' of the Court referred to in the English text of that Article does not include the *consideranda* of the judgement'. See *Continental Shelf (Tunisia/Libyan Arab Jamahiriya), Application for Permission to Intervene, ICJ Rep 1981*, p. 10, para. 15.

[25] Fitzmaurice, *Law and Procedure*, II, p. 584.

As argued above, it was not, however, the object of the saving reference in Article 38, paragraph 1 *(d)*, to Article 59 to exclude the doctrine of binding precedent[26] in the sense that, in the absence of that reference, the doctrine would have applied. Even without Article 59, and therefore even without the saving reference to it in Article 38, paragraph 1 *(d)*, there was nothing in the draft Statute which could operate to attract the doctrine. McNair's views seem consistent with this. He says:

At first sight it might appear that Article 59 of the Statute of the Court might have been designed to exclude the binding force of precedents. . . .

But an examination of the drafting of the Statute negatives any such design, whatever may have been its effect. It appears that this article is closely linked with Article 63 (giving a right of intervention), is to some extent complementary to it, and has a history that goes back at least to 1899. It does not appear to have originated as a Continental protest and safeguard against the English doctrine of judicial precedent but to have been inspired by a wider (though not entirely dissimilar) purpose; namely, to prevent a State which has not intervened in a suit from being bound by the decision given in it 'and any ulterior conclusions to which that decision may seem to point'.[27]

In sum, Article 59 was not directed to the possible precedential value of a decision; *a fortiori*, there can be no question of the provision being directed to excluding the doctrine of binding precedent. The provision simply had no bearing on the question whether the doctrine was applicable or inapplicable. The doctrine is, indeed, inapplicable, but the provision is not the reason. The doctrine was peculiar to a particular municipal legal system; it was not part of the thinking on which the Court was constructed.

To hold that the Court can create law does not imply that *stare decisis* applies

Some part of the hesitation to regard a decision adopting a new principle as creative of new law seems to stem from apprehension

---

[26] Cf. S. Rosenne, 'Article 27 of the Statute of the International Court of Justice', *Virg JIL*, 32 (1991), p. 229.

[27] Sir Arnold Duncan McNair, *The Development of International Justice* (New York, 1954), p. 13. A footnote to the passage refers to Lauterpacht, 'Schools of Thought in International Law', pp. 52–61; Mr Balfour and M. Leon Bourgeois in *Documents concerning the Action Taken by the Council of the League of Nations*, 1921, at pp. 38 and 50; Stauffenberg, Cross and De Janasz, *Statut et règlement de la Cour Permanente de Justice Internationale* (Institut für ausländisches öffentliches

that to take that view is necessarily to imply that the doctrine of *stare decisis* applies in relation to the Court. It is submitted that this would not follow. A precedent may well be law even if *stare decisis* does not apply on the common law model.

First, the existence of *stare decisis* is not a precondition to the creation of judge-made law. Even in England, the doctrine did not always have the rigidity which came to be associated with it in the late nineteenth and early twentieth centuries;[28] over the greater part of its history, it seems to have rested merely on a practice of following previous decisions, and not on a rule of law requiring previous decisions to be followed.[29] The crystallisation of the strict rule was a relatively late occurrence; by contrast, the existence of judge-made law went further back. The doctrine, which is not at variance with judicial impartiality or independence,[30] still of course applies in England, but subject to a considerable modification effected at the top by the 1966 House of Lords Practice Statement. In fact, signs of a relaxation of the doctrine, as it operated in the House, had been in evidence in the period running up to the issuing of the Practice Statement.[31] Speaking, at an even earlier stage, of the 'extreme doctrine whereby a decision once given can never be overruled', Fachiri was able to observe that even 'in Common-Law countries this only applies to decisions of the House of Lords, and not to those of the Privy Council or the Supreme Court of the United States'.[32] According to the 1966 Practice Statement, previous decisions of the House are treated by it 'as normally binding', but this is subject to a right 'to depart from a previous decision

Recht und Völkerrecht of Berlin, 1934), pp. 419–24; and Hudson, *The Permanent Court*, p. 207.

[28] See W. S. Holdsworth, *A History of English Law*, 3rd edn, (London, 1924), IV, pp. 220 ff; T. F. T. Plucknett, *A Concise History of the Common Law*, 4th edn (London, 1948), pp. 324–332; and Cross and Harris, *Precedent*, p. 24.

[29] See and compare Laurence Goldstein, 'Some Problems about Precedent', *CLJ*, 43 (1984), p. 88; Jim Evans, 'The Status of Rules of Precedent: A Brief Reply', *ibid.*, p. 108; and Jim Evans, 'Change in the Doctrine of Precedent during the Nineteenth Century', in Laurence Goldstein (ed.), *Precedent in Law* (Oxford, 1987), at pp. 35–37 and 45.

[30] J. E. S. Fawcett, *The Application of the European Convention on Human Rights* (Oxford, 1987), p. 173.

[31] See Gerald Dworkin, '*Stare Decisis* in the House of Lords', *MLR*, 25 (1962), p. 174; and R. W. Dias, 'Precedents in the House of Lords – A much needed Reform', *CLJ*, 24 (1966), p. 123.

[32] A. P. Fachiri, *The Permanent Court of International Justice, its Constitution, Procedure and Work*, 2nd edn (London, 1932), p. 104, note 1.

when it appears right to do so'. Granted this competence, on however cautious a basis, to depart from a previous decision, it is not possible, except by a play on words, to regard such decisions as any longer strictly binding on the House. And yet, until departed from, they are law, even for the House. So judge-made law can come into being even in the absence of a strict *stare decisis* rule.

Second, if the Court has a limited power to create law, it does not exhaust the power in exercising it on a particular point on a particular occasion; for good reason, it may later reopen the point and vary its previous ruling.[33] The fact that a decision of the House of Lords is law, even for the House, does not prevent the House from later departing from it.

Thus, it is possible to hold that a decision creates law without necessarily implying that *stare decisis* applies.

The exclusion of *stare decisis* does not also exclude the precedential force of decisions of the Court

Even if the non-applicability of *stare decisis* means that decisions of the Court cannot create law, it does not mean that they do not have precedential effect. In the words of Lindsey, writing in 1931, the 'enunciation by the Court of the legal rules or principles on which its decision of the issue rests has weight as a precedent even though the principle of *stare decisis* is not regarded as obligatory on the Court'.[34]

There is a sense in which the matter tends to be misstated. This is because of a distinction between the force of the decision itself and the force of international law as authoritatively expressed in the decision. The distinction was alluded to by Judge Zoričič in the *Peace Treaties* case when stating that 'it is quite true that no international court is bound by precedents. But there is something which this Court is bound to take into account, namely the principles of international law. If a precedent is firmly based on such a principle, the Court cannot decide an analogous case in a contrary

---

[33] See, generally, A. W. B. Simpson, 'The Ratio Decidendi of a case and the Doctrine of Binding Precedent', in A. G. Guest (ed.), *Oxford Essays in Jurisprudence* (London, 1961), p. 148; and P.J. Evans, 'The Status of the Rules of Precedent', *CLJ*, 41 (1982), pp. 172–173; and cf., in the case of the High Court of Australia, Peter Wesley Smith, 'Theories of Adjudication and the Status of *Stare Decisis*', in Laurence Goldstein (ed.), *Precedent in Law* (Oxford, 1987), pp. 75–76.

[34] Edward Lindsey, *The International Court* (New York, 1931), p. 268.

sense, so long as the principle retains its value.'[35] As was noticed earlier, in 1961 the Court itself had occasion to mark the distinction between the fact that the binding force of a decision is limited to the parties and the fact that the decision may be '[c]onsidered however as a statement of what the Court regarded as the correct legal position'.[36]

Speaking of the *Continental Shelf (Tunisia/Libyan Arab Jamahiriya), Application for Permission to Intervene*,[37] counsel likewise later remarked that 'reliance upon Article 59 is too narrow a basis on which to rest the binding force of a judgment of the Court. The judgment of the Court – and its advisory opinion – bind all states by virtue of their quality as authoritative statements of the law. This is a point of the greatest importance.'[38] In that case, the Court indicated that the 'findings at which it arrives and the reasoning by which it reaches those findings in the case between Tunisia and Libya' would not apply to non-parties.[39] That remark was directed to the fact that Malta's concern was over specific aspects of the possible judicial treatment of the physical features of an area in which it was also asserting an interest;[40] the remark could not operate to suppress the potential precedential influence of the decision. Nor should Malta be thought to have considered otherwise; as has already been seen, it had made it clear that it did not 'base its request for permission to intervene simply on an interest in the Court's pronouncements in the case regarding the applicable general principles and rules of international law'.[41] The judgment of the Court is not at variance with the view that its pronouncements on legal principles could form part of the general law.

A similar conclusion would apply in relation to the Court's holding in *Continental Shelf (Libyan Arab Jamahiriya/Malta), Application for Permission to Intervene*, 'that the principles and rules of international

---

[35] *Interpretation of Peace Treaties with Bulgaria, Hungary and Romania, ICJ Rep 1950*, p. 104, Judge Zoričič, dissenting opinion.

[36] *Temple of Preah Vihear, Preliminary Objections, ICJ Rep 1961*, p. 27.

[37] *ICJ Rep 1981*, p. 10, para. 15.

[38] *Proceedings of the American Society of International Law*, 75 (1981), p. 61, Mr E. Lauterpacht. In a later case before a chamber of the Court he submitted that 'almost by definition, what the Court has said is the law'. See *Land, Island and Maritime Frontier Dispute (El Salvador/Honduras), Application by Nicaragua for Permission to Intervene*, Verbatim Record, C 4/CR 90/3, p. 82, afternoon.

[39] *ICJ Rep 1981*, p. 20, para. 35.

[40] *Ibid.*, p. 12, para. 19, and pp. 16–18, paras. 28–33.

[41] *Ibid.*, p. 17, para. 30.

law found by the Court to be applicable to the delimitation between Libya and Malta, and the indications given by the Court as to their application in practice, cannot be relied on by the Parties against any other State'.[42] The concern there was to make it clear that the fact that certain 'principles and rules of international law' were found to be applicable as between the parties did not mean that a party was entitled to extend the applicability of those principles and rules as between itself and a non-party which was interested in the same general area; that did not affect the question of the extent to which the legal principles set out in the judgment could exert precedential force.

In effect, seen from the point of view of the Court itself, the law as stated in a decision is regarded as part of international law; it thus applies to all States whether or not parties to the particular case. It is not then a question whether the decision *per se* applies as a binding precedent, but whether the law which it lays down is regarded as part of international law.

[42] *ICJ Rep 1984*, p. 26, para. 42.

9

Distinguishing

Introductory remarks

Charles De Visscher correctly drew attention to the 'Court's concern to assert the unity and coherence of its own decisions'.[1] That concern is noticeably expressed in the care which the Court takes in demonstrating that cases which appear to be in conflict may not involve any inconsistency as between the true principles on which each rests. Cases which rest on different principles are distinguishable; if they are distinguishable, they are not inconsistent. The attention paid by the Court to distinguishing one case from another, even though the initial impression might be that the first was applicable to the second, is an affirmation of its general policy of following its previous decisions.

It is therefore always necessary to determine what were the true principles of the earlier case; to appreciate what exactly was the holding in a case is, indeed, the necessary condition of the functioning of a system of precedent. It was for this reason that it was said at the bar of the Permanent Court of International Justice, and said early in its life, *qui bene distinguit bene docet*.[2] Even where a case is distinguished, the very process of distinguishing may aid analysis; to cite a general remark made by

---

[1] De Visscher, *Theory and Reality*, p. 360.
[2] *Certain German Interests in Polish Upper Silesia*, PCIJ, Series C, No. 9–I, p. 94, Mr Limburg; and see *Aerial Incident of 27 July 1955, ICJ Rep 1959*, p. 154, Judge Armand-Ugon, separate opinion, referring to the old rule *bene indicat qui bene distinguit*.

110

Fitzmaurice in the course of his arguments in the *Reparation* case, 'In order to ascertain what a thing is, it is sometimes very useful to begin by enquiring what it is not.'[3] Consequently, the practice of distinguishing cases is well established in the jurisprudence of the World Court. The existence of the practice was recognised in the *Third Annual Report* of the Permanent Court of International Justice.[4] Writing in 1932, Beckett was able to cite over a dozen instances.[5] The exercise often involves the Court in elaborate analyses. See its treatment of the *Status of Eastern Carelia* case in the *Mosul* case,[6] and the way in which, in the later case of *Barcelona Traction, Light and Power Company Ltd, Preliminary Objections*,[7] it distinguished the case of the *Aerial Incident of 27 July 1955 (Israel v. Bulgaria)*.[8] A common lawyer would feel at home listening to arguments in various cases, presented with equal ability by counsel of different legal traditions, on the question whether *Monetary Gold* could be distinguished or applied.[9] It is obvious that the question whether or not a previous case could be distinguished lay at the heart of several decisions.

There are two main ways of distinguishing. First, the effort could be to show that the precedent did not establish the principle later contended for. Second, it might be argued that, even if the precedent did establish the principle contended for, the principle did not apply in the circumstances of the new case.[10] It is not proposed to embark on a detailed survey of these two areas; the broad categorisation is sought to be dealt with in the sweep of the following general remarks.

---

[3] *ICJ Pleadings, Reparation for Injuries Suffered in the Service of the United Nations*, p. 111.
[4] *PCIJ, Series E, No. 3*, p. 218.
[5] Beckett, 'Jurisprudence', p. 138, footnote.
[6] *PCIJ, Series E, No. 2*, p. 164, and *No. 3*, p. 226.
[7] *ICJ Rep 1964*, pp. 28–30.
[8] *ICJ Rep 1955*, p. 127.
[9] See *Monetary Gold Removed from Rome in 1943, ICJ Rep 1954*, p. 19; *Military and Paramilitary Activities in and against Nicaragua, ICJ Rep 1984*, pp. 184–186, 429–431, and *ICJ Rep 1986*, p. 37, para. 53; *Continental Shelf (Libyan Arab Jamahiriya/Malta), ICJ Rep 1984*, pp. 25 ff; *Frontier Dispute, ICJ Rep 1986*, p. 579, para. 49; *Land, Island and Maritime Frontier Dispute, ICJ Rep 1990*, p. 92; *Certain Phosphate Lands in Nauru (Nauru v. Australia), Preliminary Objections, ICJ Rep 1992*, p. 240; and *East Timor (Portugal v. Australia), ICJ Rep 1995*, p. 90.
[10] See generally Barberis, 'La Jurisprudencia', pp. 668, 670.

The case may not have established the principle for which it is cited

The problem under this head is complicated where the evolution of thought on a decided case is allowed to proceed on a mistaken appraisal of what was in fact the holding. The *Status of Eastern Carelia* was understood in several quarters, and over a long period, as resting on non-consent by a State which was a party to an actual dispute; but the Court had expressly reserved that aspect,[11] and there was contemporary awareness of this.[12] Russia was not a member of the League of Nations and had not accepted the obligations of membership for the purposes of the dispute. In effect, the decision turned not on lack of competence of the Court as such, but, more fundamentally, on lack of competence of the Council of the League to invoke the competence of the Court. This had become apparent late in 1925, shortly after the *Mosul* case.[13] The realisation, some time later, that the Court had in fact reserved the point concerning non-consent by a State as a party to an actual dispute was to give rise to interesting discussion.[14] The true ground was recognised by Henri Rolin at the 1926 Geneva Conference of States Signatories to the Protocol of Signature of the Statute of the Permanent Court of International Justice. Speaking for Belgium, he was recorded as saying:

[I]n the well-known case of Eastern Carelia, which concerned Finland and the Soviet Government, the Permanent Court of International Justice had refused to give an advisory opinion at the request of the Council, considering that, as the Soviet Government was not a Member of the League and had not accepted the compulsory jurisdiction of the Court, it could not agree to the Court pronouncing judgment by a roundabout method, and by default, on a matter regarding which it was not in any way bound to accept that jurisdiction.[15]

---

[11] *PCIJ, Series B, No. 5*, p. 27.

[12] Arnold D. McNair, 'The Council's Request for an Advisory Opinion from the Permanent Court of International Justice', *BYBIL*, 7 (1926), p. 7; and see P. C. Jessup, *The United States and the World Court* (Boston, 1929), pp. 31–32.

[13] Michael Dunne, *The United States and the World Court, 1920–1935* (London, 1988), pp. 110–111.

[14] See K. J. Keith, *The Extent of the Advisory Jurisdiction of the International Court of Justice* (Leiden, 1971), pp. 88 ff; *ICJ Pleadings, Western Sahara*, IV, p. 347, Professor Salmon, 25 June 1975; and Waldock, *Advisory Jurisdiction*, p. 3.

[15] *Minutes of the Conference of States Signatories to the Protocol of Signature of the Statute of the Permanent Court of International Justice, held at Geneva from September 1st to 23rd, 1926*, (Geneva, 1926) p. 22. And see, *ibid.*, by him, at pp. 37–38.

The Court's decision rested on Russia's non-membership of the League and non-acceptance of the authority of the Court, and not on its lack of consent to a decision being given by the Court on a dispute to which it was a party. This distinction was used by the present Court in *Namibia* to answer arguments that in the *Status of Eastern Carelia* the Permanent Court of International Justice 'declined to rule on the question referred to it because it was directly related to the main point of a dispute actually pending between two States'.[16] The distinction is helpful in following arguments as to whether the *Status of Eastern Carelia* is still law and, if so, to what extent.

There are other cases which show that there could be difficulty in determining what was the precise holding of a case. The *Reparation* case may be used as an illustration. There, Judge Badawi Pasha sought unsuccessfully to show that the asserted principle was not established by the cited precedent. His views related to the following holding by the Court:

Under international law, the Organization must be deemed to have those powers which, though not expressly provided in the Charter, are conferred upon it by necessary implication as being essential to the performance of its duties. This principle of law was applied by the Permanent Court of International Justice to the International Labour Organization in its Advisory Opinion No. 13 of July 23rd, 1926 (Series B, No. 13, p. 18), and must be applied to the United Nations.[17]

Judge Badawi Pasha dissented. In his view:

In the first place, I do not think that Opinion No. 13 of the P.C.I.J. concerning the competence of the International Labour Organization lays down the principle so categorically and absolutely as a principle of international law, as the Court states. The Permanent Court had to give an opinion on the question whether a certain measure recommended by the International Labour Organization was or was not within the Organization's competence; and it stated that 'the terms in which the objects committed to the International Labour Organization are stated are so general that language could hardly be more comprehensive', and that 'while the competence ... so far as concerns the investigation and discussion of labour questions and the formulation of proposals ... is exceedingly broad,

---

[16] See *ICJ Rep 1971*, p. 23, paras. 30 and 31, and *ICJ Pleadings, Namibia*, I, pp. 442 ff, and II, pp. 32 ff, pp. 186 ff, and p. 500.

[17] *Reparation for Injuries Suffered in the Service of the United Nations, ICJ Rep 1949*, pp. 182–183.

its competence is almost entirely limited to that form of auxiliary activity.'
The Permanent Court therefore concluded in the following terms:

> 'It results from the consideration of the provisions of the Treaty
> that the High Contracting Parties clearly intended to give to the
> International Labour Organization a very broad power of co-
> operating with them in respect of measures to be taken in order to
> assure humane conditions of labour and the protection of workers.
> It is not conceivable that they intended to prevent the Organization
> from drawing up and proposing measures essential to the
> accomplishment of that end. The Organization, however, would be
> so prevented if it were incompetent to propose for the protection of
> wage earners a regulative measure to the efficacious working of
> which it was found to be essential to include to some extent work
> done by employers.'

This Opinion therefore laid down no general principle. It only interprets
the intention of the Parties as to Part XIII of the Treaty of Versailles in
the light of the terms generally used therein.[18]

Judge Badawi Pasha was right in holding that the Advisory Opinion
of the Permanent Court of International Justice 'only interprets the
intention of the Parties as to Part XIII of the Treaty of Versailles in
the light of the terms generally used therein'. It was, nevertheless,
open to the present Court to interpret the basis on which its predecessor proceeded to make its interpretation of the intention of the
Parties to the Treaty, and it seemed reasonable to understand the
Permanent Court as in fact proceeding on the basis that under
'international law, the Organization must be deemed to have those
powers which, though not expressly provided in the [relevant instru-
ment], are conferred upon it by necessary implication as being
essential to the performance of its duties'.

The principle of the case may be qualified by later legal developments

A second, and related, way of distinguishing a case would be to
accept that the principle it established would ordinarily apply to
the facts of the new case, but to point to other legal developments
which interpose to exclude its applicability. Thus, in expressing the

[18] *Reparation for Injuries Suffered in the Service of the United Nations, ICJ Rep 1949*,
p. 214.

view that the precedent set in the *Status of Eastern Carelia* had been abandoned, Judge de Castro observed that 'the constitutional or organic position of the Court has changed', the Permanent Court of International Justice not being a part of the League of Nations, whereas the present Court 'is both a creation of the Charter and an organ of the United Nations'.[19]

The problem is that, while some intervening legal developments may be apparent, others may be of a subtler shade. It is important, as pointed out by Judge Gros, to bear in mind the possibility that 'colour and content' may have changed. Dissenting in the *Delimitation of the Maritime Boundary in the Gulf of Maine Area*, he said:

In the course of the present proceedings, the Parties and the Chamber have each referred to judicial decisions in support of their legal reasoning, but frequently a judicial text has been quoted without anything to indicate that colour and content have in fact changed. The present must however be seen in its own true colours: the jurisprudence of the subject is no longer viewed as in 1969 and 1977, but has taken a sudden turn of which due note must be taken, and the Judgment of the Chamber takes its place within this change.[20]

One is, of course, concerned here not with the correctness of the view that a sudden turn had taken place in the jurisprudence, but only with the approach based on the assumption that there had been such a turn.[21]

That approach points to the need to take account of changes in the legal environment when seeking to apply a precedent which may well have been decided in a different legal milieu. As the Court itself said, 'the Court has to bear in mind the continuous evolution of international law'.[22] It is possible, for example, that a definition of a concept, as laid down in an earlier case, may need to be reviewed in the light of later judicial thinking on the subject.[23] It

---

[19] *Namibia, ICJ Rep 1971*, p. 172. Whether that was by itself a sufficient distinction is not considered here.

[20] *ICJ Rep 1984*, para. 2, p. 360. For possible obsolescence of holdings, see Emmanuel Roucounas, 'Rapport entre "moyens auxiliaires" de détermination du droit international', in *Thesaurus Acroasium*, 19 (1992), p. 270, para. 26, referring to the approach taken in *Texaco-Calasiatic*.

[21] See the parallel position taken in argument by Mr. de Villiers in *ICJ Pleadings, South West Africa*, X, p. 226.

[22] *Barcelona Traction, Light and Power Company, Limited, ICJ Rep 1970*, p. 33, para. 37.

[23] See, as to the concept of a dispute, Judge Morelli's dissenting opinion in *South West Africa, ICJ Rep 1962*, p. 566.

may be recalled that even where *stare decisis* applies, it does not prevent the Court from leaving aside the old case law for new legal developments even in the international field. In *Trendtex Trading Corporation* v. *Central Bank of Nigeria* Shaw LJ put it this way:

[T]he rule of stare decisis operates to preclude a court from overriding a decision which binds it in regard to a particular rule of (international) law, it does not prevent a court from applying a rule which did not exist when the earlier decision was made if the new rule has had the effect in international law of extinguishing the old rule.[24]

There is the connected, though more difficult, point that the orientation of the Court may itself have changed in the course of time. Speaking of the phenomenon sometimes described in sociology as 'a heterogeny of aims', Hersch Lauterpacht observed that institutions 'set up for the achievement of definite purposes grow to fulfil tasks not wholly identical with those which were in the minds of their authors at the time of their creation'.[25] Referring to this passage, Rosenne in turn remarked that the 'joint history of the two Courts is a convincing confirmation of this thesis; for the Court of 1965 is not that of 1946, and the Court of 1946 was not that of 1939, and the Court of 1939 was not that envisaged by its founders in 1921. International law, and its organs, move in sympathy with universal trends, and the value of "precedents" oscillates accordingly.'[26] Were that written today, it might well have been added that the Court of 1995 is not that of 1965; some change has taken place in its composition, and possibly some also in its general outlook. The underlying phenomenon explains the observation made by Judge Padilla Nervo when, speaking of the mandate in *South West Africa*, he said that 'for a just interpretation of its terms and spirit, it is important to keep in mind that such interpretation is being made today; that this Court is sitting in 1966 and not in 1920, and that the international community of today, the

---

[24] [1977] 1 QB 529, at p. 579, CA, referred to in Rosalyn Higgins, 'The Death Throes of Absolute Immunity: The Government of Uganda before the English Courts', *AJIL*, 73 (1979), p. 468. See too *Thomson* v. *Moyse*, [1961] AC 967; Hermann Mosler, 'Supra-National Judicial Decisions and National Courts', *Hastings International and Comparative Law Review*, 4 (1981), p. 472; and Gerald Dworkin, 'Stare Decisis in the House of Lords', *MLR*, 25 (1962), p. 175.

[25] Lauterpacht, *Development*, p. 5; and see, also by him, *The Development of International Law by the Permanent Court of International Justice* (London, 1934), p. 2.

[26] Rosenne, *Law and Practice* (1965), I, p. 57.

United Nations, has the right and the duty to see that the sacred trust is performed'.[27] It is difficult to say with confidence that the attitude of the Permanent Court of International Justice in the 1920s would have been the same as that later taken by the International Court of Justice in 1971.[28] As remarked by Judge Jennings, 'Law develops by precedent, and it is that which gives it consistency and predictability. But legal precedents like any other must be seen in the light of history and of changing times.'[29]

The point involved takes strength from the fact that the present Court has a relationship to the general world body which is different from that which the Permanent Court of International Justice had to the League of Nations. Though closely related to the League, the Permanent Court was not part of it. The International Court of Justice is constitutionally both a principal organ of the United Nations and its principal judicial organ. Subject to preservation of its independence, and functioning within its allotted field, the Court shares in the fulfilment of the purposes of the United Nations; those purposes are thought to be, in some ways, wider and more challenging than those of the League.[30]

The point about possible changes in the orientation of the World Court is a delicate one; to ascertain how it translates out in concrete terms could be an interesting exercise in itself. For present purposes, it may be recognised as raising a general consideration affecting the framework in which precedents have their being and live out their useful lives, in the case of the World Court as no doubt in the case of national courts also.

The legal or factual framework may be significantly different

A third, and usual, way of distinguishing a case is to accept that it established the principle contended for but to argue that the principle does not apply in the circumstances of the new case. An early

---

[27] *ICJ Rep 1966*, p. 456, dissenting opinion; and see *Namibia, ICJ Rep 1971*, p. 112, for a similar remark in his separate opinion.
[28] See the remarks of Judge Fitzmaurice, dissenting, in *Namibia, ICJ Rep 1971*, p. 223, para. 7.
[29] *Military and Paramilitary Activities in and against Nicaragua, ICJ Rep 1984*, p. 547, Judge Jennings, dissenting opinion.
[30] See statement by President Bedjaoui before the General Assembly, 13 October 1994.

example in the jurisprudence of the two Courts of a relevant factual difference operating to trigger a distinction is to be found in the 'Lotus', in which the Permanent Court of International Justice observed:

In regard to precedents, it should first be observed that, leaving aside the collision cases which will be alluded to later, none of them relates to offences affecting two ships flying the flags of two different countries, and that consequently they are not of much importance in the case before the Court. The case of the *Costa Rica Packet* is no exception, for the prauw on which the alleged depredations took place was adrift without flag or crew, and this circumstance certainly influenced, perhaps decisively, the conclusion arrived at by the arbitrator.[31]

Thus, the framework in which a judicial pronouncement was made is important; the care with which the Court considered this aspect is apparent.

Regard must be had too to the exact issues involved in the cited case. In *Certain Norwegian Loans*, Judge Lauterpacht was considering the validity of the 'automatic reservation' in France's optional clause declaration. Was the validity of the reservation supported by *Rights of Nationals of the United States of America in Morocco?*[32] Answering in the negative, he observed that in that case 'the jurisdiction of the Court was not challenged by the defendant State; the latter did not invoke the "automatic reservation". There was, therefore, no direct occasion for the Court to embark upon an examination of the validity of that reservation and of the Acceptance as a whole.'[33] He pointed out that

although in [the *Morocco*] case France relied in her Application upon the Optional Clause of Article 36(2) of the Statute, the jurisdiction of the Court was in fact exercised not on the basis of the Optional Clause but on the principle of *forum prorogatum*, i.e. on what was actually a voluntary submission independent of the source of jurisdiction originally invoked by the applicant party.[34]

Concluding, he said:

It is thus clear that in that case the Court exercised jurisdiction not only because – unlike in the present case – the defendant Party agreed to it

---

[31] *1927, PCIJ, Series A, No. 10*, p. 26. But see the position taken later in Article 1 of the Brussels Convention on Penal Jurisdiction in Matters of Collision, 1952.

[32] *ICJ Rep 1951*, p. 109; and *ICJ Rep 1952*, p. 176.

[33] *ICJ Rep 1957*, p. 59.

[34] *Ibid.*, p. 60.

but also because it agreed to it on the basis other than the Declaration of Acceptance. The dispute now before the Court is the first case – an entirely novel case – in which a Party has claimed the right, denied to it by Article 36(6) of the Statute, to substitute itself for the Court in the matter of a decision as to its jurisdiction. This being so, I need not discuss the question as to the extent to which the Court would be bound by the precedent of the case of the *United States Nationals in Morocco*, if that case were relevant to the issue now before the Court.[35]

Thus, one way of distinguishing a precedent is to show that, although the decision might appear on the surface to be applicable, it was nevertheless one in which the specific legal point was not the subject of consideration.

But differences do not always preclude recourse to a precedent

The ideal situation is of course one in which all relevant elements in the context of the new case match those of the old, where one case 'runs upon all four feet with another' so as to raise the same precise question. In principle, that is a prerequisite for the application of precedent. Thus, in the *Barcelona Traction, Light and Power Company* case, the Court carefully observed that the relevant provision of its Rules of Court 'repeats verbatim the like provision in the 1936 Rules of the Permanent Court of International Justice' before it proceeded 'to take note of the various reasons which that Court gave for deciding to join a preliminary objection to the merits'.[36]

But the ideal situation does not always favour counsel with its presence. As Sir Ernest Pollock pointed out to the Permanent Court of International Justice, 'All lawyers know that it is very rare to find a precise governing authority upon the new facts which arise from time to time'.[37] Another problem is that, in McNair's words, 'As in municipal law, the more elementary a proposition is, the more difficult it often is to cite judicial authority for it.'[38] For these reasons, the endeavour of counsel would be to extend the principle

---

[35] *Ibid.*

[36] *ICJ Rep 1964*, p. 41.

[37] *Avis No. 6, Colons allemands en Pologne, PCIJ, Series C, No. 3*, I, p. 569.

[38] Lord McNair, *The Law of Treaties* (Oxford, 1961), p. 554, cited by Mr. Stavropoulos in *ICJ Pleadings, Legal Consequences for States of the Continued Presence of South Africa in Namibia (South West Africa) notwithstanding Security Council Resolution 276 (1970)*, II, p. 54.

of a precedent to facts other than those belonging exactly to the type of facts upon which the precedent is based. As remarked by the agent for Canada in the Canada–France Arbitration of 1992 (echoing Pollock) 'quand donc deux situations sont-elles identiques en tous points? Ces coïncidences parfaites n'existent pas.'[39] As he implied, differences do not necessarily preclude recourse to a precedent. But, if differences can be disregarded, on what basis is this done, and to what extent?

The use of precedents involves a method of reasoning by analogy;[40] the latter, despite the need for 'reserve and circumspection' in its use in international law,[41] is the logical process whereby the law develops through precedents. According to Levi, it is the basic pattern of legal reasoning.[42] But, as he also remarks, 'The problem for the law is: When will it be just to treat different cases as though they were the same? A working legal system must therefore be willing to pick out key similarities and to reason from them to the justice of applying a common classification.'[43]

The question which this in turn poses is, 'Quels sont les traits propres au cas particulier qu'il y a lieu de négliger, parce que accidentels et non représentatifs?'[44] It is not always easy to answer; in Cardozo's words, 'Cases do not unfold their principles for the asking.'[45] What matters is not mechanical identity between situations, but identity from some relevant point of view. Speaking of certain provisions of the Statute of the Court, Judge Tanaka expressed the idea as follows:

In a matter of this kind we cannot assert absolutely that one thing is identical with or different from the other. There may be found many elements of similarity and difference. What matters is from what viewpoint they are identical or different. The decision as to whether one thing is identical or not with the other depends upon the position from which one regards the matter. Therefore, the decision is relative to the viewpoint one adopts.[46]

---

[39] Transcript of the Canadian Pleadings, II, p. 51, Mr. Mathys.
[40] Jerome Frank, *Courts on Trial, Myth and Reality in American Justice* (New Jersey, 1963), p. 275.
[41] *Reparation, ICJ Rep 1949*, p. 211, Judge Badawi Pasha, dissenting opinion; for dangers in reasoning by analogy, see Cross and Harris, *Precedent*, pp. 196–199.
[42] Edward H. Levi, *An Introduction to Legal Reasoning* (Chicago, 1949), p. 1.
[43] *Ibid.*, p. 2.
[44] Ch. Perelman, *Logique juridique, Nouvelle rhétorique* (Paris, 1976), p. 129, para. 67.
[45] Benjamin N. Cardozo, *The Nature of the Judicial Process* (New Haven, 1921), p. 29.
[46] *Barcelona Traction, Light and Power Company, Limited, ICJ Rep 1964*, p. 71, Judge Tanaka, separate opinion.

Thus, it is not always sufficient to assert a difference in the legal or factual situations in order to distinguish a precedent; it would be necessary to show that the difference involves the absence of a significant element which operates to exclude the reasoning behind the principles established by the precedent. An illustration is furnished by the position taken by Judge Armand-Ugon, dissenting in the *Barcelona Traction* case. Referring to the interpretation placed by the Court on Article 36, paragraph 5, of its Statute in the *Aerial Incident* case, he observed:

It must therefore be shown why that interpretation is not applicable with regard to Article 37. In the absence of such proof, the decision in the *Aerial Incident* case would be applicable and the Belgian contention must be abandoned. It is only the legal differences between these two texts that concern us. Factual differences between the present case and that of the *Aerial Incident* are of less importance, for they have no bearing on the legal problem concerning the two texts.[47]

The context is obviously important. In the *ICAO* case, Judge de Castro observed that 'the observations to be found in the [*Namibia*] Opinion must not be taken out of context'.[48] Yet, for the reasons given above, not every difference in context is enough to found a distinction on the ground that a different legal issue is involved. In *Interpretation of the Convention of 1919 concerning Employment of Women during the Night*, the Permanent Court of International Justice observed:

The Court has already had occasion to consider some aspects of the question concerning the limits of the sphere of activity of the International Labour Organization in its Advisory Opinions Nos. 2 and 3 of August 12th, 1922, and No. 13 of July 23rd, 1926. These Opinions, it is true, dealt with questions relating to the competence of the Organization, whereas the point which is under consideration at the moment relates to the interpretation of an instrument whose validity is not questioned; but the principles underlying these earlier decisions throw light on the question whether there is any solid foundation for the suggested rule of interpretation.[49]

The questions before the Court were admittedly different, but the principles underlying the earlier decisions would still 'throw light' on the new problem.

---

[47] *ICJ Rep 1964*, p. 135, dissenting opinion.
[48] *Appeal Relating to the Jurisdiction of the ICAO Council, ICJ Rep 1972*, p. 130, note 1, separate opinion.
[49] *1932, PCIJ Series A/B, No. 50*, pp. 374–375.

Take also *Application for Review of Judgment No. 158 of the United Nations Administrative Tribunal*. There, the Court said, 'Despite the different context, the views then expressed by the Court in its Opinion concerning *Judgments of the Administrative Tribunal of the ILO upon Complaints Made against Unesco (I.C.J. Reports 1956*, p. 77) are, in certain respects, apposite for the purpose of the present Opinion.'[50] Reference may also be made to *Western Sahara*. The point arose as to whether a 'legal question' within the meaning of Article 65, paragraph 1, of the Statute of the Court was limited to 'legal questions relating to existing rights or obligations'. Referring to certain cases which suggested that no such limitation existed, the Court said, 'Although these pronouncements were made in somewhat different contexts, they indicate that the references to "any legal question" in the above-mentioned provisions of the Charter and Statute are not to be interpreted restrictively.'[51]

Thus, as was remarked by Henri Rolin, both Courts have repeatedly used cases though the context might not have been exactly similar; it is the reasoning which the Court evaluates, and the evaluation is not necessarily affected by any and every difference in context.[52] It is useful to note also that the fact that a judgment does not explicitly state that a precedent is being applied does not necessarily mean that the precedent has been distinguished; on analysis, the operation of the principle of the decision may be apparent in the shape taken by the judgment, as in the case of a limitation of the latter which is intended to take account of the precedent.[53]

Case law is not statute law

It is obviously necessary to avoid rigidity in judicial formulations of legal principles. Each case represents a unique combination of fac-

---

[50] *ICJ Rep 1973*, p. 179, para. 33.
[51] *ICJ Rep 1975*, p. 20, para. 18.
[52] *ICJ Pleadings, Application of the Convention of 1902 Governing the Guardianship of Infants*, p. 267.
[53] See, as to the possible application of the *Monetary Gold* principle, *Continental Shelf (Tunisia/Libyan Arab Jamahiriya), Application for Permission to Intervene, ICJ Rep 1981*, p. 10, para. 15, and p. 20, para. 35; *Continental Shelf (Tunisia/Libyan Arab Jamahiriya), ICJ Rep 1982*, pp. 61–62, para. 75, and p. 94, para. 133, subparagraph C(3), last sentence; *Continental Shelf (Libyan Arab Jamahiriya/Malta), Application*

tual and legal elements.[54] This is true of cases before a municipal court; it is not less true of cases before an international court. Indeed, stressing 'the predominance of particular over general situations' in international relations, Charles De Visscher adumbrated an important difference between the application of the law by an international court and the application of the law by national courts when he observed:

Thus, from the beginning and in much greater degree than the national judge, the international judge is faced with a fundamental question: On what level of generalization or individualization must the actual case before him be approached? An objective analysis of the details of the matter in dispute, preceding any recourse to technical construction, guides this first confrontation of the case with the norms. It is made particularly delicate in international law by the frequent want of an exact adaptation of norms to the variety of cases. The influence of this initial orientation, though it is at times only implicit in the text of the judgment, is of considerable importance not only in the decision of the concrete case, but also in the development of case law by the establishment of judicial precedents.[55]

For these reasons, a principle established by the decision of an international court is likely to be somewhat more plastic than one established by the decision of a common law court. This naturally has a bearing on the question of distinguishing.

As has been remarked at the municipal level, case law is not statute law and the approach to its interpretation should not be the same as the approach to the interpretation of the latter.[56] The common lawyer will naturally recall the remarks of Lord Reid in *Cassell and Co.* v. *Broome* relating to the need 'to avoid treating sentences and phrases in a single speech as if they were provisions in an Act of Parliament',[57] or his earlier words in *Goodrich* v. *Paisner* to the effect 'that the words used by the Court of Appeal are [not]

---

    for Permission to Intervene, ICJ Rep 1984, pp. 25–27, paras. 40–43; *Continental Shelf (Libyan Arab Jamahiriya/Malta), ICJ Rep 1985*, pp. 25–28, paras. 21–23; and *East Timor (Portugal* v. *Australia), ICJ Rep 1995*, p. 121, separate opinion of Judge Shahabuddeen.

[54] *Continental Shelf (Tunisia/Libya), ICJ Rep 1982*, p. 152, para. 16, Judge Gros, dissenting opinion.

[55] De Visscher, *Theory and Reality* (1968), pp. 391–392.

[56] See, in English law, Cross and Harris, *Precedent*, pp. 95 and 179.

[57] [1972] AC 1027, HL, at p. 1085.

to be treated as if they were words in an Act of Parliament'.[58] A greater degree of flexibility is available in relation to case law than in relation to statute law. Lawyers of all legal traditions would recognise that a similar approach is valid in the case of international law. In the words of Judge Gros, '[P]recedents should not be confused with mandatory rules; each case has its own particular features and it is mere mechanical justice which contents itself with reproducing the decisions of previous proceedings.'[59] At the same time, however, there is a correspondingly greater propensity to impose on the material to be interpreted a reading sympathetic to the particular thesis being espoused. Speaking of one possible interpretation of the Court's judgment in the case of *South West Africa, Preliminary Objections*,[60] Judge Morelli observed in 1966 that to 'read the decision in that way would be, not to interpret it with a view to ascertaining the Court's real intention, but rather to modify and systematize it with a view to fitting it into a particular logical construction'.[61]

The relevance of arguments

In determining what was the issue in the mind of the Court when it gave the decision being construed, it is not permissible to use the personal knowledge of a member of the Court 'as to the state of his – or his colleagues' – minds at the time when the' decision was given.[62] But it is, of course, useful to consider what were the arguments before the Court; indeed, there is a certain imprudence in attempting to understand a judicial decision in isolation from the pleadings and arguments of the parties and their counsel out of which it arose. The importance of consulting this material was emphasised by Charles De Visscher; in his words:

Much more than the judgments of national tribunals, those of the International Court, if they are to be understood, demand an examination and

---

[58] [1957] AC 65, HL, at p. 88; and see *Mills* v. *The Queen, The Times,* PC, 1 March 1995, p. 38, in which the Privy Council stated that *R.* v. *Turnbull,* [1977] QB 224, 'was not a statute'.

[59] *Nuclear Tests (Australia* v. *France), ICJ Rep 1974,* p. 291, para. 26, separate opinion.

[60] *ICJ Rep 1962,* p. 319.

[61] *South West Africa, ICJ Rep 1966,* p. 60, separate opinion.

[62] *Voting Procedure on Questions relating to Reports and Petitions concerning the Territory of South West Africa, ICJ Rep 1955,* p. 96, Judge Lauterpacht, separate opinion.

exact knowledge of the written proceedings and oral arguments of the Parties. These reveal the nature of the collaboration between the Court and the governments represented before it in the development of international law; the use the Court makes of a generally abundant and well studied documentation; the arguments that hold its special attention; the order in which it ranges those which it sees fit to accept. This side of its judicial work is rich in instruction and in every way deserved to be better known.[63]

The positions taken in the arguments of counsel cannot of course be mechanically imputed to the Court, particularly where it has not spoken on the particular matter in debate. But De Visscher's point is obviously right; it is often the case that in order to understand what the Court was in fact doing it is necessary to consider the arguments advanced by counsel at the bar.[64] Speaking of the *Continental Shelf (Tunisia/Libyan Arab Jamahiriya), Application for Permission to Intervene*,[65] one practitioner had occasion to say, 'This is not a judgment the significance of which can be assessed by reference to its terms alone. It must be read in conjunction with the arguments addressed to the Court by the parties.'[66]

Limits to the utility of distinguishing as a method of developing the law

To conclude this branch, the individualistic nature of matters being litigated before the World Court tends to facilitate the process of distinguishing; but this is offset to some extent by the circumstance that differences in context do not always suffice to exclude the application to the new case of the principle underlying the old. The law is not stated once and for all in a particular case; it may need to be progressively clarified. Thus, speaking of the definition of a 'dispute' given in the *Mavrommatis Palestine Concessions* case,[67] the Court observed that this 'definition has since been applied and clarified on a number of occasions'.[68] This process of clarification

---

[63] De Visscher, *Theory and Reality* (1968), p. 403.
[64] *Passage through the Great Belt (Finland v. Denmark), ICJ Rep 1991*, pp. 28 ff, separate opinion.
[65] *ICJ Rep 1981*, p. 3.
[66] *Proceedings of the American Society of International Law*, 75 (1981), p. 61, Mr. E. Lauterpacht.
[67] *1924, PCIJ, Series A, No. 2*, p. 11.
[68] *Applicability of the Obligation to Arbitrate under Section 21 of the United Nations Headquarters Agreement of 24 June 1947, ICJ Rep 1988*, p. 27, para. 35.

might well lead, if insensibly, to an extension of the reasoning of a case to situations which are not exactly on par with the original. It is largely through the dual process of distinguishing, on the one hand, and of gradually extending the reasoning of a case to similar but not identical situations, on the other, that the law develops through precedent.[69]

As Hersch Lauterpacht remarked, although no formal provision can prevent its use, 'the power of judicial precedent is in the long run not greater than the inherent value of the legal substance embodied in it'.[70] Thus, even where the common law doctrine of binding precedent applies, a judge who is convinced that a precedent is wrong can frequently (if not always) distinguish it and so not follow it. Where, as in the case of the International Court of Justice, *stare decisis* does not apply, the room for movement is greater.

But the effort, however admirable, to serve the cause of the law through the art of distinguishing has limits. They were elegantly portrayed by Cardozo; speaking of a somewhat quaint rule, he said:

In our day, when the perfunctory initials 'L.S.' have replaced the heraldic devices, the law is conscious of its own absurdity when it preserves the rubrics of a vanished era. Judges have made worthy, if shamefaced, efforts, while giving lip service to the rule, to riddle it with exceptions and by distinctions reduce it to a shadow. A recent case suggests that timidity, and not reverence, has postponed the hour of dissolution. The law will have cause for gratitude to the deliverer who will strike the fatal blow.[71]

This over-employment of the art of distinguishing in an endeavour to reconcile what Pound called 'the conflicting demands of the need of stability and of the need of change'[72] goes some way to explain Holmes's epigram that the 'life of the law has not been logic: it has been experience'.[73] Strict logic would fault many an exercise in distinguishing one case from another; and yet, from the point of view of reconciling 'the need of stability' with 'the need of change',

---

[69] Edward Levi, *An Introduction to Legal Reasoning* (Chicago, 1949), p. 1; and Ch. Perelman, *Logique juridique, Nouvelle rhétorique* (Paris, 1976), pp. 128–129, paragraphs 67–68.

[70] Lauterpacht, 'Schools of Thought in International Law', p. 52.

[71] Benjamin Cardozo, *The Nature of the Judicial Process*, 7th printing (New Haven/London, 1931), p. 155.

[72] Roscoe Pound, *Interpretations of Legal History* (Cambridge, 1930), p. 1.

[73] O. W. Holmes, *The Common Law* (Boston, 1881), p. 1.

that is to say, from the point of view of actual experience, the objective tendency of the jurisprudence so produced is rational enough, even if not always formally logical.[74] But the artificiality which is often involved in the process may properly be dispensed with by recourse to the more surgical method of departing, a subject dealt with in the following chapter.

[74] See W. Friedmann, *Legal Theory*, 5th edn (London, 1967), p. 469, citing Edward Levi, *An Introduction to Legal Reasoning* (Chicago, 1949); Dennis Lloyd, 'Reason and Logic in the Common Law', *LQR*, 64 (1948), pp. 468 ff; and A. G. Guest, 'Logic in Law', in A. G. Guest (ed.), *Oxford Essays in Jurisprudence* (London, 1961), p. 179.

10

Departing from a previous decision

Existence of the power to depart from a previous decision

Although *stare decisis* does not apply, yet, as has been seen in chapter 2, the decision of the Court in one case may be so highly persuasive in another as to excuse language which a lawyer of the common law school may find familiar. In Hersch Lauterpacht's view:

Undoubtedly, so long as the Court itself has not overruled its former pronouncement or so long as States have not, by a treaty of a general character, adopted a different formulation of the law, the ruling formally given by the Court on any question of international law must be considered as having settled, for the time being, the particular question at issue.[1]

That statement, while emphasising that the law on a point must ordinarily be considered as having been settled by a former pronouncement by the Court, makes it clear, however, that such a pronouncement can be 'overruled'. It is not open to doubt that the Court is at any rate competent to 'depart' from a previous decision. Unless it can do so, precedent serves not to broaden but to narrow the development of the law.[2] In the words of Judge Hackworth, 'It is common knowledge that courts of law and other tribunals, however praiseworthy their intentions may be, are not infallible. In recognition of this fact appellate tribunals are usually provided.'[3] As there is no appellate tribunal to which an aggrieved litigant can go from the Court, it is important that the latter should have a power to depart from its previous holding.

[1] Lauterpacht, *Development*, p. 62.
[2] See, in the case of a municipal court, Lord Macmillan, *Law and Other Things* (1937), p. 85.
[3] *Effect of Awards, ICJ Rep 1954*, p. 86, dissenting opinion.

There are several cases in which the Court has used language recognising the existence of a power of departure, even though not exercising it. Thus, in 1953 it said, 'The Court is not departing from the principle, which is well-established in international law and accepted by its own jurisprudence as well as that of the Permanent Court of International Justice, to the effect that a State may not be compelled to submit its disputes to arbitration without its consent.'[4] In 1962 it remarked, 'The unanimous holding of the Court in 1950 . . . continues to reflect the Court's opinion today. Nothing has since occurred which would warrant the Court reconsidering it.'[5] In 1971 it said that 'the Court found no reason to depart in the present advisory proceedings from the decision adopted by the Court in the Order of 18 March 1965 in the *South West Africa* cases (Ethiopia *v.* South Africa; Liberia *v.* South Africa) after hearing the same contentions as have now been advanced by South Africa'.[6] In 1973, referring to earlier decisions made by it in 1954 and 1956, it said, 'The Court sees no reason to depart from the position which it adopted in these cases.'[7] The implication of these references, direct or indirect, to the concept of a departure would seem to be that, if the Court saw sufficient reason, it would depart. The existence of the power to do so was impliedly recognised very early in the publications of the Permanent Court of International Justice, its *Third Annual Report* stating that 'the Court has in practice been careful not to reverse precedents established by itself in previous judgments and opinions, and to explain apparent departures from such precedents'.[8] True, the *Annual Reports* did not represent the authoritative views of the Court;[9] there could be little doubt, however, that the implication that the Court had the power to 'reverse' its previous decisions was a correct representation of the law.

Giving the justification for a power to 'overrule', in his separate opinion in the *Barcelona Traction* case, Judge Tanaka observed that 'the real life of a decision should be found in the reasoning rather

---

[4] *Ambatielos, ICJ Rep 1953*, p. 19.
[5] *South West Africa, Preliminary Objections, ICJ Rep 1962*, p. 334.
[6] *Namibia, ICJ Rep 1971*, p. 18, para. 9.
[7] *Application for Review of Judgment No. 158 of the United Nations Administrative Tribunal, ICJ Rep 1973*, p. 172, para. 14.
[8] *PCIJ, Series E, No. 3*, p. 218.
[9] See *Military and Paramilitary Activities in and against Nicaragua (Nicaragua v. United States of America), Jurisdiction and Admissibility, ICJ Rep 1984*, p. 403, para. 23, and pp. 408–409, paras. 36–37.

than in the conclusion'.[10] Hence, 'the requirement of the consistency of jurisprudence is never absolute. It cannot be maintained at the sacrifice of the requirements of justice and reason. The Court should not hesitate to overrule the precedents and should not be too preoccupied with the authority of its past decisions.'[11] Making a distinction suggested by Lauterpacht[12] between the formal authority of a decision and its substantive authority, he added: 'The formal authority of the Court's decision must not be maintained to the detriment of its substantive authority.' In the view of Judge *ad hoc* Van Wyk, 'the Court is not bound to perpetuate faulty reasoning'.[13] This would apply with particular force to decisions made *per incuriam*.[14] The power of the Court to re-examine a previous decision extends also to previous advisory opinions.[15]

Undesirability of a departure *sub silentio*

A departure is obviously a matter of importance. The Court should not effect it except on the basis that it recognises that it is in fact departing; it should not do so obliquely, or through a side-wind. Speaking of *Aerial Incident of 27 July 1955*,[16] Judge Ago reached the conclusion, in *Military and Paramilitary Activities in and against Nicaragua*, that 'the present Judgment undeniably represents a break with the 1959 precedent', and added, 'Of course, there is nothing to hinder this, but it is as well to be fully aware of it.'[17] Reluctant though the Court may be to acknowledge that a change has occurred, reticence to make an acknowledgment which is due does not serve the cause of legal development. This was probably the broad concern which moved Judge Gros in 1982 to remark that while 'the Court is entitled to change its conception of equity in

[10] *ICJ Rep 1964*, p. 66, separate opinion. And see, *ibid.*, by him, at p. 69.
[11] *Ibid.*, p. 65. And see his dissenting opinion in *South West Africa, ICJ Rep 1966*, p. 250, accepting 'the power of the Court to re-examine jurisdictional and other preliminary matters at any stage of proceedings *proprio motu*'.
[12] See Lauterpacht, *Development*, p. 66.
[13] *South West Africa, ICJ Rep 1966*, p. 67, separate opinion.
[14] *Ibid.*, p. 68. As to whether this ground of review is available in the case of the European Court of Justice, see Koopmans, '*Stare decisis* in European Law', p. 22.
[15] See, generally, arguments in *ICJ Pleadings, South West Africa*, II, pp. 98–99, and VII, pp. 21–22; *South West Africa, ICJ Rep 1962*, p. 576, Judge *ad hoc* Van Wyk, dissenting; and *Namibia, ICJ Rep 1971*, p. 18, para. 9.
[16] *ICJ Rep 1959*, p. 127.
[17] *ICJ Rep 1984*, p. 526, para. 26.

comparison with the 1969 Judgment, the use of a few quotations from that Judgment does not suffice to prove that no such change has taken place'.[18] In *Aerial Incident of 3 July 1988 (Islamic Republic of Iran* v. *United States of America)*[19] the question was considered in two of the separate opinions whether the Court was departing, *sub silentio*, from its previous position on a point of procedure; the decision probably falls to be construed as meaning that it was not.[20]

Can the Court, though making it clear that it is departing from a precedent, omit to give reasons for the departure? The Court of Justice of the European Communities is free to depart from its previous decisions without giving reasons for so doing.[21] It is unlikely that the International Court of Justice will give no reason for a departure – not, at any rate, where it accepts that it is departing. As remarked by Hersch Lauterpacht:

No legal rule or principle can bind the judge to a precedent which, in all the circumstances, he feels bound to disregard. In that case he will contrive to do what he considers to be justice through the elastic process of 'distinguishing' and in other ways. But he is not free to disregard judicial precedent altogether. He is bound to adduce reasons for departing from the obligation of consistency and of observance of settled principles. These considerations are of particular urgency in relation to international jurisdiction, which is essentially voluntary in character.[22]

In the pithy language of Rosenne, 'Precedents may be followed or discarded, but not disregarded.'[23]

The power to depart is to be exercised with caution

The desiderata of consistency, stability and predictability, which underlie a responsible legal system, suggest that the Court would not exercise its power to depart from a previous decision except with circumspection. This is of especial importance in the delicate field of applying the rule of law to inter-State relations. The nature of these relations may occasionally require some rethinking of a

---

[18] *Continental Shelf (Tunisia/Libyan Arab Jamahiriya), ICJ Rep 1982*, p. 151, para. 16.
[19] *ICJ Rep 1990*, p. 132.
[20] See *ICJ Rep 1990*, at pp. 136 and 145.
[21] L. N. Brown and F. G. Jacobs, *The Court of Justice of the European Communities*, 3rd edn (London, 1989), pp. 313–314; and Cross and Harris, *Precedent*, p. 17.
[22] Lauterpacht, *Development*, pp. 14–15.
[23] Rosenne, *Law and Practice* (1985), p. 56.

previous ruling as to the law, but more usually it would call for its maintenance. This consideration is reinforced by the reflection that the decisions of the Court are relatively small in number; there is greater freedom to overrule where a court is functioning in a system which delivers a multitude of decisions.[24] In his dissenting opinion in the *Interhandel* case, speaking of the right of a State to claim in respect of an injury to its national, Judge Lauterpacht considered that there applied, 'with some cogency, the principles which are now firmly rooted in the jurisprudence of the Court and which were clearly expressed in the Judgment of the Permanent Court in the *Chorzów Factory* case',[25] and added: 'There must exist weighty reasons for any departure from that principle so clearly formulated.'[26]

The Court accordingly pursues a judicial policy of not unnecessarily impairing the authority of its decisions. Judge Tanaka recognised the policy in *Barcelona Traction, Light and Power Company, Limited*, when stating, 'That the Court's attitude vis-à-vis the *Temple of Preah Vihear* case was influenced by the preoccupation of not impairing the authority of the Judgment in the *Aerial Incident* case is very probable. Respect for precedents and maintenance of jurisprudence are important considerations required in judicial activities.'[27] In the same case Judge Armand-Ugon, dissenting, also testified to the existence of the policy in observing that a 'change of jurisprudence on a question of jurisdiction must have a very solid basis. It is important that decisions should be consistent in order to maintain the authoritative character of the texts interpreted.'[28]

On at least eight occasions the House of Lords has departed from its previous decisions, and has accepted that it has, since the issuing of its 1966 Practice Statement.[29] Although it is arguable that the World Court has also departed from its previous decisions, it has so far not conceded that it has done so, preferring always to explain any departures in terms of distinguishing. That preference was dis-

[24] Michel Dubisson, *La Cour internationale de Justice* (Paris, 1964), p. 117, citing J.-P. Cot, *AFDI*, 1961, p. 237.
[25] *Series A, No. 17*, p. 28
[26] *ICJ Rep 1959*, p. 120.
[27] *ICJ Rep 1964*, p. 69, separate opinion.
[28] *Ibid.*, p. 148.
[29] Cross and Harris, *Precedent*, p. 135; and see *Halsbury's Laws of England*, 4th edn, XXVI, p. 296, para. 577.

cernible as early as 1927, as is shown by the statement quoted above from the *Third Annual Report* of the Permanent Court of International Justice.[30] An illustration from the practice of the present Court relates to its treatment of equity in the law of maritime delimitation. Considering that *Tunisia/Libya*[31] was 'diametrically opposed' to the Court's previous jurisprudence, Prosper Weil remarks that far 'from trying to obscure the fact of the U-turn, [the Court] has rejected, in the clearest of terms, the previous concept of equity as a corrective in favour of equity as directly generating the outcome'.[32] And he observes that although 'the Court adds that "this was the view of the Court" in its 1969 judgment, what we in fact have is the complete opposite'.[33] The fact that the Court has never acknowledged that it was departing even when it might have done so may be criticised on other grounds, but it is by itself an indicium of the tenacity with which it considers that it should adhere, and be seen to be adhering, to its previous holdings.

This well-known disposition of the Court corresponds interestingly to the circumstance that, as it happens, there have not been many cases in which counsel have actually asked the Court to depart from one of its previous decisions. In *Namibia*, South Africa submitted that 'although the Court would not lightly depart from a previous opinion, it would do so if good reasons existed', and that on pure questions of law 'the Court would not follow a previous [advisory] opinion clearly based on faulty reasoning';[34] more particularly, it 'contended that the Court should not follow the 1950 majority opinion but should hold that the said Opinion was incorrectly decided in the respect now in question'.[35] The Court in turn recognised that South Africa was 'asking [it] to reappraise the 1950 Advisory Opinion'.[36] It did go afresh into certain aspects, but ended

---

[30] See p. 129 above and *Third Annual Report, PCIJ, Series E, No. 3*, p. 218; and see Sørensen, *Les Sources*, p. 166.

[31] *ICJ Rep 1982*, p. 18.

[32] Prosper Weil, *The Law of Maritime Delimitation – Reflections* (Cambridge, 1989), p. 172.

[33] *Ibid.*, p. 173. And see the remarks of Judge Gros, dissenting, in *Continental Shelf (Tunisia/Libyan Arab Jamahiriya), ICJ Rep 1982*, p. 151, para. 16.

[34] *ICJ Pleadings, Legal Consequences for States of the Continued Presence of South Africa in Namibia (South West Africa) notwithstanding Security Council Resolution 276 (1970)*, I, p. 677, para. 3.

[35] *Ibid.*, I, p. 716, para. 69; and see, *ibid.*, II, p. 375.

[36] *Namibia, ICJ Rep 1971*, p. 35, para. 65.

by noting that the 'Court rightly concluded in 1950' as to what was the legal position on the particular point.[37] In 1962 South Africa had also sought to reopen legal issues previously decided; citing the 1950 advisory opinion, the Court said, 'The findings of the Court on the obligation of the Union Government to submit to international supervision are thus crystal clear.'[38]

Thus, if asked to reconsider a previous holding, the Court would do so; but it has not so far upheld any of the few contentions which have been made to the effect that a previous ruling was wrong in law. In the recent *Jan Mayen* case,[39] some of the arguments for Denmark were suggestive of dissatisfaction with the course taken latterly by the Court's jurisprudence on the subject of maritime delimitation; but there was no explicit submission that the Court should depart from its previous holdings.

The extent to which the power to depart is exercisable

Judge Nagendra Singh was of the view that 'the Court ... would be unlikely to disown a previous decision unless it was satisfied that the legal rule or principle in question had undergone a subsequent modification'.[40] As an indication of general tendency, that no doubt is largely correct. It does not, however, exclude the possibility of the Court departing from its previous decision not merely because the legal rule or principle in question has undergone a subsequent modification, but also because the Court may think that the original decision was in the first place wrong (including decisions given *per incuriam*),[41] or that it no longer corresponds to the requirements of the international community.

In view of the need for caution, the question, however, arises how far the Court is at liberty to overrule a decision which it considers erroneous. A general view put forward by Hersch Lauterpacht is that subject 'to the overriding principle of *res judicata*, the Court is free at any time to reconsider the substance of the law as embodied

---

[37] *Namibia, ICJ Rep 1971*, p. 37, para. 72.
[38] *South West Africa, ICJ Rep 1962*, p. 334.
[39] *ICJ Rep 1993*, p. 38.
[40] Nagendra Singh, *The Role and Record of the International Court of Justice* (Calcutta, 1989), p. 138.
[41] Consider *South West Africa, ICJ Rep 1966*, p. 68, Judge *ad hoc* Van Wyk, separate opinion.

in a previous decision ... it will not do so lightly and without good reason. But it may do so, and it has done so.'[42] What should not acting 'lightly and without good reason' mean? May there be cases in which the Court may be disposed to see the law differently from the way it was stated in a previous case but in which it may nevertheless feel that a reversal of the previous ruling would not be right? If there could be such cases, on what criteria should the Court base its refusal not to reverse?

In some national jurisdictions a court of last resort would reverse only if satisfied by the twin tests of clear error and public mischief. As to the first criterion, there should be clear error in the sense that the Court must be satisfied that the alleged error has been demonstrated not marginally but conclusively. As to the second criterion, the Court must be satisfied that the injustice created by the legal position as laid down by the challenged precedent decisively outweighs the injustice that may be created by disturbing settled expectations based on an assumption of continuance of that position.[43]

In this respect, there could be practical differences in the approach to problems relating to different branches of the law. In procedural matters, the argument for stability may outweigh arguments based on theoretical correctness. In the event of conflict, a practice of the Court, especially if only accidentally adopted, must no doubt yield to a controlling provision of the Statute or the Rules of Court.[44] However, when the practice is based on a previous judicial interpretation of such a controlling provision, difficult questions can arise as to whether a reversal of that interpretation is justified in all circumstances of proven error; the injustice arising from the defeat of settled expectations based on the interpretation may well tip the scales in favour of non-interference.

By contrast, where the previous error of interpretation relates to a provision of a constitutional character, the necessity for re-interpreting the essential message of the provision, as read by a

---

[42] Lauterpacht, *Development*, p. 19. See also *ibid.*, p. 20.

[43] See *Aerial Incident of 3 July 1988, ICJ Rep 1989*, p. 158, separate opinion.

[44] See *Land, Island and Maritime Frontier Dispute (El Salvador/Honduras), ICJ Rep 1990*, pp. 52–53, separate opinion. And see, in English law, *Langdale* v. *Danby* [1982], 3 All ER 129, HL, and *The Supreme Court Practice 1993* (London, 1992), I, Pt 1, Order 14/3–4/38, at p. 164.

contemporary mind contemplating the unfolding conditions of the times, may be the major consideration.[45] No doubt this was the view underlying the United States argument in *Aerial Incident of 27 July 1955*, reading:

The Judgment of the Court on May 26, 1959 in the case between Israel and Bulgaria does not conclude the Parties in the present case. This is made clear by Article 59 of the Statute of the Court. Particularly, where the interpretation of a constitutional text (Article 36, paragraph 5) is in question, no doctrine of *stare decisis* precludes reexamination of the holding in a previous case in this Court.[46]

That contention drew on United States constitutional jurisprudence; it would seem to be equally applicable to the International Court of Justice.[47] A qualification may, however, be appropriate in so far as some elements of the Statute of the Court are more procedural than substantive.

As to how the Court may comport itself on the question of its power to depart, if it decides openly to exercise it, one must still look to the future. It may, however, be useful to consider the possible play of certain factors.

Absence of argument

Apart from the need to appreciate what was the issue before the Court, a question may arise as to the weight to be assigned to a holding when the arguments were less than full. In the case of a decision by a common law court, the extent of the arguments presented is relevant in evaluating a decision.[48] The relevance is slight, though possibly not altogether non-existent, in the case of the International Court of Justice. As observed by Rosenne, 'The conception sometimes encountered in municipal jurisprudence, that the value of a judicial precedent may vary according as the

---

[45] See, generally, Cross and Harris, *Precedent*, pp. 18, 22; Julius Stone, *Precedent and Law, Dynamics of Common Law Growth* (Sydney, 1985), p. 177; and H. M. Seervai, *Constitutional Law of India: A Critical Commentary* (Bombay, 1967), pp. 1020–1022.

[46] *ICJ Pleadings, Aerial Incident of 27 July 1955*, p. 307, para. 1.

[47] As to argument about the kinds of issues with respect to which the House of Lords would exercise its power to depart from its previous holding, see Julius Stone, 'The Lords at the Cross Roads – When to "Depart" and How!', *Australian Law Journal*, 46 (1972), p. 486.

[48] See, in English law, Cross and Harris, *Precedent*, pp. 158–159.

case was defended or undefended, is not prominent in the work of the International Court.'[49] The municipal approach is explained by the possibility that, in the absence of argument, the court, particularly in an adversarial system, might simply have assumed the correctness of the legal proposition in question. The World Court can make no easy assumptions; whether or not there has been argument, the principle *jura novit curia* requires it to satisfy itself of the correctness of a legal proposition before announcing it or acting on it.

However, the question whether the Court had the benefit of full argument is not without some trace in the thinking of judges. In the *South West Africa* cases, Judge Jessup considered it important to dissociate himself from the 'thought that in advisory proceedings the Court does not receive as full a statement or argument as is presented in contentious proceedings'.[50] In the *Peace Treaties* case, Judge Winiarski also referred to the need for full argument in advisory proceedings.[51]

The necessity for full argument in contentious cases cannot be less. The principle *jura novit curia*, which is of municipal origin,[52] does not relieve a party from the duty to present full argument directed to supporting the legal propositions on which its case rests. All it means is that arguments so presented are by way of assistance to the Court; in case of deficiency, the Court has the duty to fill the gap out of its own knowledge of the law.[53] The importance of ensuring full discussion by the parties is obvious.[54] The maxim is a statement of the responsibility of the Court to ascertain the law of its own accord;[55] it is not an assertion of its

---

[49] Rosenne, *Law and Practice* (1965), I, p. 49.

[50] *ICJ Rep 1966*, p. 350, dissenting opinion; and see *ICJ Pleadings, Namibia*, I, p. 677.

[51] *ICJ Rep 1950*, pp. 91–92, dissenting opinion.

[52] Bin Cheng, *General Principles of Law as Applied by International Courts and Tribunals* (London, 1953), p. 299.

[53] See *Fisheries Jurisdiction (United Kingdom v. Iceland), Merits, ICJ Rep 1974*, pp. 9–10, para. 17, and, at p. 63, Judge Dillard, separate opinion; *ICJ Pleadings, Fisheries*, IV, p. 32, Sir Eric Beckett, and p. 394, Professor Waldock; and Sir Gerald Fitzmaurice, 'The Problem of the "Non-Appearing" Defendant Government', *BYBIL*, 51 (1980), p. 108.

[54] See *ICJ Pleadings, South West Africa*, X, p. 226.

[55] But the Court is not obliged to institute research necessary for finding any applicable municipal law on which a party relies; see *Société Commerciale de Belgique, PCIJ, Series A/B, No. 78*, p. 184, Judge Hudson, separate opinion.

ability in all circumstances to do so completely unaided.[56] Judge *ad hoc* Barwick put it this way:

Whilst it is true that it is for the Court to determine what the fact is and what the law is, there is to my mind, to say the least, a degree of judicial novelty in the proposition that, in deciding matters of fact, the Court can properly spurn the participation of the parties. Even as to matters of law, a claim to judicial omniscience which can derive no assistance from the submissions of learned counsel would be to my mind an unfamiliar, indeed, a quaint but unconvincing affectation.[57]

Looking at the matter from the point of view held by the Bar of its own responsibilities, one might call to mind the following remarks by Sir Frank Soskice in the *Corfu Channel* case:

I think no impartial observer would deny that the case for Albania has been well presented by Professor Cot and Me. Nordmann. I say this, not out of compliment to them but because I feel that the Court may agree that it can rest assured that every conceivable argument which could be used in Albania's defence has been brought to the notice of the Court.[58]

The question of the precedential weight to be assigned to a decision made without argument is tied up with the associated question of the permissibility or propriety of such a decision. There is opinion to the effect that the 'maxim *jura novit curia* does not mean that the Court may adjudicate on points of law in a case without hearing the legal arguments of the parties'.[59] Speaking in 1986 in connection with the question whether there is a right of intervention in furtherance of 'the process of decolonization', and of his understanding of the position taken by the Court on the question as contrasted with the view taken by 'leading States', Judge Schwebel remarked, 'It is not to be expected that their view of the law, or the content of the law, will be influenced by an acknowledged and ambiguous *dictum* of the Court on a topic of which no trace can be found in the pleadings of the Parties.'[60] In the *Ambatielos* case, the Court itself stated, 'The point raised here has not yet been fully argued by the Parties, and cannot, there-

---

[56] See the remark made in Sir Gerald Fitzmaurice, 'The Problem of the "Non-Appearing" Defendant Government', *BYBIL*, 51 (1980), p. 108.

[57] *Nuclear Tests (Australia v. France)*, *ICJ Rep 1974*, p. 442, dissenting opinion.

[58] *ICJ Pleadings, The Corfu Channel*, IV, p. 471.

[59] *Nuclear Tests (Australia v. France)*, *ICJ Rep 1974*, p. 365, joint dissenting opinion.

[60] *Military and Paramilitary Activities in and against Nicaragua*, *ICJ Rep 1986*, p. 351, para. 181, dissenting opinion.

fore, be decided at this stage."[61] This statement was recalled by Judge Read in *Monetary Gold Removed from Rome in 1943, Preliminary Question*. Relying on it, he considered that a certain point, which had not been fully argued, should not be decided at the particular stage of the proceedings; it was only because the point was nevertheless decided by the Court that he proceeded to give his views on it in a separate opinion.[62] In principle, he adhered to that position in *Nottebohm*.[63]

There is much to recommend the view that a point not argued should not be decided.[64] But there is room for qualification. Speaking in *Certain Norwegian Loans* on France's position on the question of jurisdiction under the General Act for the Pacific Settlement of Disputes of 1928, Judge Basdevant, dissenting, said:

Even if [France] had maintained silence with regard to it, the Court 'whose function it is to decide in accordance with international law such disputes as are submitted to it' could not ignore it. When it is a matter of determining its jurisdiction and, above all, of determining the effect of an objection to its compulsory jurisdiction, the principle of which has been admitted as between the Parties, the Court must, of itself, seek with all the means at its disposal to ascertain what is the law.[65]

Is there some way of reconciling the different positions on the question whether the Court may decide a point without hearing legal argument on it? A solution may lie through a distinction between a situation in which an issue has not been raised and one in which it has been raised but in which some particular argument has not been advanced or legal authorities presented.[66] Except in the case of jurisdiction (as to which the Court has a duty *ex officio* to satisfy itself), and possibly also in matters of fundamental importance to the organisation and functioning of the Court, it

---

[61] *Ambatielos, Preliminary Objection, ICJ Rep 1952*, p. 45.

[62] *ICJ Rep 1954*, p. 37.

[63] *ICJ Rep 1955*, p. 38.

[64] Sir Gerald Fitzmaurice, 'Judicial Innovation – Its Uses and its Perils – As Exemplified in some of the Work of the International Court of Justice during Lord McNair's Period of Office', in *Cambridge Essays in International Law* (London/New York, 1965), p. 26. And see *Barcelona Traction, Light and Power Company Limited, Second Phase, ICJ Rep 1970*, p. 80, para. 28, Judge Fitzmaurice, separate opinion; and Hugh Thirlway, 'Reflections on the Articulation of International Decisions and the Problem of "Mootness" ', in R. St J. Macdonald (ed.), *Essays in Honour of Wang Tieya* (Dordrecht, 1994), p. 790.

[65] *ICJ Rep 1957*, p. 74.

[66] Fitzmaurice, *Law and Procedure*, II, pp. 531 and 755.

would not seem proper for the Court to consider an issue not raised by either party;[67] even in such exceptional cases, whenever practicable the parties might be recalled for further argument. Be that as it may, it is clear that, where an issue has been raised, the Court may competently consider all pertinent arguments and authorities, even if not presented by the parties. In the 'Lotus', speaking of the possible existence of a principle of international law precluding Turkey from instituting the prosecution, the Permanent Court of International Justice observed

that in the fulfilment of its task of itself ascertaining what the international law is, it has not confined itself to a consideration of the arguments put forward, but has included in its researches all precedents, teachings and facts to which it had access and which might possibly have revealed the existence of one of the principles of international law contemplated in the special agreement. The result of these researches has not been to establish the existence of any such principle.[68]

A tenable conclusion would seem to be that the absence of argument on a point does not preclude the Court from pronouncing on it or diminish the quality of the pronouncement as a judicial statement of the law; it may, however, operate subsidiarily in aid of a contention that the holding was wrong and should be reconsidered.

A question which may be incidentally noticed concerns the extent of the duty of counsel to bring relevant precedents to the attention of the Court. It seems that, in the case of the European Court of Justice, it is not recognised that counsel is under a duty to cite adverse decisions.[69] But that Court enjoys the assistance of an advocate general. It has been observed that in 'some respects, the assistance which the Court is given by the advocate general may be compared with that which an English or Scottish court obtains from the Bar'.[70] Statements have been made at the bar of the International Court of Justice to the effect that counsel have a duty of honour to collaborate with the Court in its search for truth.[71] The Court itself

---

[67] See the controversy relating to *Nuclear Tests (Australia v. France), ICJ Rep 1974*, p. 391, Judge *ad hoc* Barwick, dissenting opinion.

[68] *1927, PCIJ, Series A, No. 10*, p. 31.

[69] L. N. Brown and F. G. Jacobs, *The Court of Justice of the European Community*, 3rd edn (London, 1989), p. 58.

[70] *Ibid.*

[71] *ICJ Pleadings, Corfu Channel*, III, p. 302, Mr. Kahreman Ylli, referring to a decision by the Permanent Court of International Justice, and at p. 354, Pro-

expects to be assisted by the parties or their counsel, and individual judges have been critical of inadequacies.[72] But more normally the Court will have reason to be grateful. In *Ambatielos*, Sir Frank Soskice, having cited the case of *George W. Cook*, went on to say:

I think I should disclose this as a matter of frankness to the Court in pursuing my researches last night and looking again at that case as reported, I found that the case immediately before that case contained expressions in a contrary sense by the judge that tried it. If the Court would desire to look at that case, I will give the reference which is in the *Annual Digest of Public International Law Cases*, years 1927 and 1928, and the case in which the doctrine was recognized is on page 263, *Saropoulous against the Bulgarian State*. There is a case which Mr. Fawcett did not cite, but I feel that in candour I ought to call the attention of the Court to it because I lighted upon it by accident, but in spite of that one contrary statement, the whole current of authority, as Mr. Fawcett no doubt agrees, is categorically in favour of the view that prescription finds no place in international law.[73]

The position so taken is probably reflective of a more generally accepted view of the duty of counsel to the Court. The transcripts occasionally show criticism by one side of the failure of the other to cite relevant decisions or particular passages from relevant decisions. The duty to assist could be particularly important where the other side does not appear. In the *Treaty of Lausanne* case Attorney General Sir Douglas Hogg, regretting the absence of Turkey, remarked that 'it is a real embarrassment to an Advocate not to be able to hear what his opponent has to say and to deal with the contentions upon which he lays stress'.[74] The disadvantage is equally felt by the Court. To their credit, counsel have tried in such circumstances to be of assistance.[75]

The standing of a particular bench

Common law courts occasionally make reference to the standing of the particular judge or the strength of the bench by which a previous

---

fessor Pierre Cot; and *ICJ Pleadings, Aerial Incident of 27 July 1955*, p. 539, Professor Pierre Cot.

[72] *South West Africa, ICJ Rep 1966*, p. 421 and p. 435, footnote (1), dissenting opinion of Judge Jessup.

[73] *ICJ Pleadings, Ambatielos*, pp. 449–450.

[74] *PCIJ, Series C, No. 10*, p. 18.

[75] See *ICJ Pleadings, Fisheries Jurisdiction*, I, p. 94, Sir Peter Rawlinson; *ibid.*, pp. 440–441, Mr. Silkin; and *ICJ Pleadings, Nuclear Tests (New Zealand v. France)*, II, p. 252, Dr Finlay.

case was decided. The habit is not apparent in the International Court of Justice. It is nevertheless possible to see, in the opinions of individual judges, special deference being paid to the views expressed by some judges. An opinion by Anzilotti as Judge, or by Huber as Judge or Arbitrator, carries noticeable weight. So too in the case of the proceedings of the Permanent Court of International Justice sitting in its rule-making capacity.[76] Views expressed in the course of such proceedings have practically the same weight as individual views expressed on the bench; but, even in this area, special respect is accorded to the opinions of some. Referring to one aspect of the operation of Article 53 of the Statute, Judge Gros noted that the 'matter was clarified in only one respect by the Court's 1922 discussion, on account of the personality of the judges who expressed their views'.[77] The names which he proceeded to call were those of Judges Anzilotti, Huber and Finlay. In principle it can, however, be safely stated that the identities of the particular judges composing the bench which decides a case are not material to the precedential weight of a decision.

Unanimity and the question of authority

In minority opinions there are occasional characterizations of the judgment of the Court as 'the majority decision of the Court'.[78] Parties would sometimes use similar language.[79] Judge Jessup essayed a useful correction in these terms:

In my view, whenever the Court renders judgment in accordance with its Statute, the judgment is the judgment *of the Court* and not merely a bundle of opinions of individual judges. This is equally true when, in accordance with Article 55 of the Statute, the judgment results from the casting vote of the President. I do not consider it justifiable or proper to disparage opinions or judgments of the Court by stressing the size of the majority. If the Court followed the prevailing European system, the size of the majority would not be known.[80]

[76] The rule-making proceedings of the International Court of Justice have not been published.
[77] *Nuclear Tests (Australia v. France), ICJ Rep 1974*, p. 292.
[78] *Continental Shelf (Libyan Arab Jamahiriya/Malta), Application for Permission to Intervene, ICJ Rep 1984*, p. 115, Judge Ago, dissenting.
[79] See *ICJ Pleadings, Namibia*, I, p. 716, para. 69, referring to 'the 1950 majority opinion'.
[80] *South West Africa cases (Ethiopia v. South Africa; Liberia v. South Africa), ICJ Rep 1966*, p. 325, footnote.

Criticism is most likely to be attracted where the decision is the result of the President's casting vote.[81] There might be situations in which the casting vote could properly be used to the opposite effect of the original vote.[82] In several cases in which the decision concerned the preservation or discontinuance of the status quo in regulatory matters, it was used in that way by the President of the Permanent Court of International Justice.[83] But it is difficult to see how it could be so used in the case of adjudicating. In collegiate courts of appeal operating without a casting vote, the result of an equal division is a decision of the court dismissing the appeal.[84] Such a decision, taken on the principle *semper praesumitur pro negate*, is as valid a decision as one reached by a majority.[85] Disparagement on the ground of the size of the majority is therefore not right.

But disparagement is one thing, precedential weight another. In 1932 Beckett distinguished between the effect of the size of the majority on the judgment as *chose jugée* and the effect of it on the judgment as precedent. The judgment as *chose jugée* was not of course affected; but, in his view, it was natural to give greater weight to a unanimous holding on the law than to one made by a small majority. In his words:

Aux termes des articles 59 et 60, l'arrêt de la Cour a également la force de chose jugée entre les Parties et n'a aucune force obligatoire pour des Etats non Parties à l'affaire, que la décision soit rendue à la majorité ou

---

[81] Cf. John Selden's remark about the marginal voter: 'They talk (but blasphemously enough) that the Holy Ghost is President of their General Council; when the truth is the odd man is still the Holy Ghost.' See Sir John Fischer Williams, *Some Aspects of the Covenant of the League of Nations* (Oxford, 1934), p. 58.

[82] See Georg Schwarzenberger, *International Law as Applied by International Courts and Tribunals* (London, 1986), IV, p. 178.

[83] See *PCIJ, Series E, No. 9*, p. 174; *No. 12*, p. 197; and *No. 16*, pp. 197–198.

[84] A decision of that kind is sometimes referred to as the *calculus minervae*. See, by the present writer, *The Legal System of Guyana* (Georgetown, 1973), p. 23, footnote 80. The practice was applied by the Permanent Court of International Justice in 1934, although it is not clear whether the matter concerned was of a judicial character. See *PCIJ, Series E, No. 10*, p. 163, and *PCIJ, Series E, No. 16*, p. 198.

[85] See R. E. Megarry, 'Decisions by equally divided Courts as Precedents', *LQR*, 70 (1954), pp. 319–321. For an interesting example of the way in which the decision-making procedure may affect the substantive result, see, also by him, *A Second Miscellany-at-Law* (London, 1973), pp. 144–145, cited in Hugh Thirlway, 'Reflections on the Articulation of International Decisions and the Problem of "Mootness" ', in R. St J. Macdonald (ed.), *Essays in Honour of Wang Tieya* (Dordrecht, 1994), at p. 802.

à l'unanimité. D'autre part, si l'on considère l'autorité d'une déclaration de la Cour sur un point de droit en tant que précédent, il est naturel de lui en accorder davantage si l'arrêt a été rendu à l'unanimité que s'il n'a été rendu qu'à une faible majorité.[86]

In *South West Africa, Preliminary Objections*, the Court said, 'It is also to be recalled that while the Court was divided on the other points involved in the questions put to it for an Advisory Opinion, it was unanimous on the finding that Article 7 of the Mandate relating to the obligation of the Union of South Africa to submit to the compulsory jurisdiction of this Court is still "in force".'[87] There is at least the glimmering of a disposition on the part of the Court itself to attach more persuasiveness to a unanimous decision than to a majority one. The fact that a decision was not unanimous would not by itself give ground for questioning it;[88] but it could lead to greater willingness to reconsider it in the light of other relevant factors. It cannot be put higher than that; but it can be fairly said that individual judges themselves see value in a decision of the Court being unanimous and will endeavour to achieve that result.[89]

It is possible that the Court may be more disposed to reconsider a decision where, as could happen,[90] the decision includes a statement of law which was in fact rejected by the majority. Beckett, Hambro, Rosenne and Judge Petrén have all adverted to such situations: the pursuit of consensus on the overall outcome could lead to a false consensus on a specific point.[91] Such a holding is still a holding by the Court as a judicial institution; however, in Beckett's view, it could not be considered as a precedent.[92] It is a fine point. With submission, the view is offered that the holding is not deprived of the precedential force exerted by a decision made by and in the

---

[86] Beckett, 'Jurisprudence', p. 143.

[87] *ICJ Rep 1962*, p. 334.

[88] See, in English law, *Fitzleet Estates Ltd* v. *Cherry (Inspector of Taxes)*, [1977] 3 All ER 996 at 999, HL, per Lord Wilberforce.

[89] See *Continental Shelf (Libyan Arab Jamahiriya/Malta)*, *ICJ Rep 1985*, p. 59, declaration of Judge El-Khani. For an interesting way in which Judge Fitzmaurice was prepared, on the question of costs, to take account of the fact that a judgment of the European Court of Human Rights was rendered by a 'narrow majority', see his dissenting opinion in the *Sunday Times* case, *ECHR*, Series A, XXXVIII, p. 20.

[90] See p. 180 below.

[91] See pp. 180–181 below.

[92] Beckett, 'Jurisprudence', p. 43.

name of the Court; but, in estimating the weight of that force, regard may be reasonably had to the circumstance that the holding did not reflect majority thinking.

Changes in the composition of the Court

It is convenient at this stage to notice the possibility that changes in the composition of the Court due to the system of triennial elections can produce problems in the area of jurisprudential consistency.[93] In the case of the Permanent Court of International Justice, general elections were held after a common nine-year term; and, of course, the potential for creating difficulties also existed.[94] Comparing the two systems, President Winiarski stated that the 'system of partial renewal of the Court better secures its unity and that esprit de corps which welds into a single sense the personal responsibility of the Judges and that of the Court'.[95] Although there is room for differences of opinion, a sense of the working of the Court does not contradict that statement; Hersch Lauterpacht had a similar view.[96] But the improvement achieved has not of course eliminated difficulties. The problem is not peculiar to the World Court; it is known to national courts as well, in which personnel changes constantly occur both over time and as between divisions or panels where these may be used. It is useful to recall some of the views expressed on it at the municipal level.

Justice Cardozo, speaking of the New York Court of Appeals, remarked that it 'happens again and again, where the question is a close one, that a case which one week is decided one way might be decided another way the next if it were then heard for the first time. The situation would, however, be intolerable if the weekly

---

[93] *South West Africa, ICJ Rep 1966*, p. 425, Judge Jessup, dissenting opinion, and p. 447, Judge Padilla Nervo, dissenting opinion; *Legal Consequences for States of the Continued Presence of South Africa in Namibia (South West Africa) notwithstanding Security Council Resolution 276 (1970), ICJ Rep 1971*, p. 222, note 3, and p. 283, note 63, Judge Fitzmaurice, dissenting; and see Hermann Mosler, 'The International Court of Justice at its Present Stage of Development', *Dalhousie Law Journal*, 5 (1979), p. 559.

[94] *Free Zones of Upper Savoy and the District of Gex, PCIJ, Series A, No. 24*, p. 20, joint dissenting opinion.

[95] *ICJ Pleadings, Temple of Preah Vihear*, II, p. 122.

[96] Lauterpacht, *Development*, p. 283. Cf. Rosenne, *Law and Practice* (1985), p. 184.

changes in the composition of the Court were accompanied by changes in its rulings.'[97] In the words of Justice Frankfurter, speaking of the Supreme Court of the United States of America, 'Especially ought the Court not reenforce needlessly the instabilities of our day by giving fair ground for the belief that Law is the expression of chance – for instance, of unexpected changes in the Court's composition and the contingencies in the choice of successors.'[98] In the words of Justice Venkatarama Iyer, speaking of issues already dealt with by the Supreme Court of India:

If they are allowed to be reopened because a different view appears to be the better one then ... the prospect will have been opened of litigants subjecting our decisions to a continuous process of attack before successive Benches in the hope that with changes in the personnel of the Court which time must inevitably bring, a different view might find acceptance ... I can imagine nothing more damaging to the prestige of the Court or to the value of its pronouncements.[99]

In 1977 Lord Wilberforce put it this way in the House of Lords:

Nothing could be more undesirable, in fact, than to permit litigants, after a decision has been given by this House with all appearance of finality, to return to this House in the hope that a differently constituted committee might be persuaded to take the view which its predecessors rejected. True that the earlier decision was by majority: I say nothing as to its correctness or as to the validity of the reasoning by which it was supported. That there were two eminently possible views is shown by the support for each by at any rate two members of the House. But doubtful issues have to be resolved and the law knows no better way of resolving them than by the considered majority opinion of the ultimate tribunal. It requires much more than doubts as to the correctness of such opinion to justify departing from it.[100]

Leaving aside the delicate issue of consistency of approach in the case of individual judges, involving questions as to whether a judge who appeared to be 'conservative' on one occasion seemed to be 'progressive' on another,[101] one may recognise that, in the case of

---

[97] Benjamin N. Cardozo, *The Nature of the Judicial Process* (New Haven, 1921), p. 150.

[98] *United States of America* v. *Rabinowitz* (1950) 339 US 56 (86).

[99] *Bengal Immunity* v. *State of Bihar* (1955) 2 SCR 603 (810).

[100] *Fitzleet Estates Ltd.* v. *Cherry (Inspector of Taxes)*, [1977] 3 All ER 996 at 999, HL.

[101] See L. Gross, *Essays in International Law and Organization* (The Hague, 1984), II, p. 847, comparing the performances of Judges Spender, Fitzmaurice, Morelli

the Court as a whole, changes in legal perspective could occur as a result of changes in its composition. The litigation concerning *South West Africa*[102] is generally thought to be illustrative of the possibility. A related situation arises where, as in *Land, Island and Maritime Frontier Dispute (El Salvador/Honduras) (Application by Nicaragua for Permission to Intervene)*,[103] a chamber is established with a membership which includes judges who had expressed dissentient opinions on a relevant issue in a previous decision of the Court; the approach taken in those opinions could turn out to be similar, at least in part, to that taken by the chamber.[104]

Can the Court overrule?

Circumscribed though it is, the Court's power to 'depart' from its holding on the law in a previous decision does exist. What is the juridical character of that power? If the Court were to 'depart' from an earlier decision, would it simply be 'not following' the decision? Or would it be 'overruling' it? It may be argued that in the former case the earlier holding would continue technically to stand, with two versions of the law being left on record, whereas in the latter case the earlier holding would be completely removed, leaving only one version on record.[105] The possibility of there being two versions of the law possessing equal authority would seem to collide with the broad meaning of Judge Anzilotti's dictum that it 'is clear that, in the same legal system, there cannot at the same time exist two rules relating to the same facts and attaching to these facts contradictory consequences'.[106] A real problem could arise were the Court to be confronted with two inconsistent decisions on the same

---

and Koretsky in the *Expenses* case, *ICJ Rep 1962*, p. 151, and in the *South West Africa* cases, *ICJ Rep 1966*, p. 6; and Georg Schwarzenberger, *International Law as Applied by Courts and Tribunals* (London, 1976), III, p. 176.

[102] *ICJ Rep 1962*, p. 319; *ICJ Rep 1966*, p. 6; and *ICJ Rep 1971*, p. 16.

[103] *ICJ Rep 1990*, p. 92.

[104] See Andrew F. Moore, '*Ad hoc* Chambers of the International Court of Justice and the Question of Intervention', *Case Western Reserve JIL*, 24 (1992), pp. 687, 697; R. M. Riquelme Cortado, *La Intervención de terceros Estados en el proceso internacional* (Madrid, 1993), p. 125; and Christine Chinkin, *Third Parties in International Law* (Oxford, 1993), pp. viii and 177.

[105] See *Salmond on Jurisprudence*, 12th edn (London, 1966), pp. 147–148, para. 26.

[106] *Electricity Company of Sofia and Bulgaria, PCIJ, Series A/B, No. 77*, p. 90. And see, *ibid.*, p. 105, Judge Urrutia. A distinguishable situation arises in respect of contradictory treaty obligations.

question.[107] From the point of view of tidiness, at any rate, there would seem to be advantage in overruling where the intention is to remove the earlier holding as a continuing statement of the law. Can the Court overrule?

Rosenne notes 'the care evinced by the Court not formally to overrule earlier decisions'.[108] However, the language of 'overruling' does occasionally appear in the literature. Thus, Lauterpacht speaks of a situation in which 'the Court itself has not overruled its former pronouncement'.[109] As one who shared the view of the joint dissenting opinion in the *Aerial Incident* case concerning the interpretation of Article 36, paragraph 5, of the Statute of the Court, Judge Tanaka considered 'that the Court should have overruled the Judgment of 1959 in the *Aerial Incident* case by the Judgment of 1961 in the *Temple of Preah Vihear* case';[110] in his view, where necessary, the Court should not hesitate 'to overrule the precedents'.[111] Which is the correct course?

The matter becomes more complicated if the view is taken that decisions of the Court can create law. If a decision of the Court creates law, it may be said that the Court in a later case must observe the law so created; it may distinguish the case but cannot overrule it.[112] The argument is plausible; but it is outweighed by the opposing argument that, once it is granted that the Court can make law, it logically follows that it can unmake any law made by it and can for this purpose resort to the mechanism of overruling.[113]

There is, however, another problem. 'Overruling is an act of superior jurisdiction', says Salmond;[114] it may therefore be thought appropriate to a hierarchical judicial framework, which is of course

---

[107] On the question whether an order fixing time-limits under Article 66, paragraph 2, of the Statute of the Court may also fix time-limits under paragraph 4 of that Article, or as to whether an order fixing the latter has to be subsequent to an order fixing the former, see and compare the orders made in the *ILO* case, *ICJ Rep 1956*, pp. 79–80; the *Fasla* case, *ICJ Rep 1973*, p. 168; the *Mortished* case, *ICJ Rep 1982*, p. 327; the *Mazilu* case, *ICJ Rep 1989*, p. 10; *Legality of the Use by a State of Nuclear Weapons in Armed Conflict*, 20 June 1994; and *Legality of the Threat or Use of Nuclear Weapons*, 1 February 1995.

[108] See Rosenne, *Law and Practice* (1965), II, p. 613.

[109] Lauterpacht, *Development*, p. 62.

[110] *Barcelona Traction, Light and Power Company, Limited, ICJ Rep 1964*, p. 77.

[111] *Ibid.*, p. 65.

[112] See, in municipal law, F. G. Kempin, 'Precedent and *Stare Decisis*: The Critical Years, 1800 to 1850', *American Journal of Legal History*, 3 (1959), p. 51.

[113] Cf., in municipal law, Benjamin N. Cardozo, *The Nature of the Judicial Process* (New Haven, 1921), pp. 149 ff.

[114] *Salmond on Jurisprudence*, 12th edn (London, 1966), p. 147.

absent as between any two decisions of the World Court. On that view, the Court may only decline to follow its own decisions, as distinguished from overruling them. But the overruling of a decision means no more than that it shall no longer be taken to represent the law.[115] Since the Court has a duty to declare the law definitively, it would seem competent to overrule its decisions for this purpose. The practice of the United States Supreme Court, the Supreme Court of Ireland and the Supreme Court of India shows that it is proper for a supreme court, which has power to differ from its previous decisions, to overrule them explicitly, as distinguished from merely not following them.[116] Breaking with the past, in its Practice Statement of 1966 the House of Lords announced its intention to 'depart' from its previous decisions when it seemed right to do so. It has been observed that the 'term "overrule" has, however, been used in this context in the House of Lords sufficiently frequently since 1966 to justify the assertion that the distinction between overruling and departing from what would normally be a binding decision is a distinction without a difference'.[117] As a matter of courtesy to a previous bench, the Court, if the time comes for it to accept that it is departing, would probably avoid the language of 'overruling'. That need not, however, obscure the possibility that an act of overruling may have occurred.

Possible cases of departure

When the case law of the Court is looked at as a whole, the aspect which is most striking is the consistency of its holdings. Writing in 1946, Sørensen pointed out that not only had the Permanent Court of International Justice never expressly disapproved of any of its precedents, but that wherever a possible departure might be thought to be involved it always took care to explain the situation in terms of a distinction.[118] That also describes the policy of the existing Court; the care taken to avoid the use of language which

---

[115] See Sir Kenneth Roberts-Wray, *Commonwealth and Colonial Law* (London, 1966), pp. 574–575.

[116] See W. W. Willoughby, *The Constitutional Law of the United States*, 2nd edn (New York, 1929), I, pp. 74 *et seq.*, and the cases therein cited; J. M. Kelly, *Fundamental Rights in the Irish Law and Constitution*, 2nd edn (New York, 1968), pp. 30 ff and p. 343; and *The Bengal Immunity Co. Ltd.* v. *The State of Bihar*, [1955] 2 SCR 603, at pp. 627–628, 692–695.

[117] Cross and Harris, *Precedent*, p. 131.

[118] Sørensen, *Les Sources*, p. 166.

might suggest that a departure has occurred is reflective of its constant preoccupation to appear to be only declaring the law or to be only bringing out its true meaning. The policy is no less familiar in municipal law, where it is bounded by limitations which would seem equally applicable in the field of international law. Douglas J. once expressed those limitations thus:

It is sometimes thought to be astute political management of a shift in position to proclaim that no change is under way. That is designed as a sedative to instill confidence and allay doubts. It has been a tool of judges as well as other officials. Precedents, though distinguished and qualified out of existence, apparently have been kept alive. The theory is that the outward appearance of stability is what is important ... But the more blunt, open and direct course is truer to democratic traditions ... The principle of full disclosure has as much place in government as it has in the market place. A judiciary that discloses what it is doing and why it does it will breed understanding. And confidence based on understanding is more enduring than confidence based on awe.[119]

Verbal stability may be secured at the price of filling words with new meanings.[120] The Court's preference for the language of distinguishing does not always conceal the fact that a change of course has taken place.

In the sense of a modification of the rigidity of previous holdings, there has probably been a departure in respect of the question of the admissibility of recourse to *travaux préparatoires*.[121] There has been argument as to whether the Court has modified its view on the question of irreparability of damage in the field of interim measures. Citing *Electricity Company of Sofia and Bulgaria (Interim Measures of Protection)*, Lauterpacht considered that 'contrary to some views expressed on the subject, the possible irreparability of the damage ceased to be the decisive criterion applied by the Court'.[122] If that is correct, then, to the extent that that factor 'ceased to be the decisive criterion', the Court's previous holdings were overruled; how far it is correct is another

---

[119] 'Stare Decisis', *Col LR*, 49 (1949), p. 735, at p. 754, cited in Jerome Frank, *Courts on Trial, Myth and Reality in American Justice*, 3rd edn (Princeton, 1973), p. 289.

[120] Jerome Frank, *Courts on Trial, Myth and Reality in American Justice*, 3rd edn (Princeton, 1973), p. 277.

[121] Lauterpacht, *Development*, pp. 121 ff; *YBILC* (1966), II, p. 223; and Röben, 'Le précédent', p. 398.

[122] Lauterpacht, *Development*, pp. 252–253.

matter.[123] Extensive discussion has also taken place on the question whether the holding in *Status of Eastern Carelia* has been overruled, or only distinguished.[124] There has likewise been argument as to the extent, if any, to which the holding in *Aerial Incident of July 27th, 1955 (Israel v. Bulgaria)*[125] has been modified in the later cases of the *Temple of Preah Vihear, Preliminary Objections,*[126] and *Barcelona Traction, Light and Power Company Limited.*[127] Other possible areas involving indirect or *de facto* departures include the litigation relating to *South West Africa,*[128] as well as the maritime delimitation decisions of the Court extending from 1969 to 1993.[129]

[123] See Jerzy Sztucki, *Interim Measures in the Hague Court, An Attempt at a Scrutiny* (Deventer, 1983), pp. 106–112.

[124] See Lauterpacht, *Development*, pp. 19–20, 248, 355–358; *ICJ Pleadings, South West Africa*, II, pp. 101–102, and VII, p. 24; Keith, *Advisory Jurisdiction*, pp. 89 ff; and Waldock, *Advisory Jurisdiction*, p. 3.

[125] *ICJ Rep 1959*, p. 127.

[126] *ICJ Rep 1961*, pp. 27–28.

[127] *ICJ Rep 1964*, p. 29. And see *Military and Paramilitary Activities in and against Nicaragua (Nicaragua v. United States of America), Jurisdiction and Admissibility, ICJ Rep 1984*, p. 405, para. 29.

[128] *ICJ Rep 1962*, p. 319, and *ICJ Rep 1966*, p. 6; and *Namibia, ICJ Rep 1971*, p. 16.

[129] *ICJ Rep 1969*, p. 3; *ICJ Rep 1982*, p. 18; *ICJ Rep 1984*, p. 246; *ICJ Rep 1985*, p. 13; and *ICJ Rep 1993*, p. 38.

11

Ratio decidendi and *obiter dictum*

Introductory remarks

From the fact that *stare decisis* is not a doctrine in force with the Court, does it follow that the Court does not need to distinguish between *ratio decidendi* and *obiter dictum*? A view, which commands respect, is that to draw that distinction 'would be to accept the doctrine of *stare decisis* at a theoretical level'.[1] Is this necessarily so in the case of the Court? What, if anything, does its practice show?

In English law one ground on which a judicial pronouncement need not be followed is that it does not form part of the *ratio decidendi*. There has been controversy as to what exactly this is.[2] The term may be taken generally to mean 'any rule of law expressedly or impliedly treated by the judge as a necessary step in reaching his conclusion';[3] theoretically, anything else is *obiter*. At the practical level, difficulties are, however, encountered in deciding how much of a judgment is *ratio decidendi* and how much is *obiter*.[4] Arguably,

---

[1] Cross and Harris, *Precedent*, p. 17.

[2] A. L. Goodhart, 'Determining the *ratio decidendi* of a case', *Yale LJ*, 40 (1930), pp. 165–182; J. L. Montrose, '*Ratio decidendi* in the House of Lords', *MLR*, 20 (1957), p. 124; and J. L. Montrose, 'The *ratio decidendi* of a Case', *MLR*, 20 (1957), pp. 593 ff.

[3] Cross and Harris, *Precedent*, p. 178. See also, *ibid.*, p. 75; and Rupert Cross, 'The *Ratio Decidendi* and a Plurality of Speeches in the House of Lords', *LQR*, 93 (1977), p. 378. According to *Halsbury's Laws of England*, 4th edn, XXVI, p. 292, para. 573, the *ratio decidendi* is the 'enunciation of the reason or principle upon which a question before a court has been decided . . . the general reasons given for the decision or the general grounds upon which it is based, detached or abstracted from the specific peculiarities of the particular case which gives rise to the decision'.

[4] A. M. Honoré, '*Ratio decidendi*: Judge and Court', *LQR*, 71 (1955), p. 197, citing Hoexter JA in *Fellner* v. *Minister of the Interior*, [1954] 4 SA 523 (AD), at p. 551.

the greater the lack of precision in the methods of ascertaining where the line is to be drawn, the greater the degree to which the doctrine of precedent can be weakened.[5] But the problem has its good side: its existence and the need to resolve it when it arises provide leeways for judicial choice.[6]

The distinction at the level of the Court

Although there is room for interpretation, a statement made by Judge Anzilotti, dissenting in 1927, may be thought to come near to denying that any distinction may be drawn between *ratio decidendi* and *obiter dictum*. The statement, which is well known, reads:

The grounds of a judgment are simply logical arguments, the aim of which is to lead up to the formulation of what the law is in the case in question. And for this purpose there is no need to distinguish between essential and non-essential grounds, a more or less arbitrary distinction which rests on no solid basis and which can only be regarded as an inaccurate way of expressing the different degree of importance which the various grounds of a judgment may possess for the interpretation of its operative part.[7]

Likewise, in the view of Hersch Lauterpacht, 'It is not conducive to clarity to apply to the work of the Court the supposedly rigid delimitation between *obiter dicta* and *ratio decidendi* applicable to a legal system based on the strict doctrine of precedent.'[8] Noting that the Rules of Court (now Article 95, paragraph 1) require a judgment to set out 'the reasons in point of law', Rosenne considers that it can be surmised that this expression did 'not contemplate such a finely drawn distinction' as that between *ratio decidendi* and *obiter dictum*.[9] The European Court of Justice probably does not make the distinction.[10]

The International Court of Justice has not had occasion to consider the subject. However, as the concept of *ratio decidendi* is the counterpart of the concept of *obiter dictum*, it would have been

---

[5] See, generally, Gerald Dworkin, '*Stare decisis* in the House of Lords', *MLR*, 25 (1962), pp. 169, 173, and *passim*.

[6] Julius Stone, *Legal System and Lawyers' Reasonings* (Stanford, California, 1964), pp. 267 ff.

[7] *Interpretation of Judgments Nos. 7 and 8 (Factory at Chorzów), 1927, PCIJ, Series A, No. 13*, p. 24.

[8] Lauterpacht, *Development*, p. 61.

[9] Rosenne, *Law and Practice* (1985), p. 614.

[10] Cross and Harris, *Precedent*, p. 23; but cf. Koopmans, '*Stare decisis* in European Law', pp. 22–23.

present to its mind when making any reference to the latter. The Court acknowledges the concept of *obiter dictum*, at least in the case of other tribunals. Speaking of a particular passage in Judgment No. 333 of the United Nations Administrative Tribunal, it considered that it 'was not essential to the argument of Judgement No. 333', and added that 'the passage in question in the Judgement is an *obiter dictum*'.[11] In his dissenting opinion in the same case, Judge Jennings remarked that 'it is not at first reading of the Judgement [of the Tribunal] easy to disentangle the *ratio decidendi* from many different ideas that are lightly adumbrated but not pursued'.[12]

It is difficult to deny that the composition of a decision could well, if only occasionally, include reasons not all of which are essential to the conclusion actually reached: the forum might itself make that clear. In *Polish Postal Service in Danzig* the Permanent Court of International Justice said that 'it is certain that the reasons contained in a decision, at least in so far as they go beyond the scope of the operative part, have no binding force as between the Parties concerned'.[13] True, the Court was there considering the question of *chose jugée* as between the parties;[14] but it seemed also to recognise that parts of the reasoning might not be necessary for the decision reached.[15] Writing in 1932,[16] Beckett considered as *obiter dicta* certain holdings in the *'Lotus'*[17] as well as some in *Treatment of Polish Nationals in Danzig*.[18] Another example is provided by the *Free Zones* case[19] in which the Permanent Court of International Justice considered the operation of a treaty stipulation in favour of a third party while recognizing that it was not necessary to decide the question.

---

[11] *Application for Review of Judgment No. 333 of the United Nations Administrative Tribunal, ICJ Rep 1987*, pp. 65–66. See further *ICJ Rep 1992*, p. 599.

[12] *Ibid.*, p. 152. See also, Jennings, 'General Course', p. 343.

[13] *1925, PCIJ, Series B, No. 11*, pp. 29–30.

[14] In this respect, there is a distinction in French law between *les motifs qui constituent le support nécessaire du dispositif* and other *motifs*. However, this distinction applies not to the precedential force of the decision but to *l'autorité de la chose jugée*: the authority of a judgment as between the parties flows not only from the *dispositif* but, if need be, from the *motifs* in so far as these explain the *dispositif*.

[15] Consider, for example, the question raised by Judge Padilla Nervo as to whether the Court needed to pass upon the objections regarding the validity of the resolutions concerned in *Namibia, ICJ Rep 1971*, p. 101, separate opinion.

[16] Beckett, 'Jurisprudence', p. 144.

[17] *1925, PCIJ, Series A, No. 10*.

[18] *1932, PCIJ, Series A/B, No. 44*.

[19] *1932, PCIJ, Series A/B, No. 46*.

Individual judges occasionally regard some of the reasons given by the Court as *rationes decidendi* and others as *obiter dicta*.[20] In *Military and Paramilitary Activities in and against Nicaragua*, the Court considered that certain acts allegedly committed by Nicaragua, even if established, could not justify intervention by a third State involving the use of force.[21] In his dissenting opinion, Judge Schwebel expressed the view that 'this conclusion may be treated as *obiter dictum* in view of the fact that there is no plea of counter-intervention before the Court'.[22] In his dissenting opinion in *Nuclear Tests (Australia v. France)*,[23] Judge de Castro referred to what he considered to be 'the *obiter* reasoning expressed' in the Court's 1970 pronouncements on the subject of 'obligations *erga omnes*'.[24] The validity of that view of the character of the pronouncement by the Court was in turn accepted by Judge Lachs, speaking extra-judicially.[25] In 1976, Judge Elias likewise recognised that the Court can and does make statements *obiter* when he spoke of the '*obiter dictum* sometimes cited from the *Legal Status of South-Eastern Greenland* case (*PCIJ, Series A/B, No. 48, 1932*, p. 268) to the effect that even action calculated to change the legal status of the territory would not in fact have irreparable consequences for which no legal remedy would be available (pp. 284 and 288)'.[26]

However, although it may otherwise be open to criticism, a pronouncement by the Court is not necessarily *obiter* merely because it relates to a point not debated between the parties. It may well be made in response to a point raised in the internal deliberations of

[20] *Anglo-Iranian Oil Co., ICJ Rep 1952*, p. 143, Judge Read, dissenting opinion, referring to decisions of the Permanent Court; *Certain Expenses of the United Nations (Article 17, paragraph 2, of the Charter), ICJ Rep 1962*, p. 193, Judge Spender, separate opinion; *Barcelona Traction, Light and Power Company, Limited, ICJ Rep 1970*, p. 280, para. 21, Judge Gros, separate opinion; and *Namibia, ICJ Rep 1971*, p. 221, para. 2(a), Judge Fitzmaurice, dissenting opinion.

[21] *ICJ Rep 1986*, p. 127, para. 249.

[22] *Ibid.*, p. 349, para. 175. See also p. 350, para. 177.

[23] *ICJ Rep 1974*, p. 387.

[24] *Barcelona Traction, Light and Power Company, Limited, Second Phase, ICJ Rep 1970*, p. 32, para. 33.

[25] Garry Sturgess and Philip Chubb, *Judging the World, Law and Politics in the World's Leading Courts* (Sydney, 1988), p. 464.

[26] *Aegean Sea Continental Shelf, ICJ Rep 1976*, p. 28. And see Edvard Hambro, 'Dissenting and Individual Opinions in the International Court of Justice', *ZöV*, 17 (1956–1957), p. 247.

the Court and of relevance to the issues,[27] particularly where the point so raised is carried forward in an appended opinion. Referring to a *dictum* of the Permanent Court of International Justice in the *'Lotus'*, Thirlway observes that, 'as so often happens, a cryptic statement in a judgment proves to be a reply to or refutation of an argument in a judge's appended opinion, and may be virtually unintelligible or even misleading taken in isolation'.[28] An example is provided by *Western Sahara*. No argument had been made to the Court that the questions on which the advisory opinion was sought were not legal questions. Yet the Court dealt with the matter, 'because doubts have been raised concerning the legal character of the questions in the particular circumstances of this case'.[29] Another illustration is furnished by *Territorial Dispute (Libyan Arab Jamahiriya/Chad)*. The judgment contains passages dealing with the question of the duration of a boundary established by a treaty terminable by either side. Neither party had raised the issue; it was however alluded to in a dissenting opinion. The judgment was obviously responding to the point suggested in the opinion.[30]

Most *dicta*, though *obiter*, stand fairly close to the decisive issues; there is little occasion to recall Lord Abinger's remark, 'It was not only an *obiter dictum*, but a very wide divaricating *dictum*.'[31] A measure of liberality may be suggested by the circumstance that, unlike a municipal system, the international legal system has relatively few mechanisms for remedying defects or lacunae in the system; it is useful to have these pointed out by international judicial tribunals. Judge Fitzmaurice put it this way:

In addition, there are a number of particular matters, not dealt with or only touched upon in the Judgment of the Court, which I should like to comment on. Although these comments can only be in the nature of *obiter dicta*, and cannot have the authority of a judgment, yet since specific legislative action with direct binding effect is not at present possible in the international legal field, judicial pronouncements of one kind or another constitute the principal method by which the law can find some concrete

---

[27] S. Rosenne, *The Practice and Methods of International Law* (London, 1984), pp. 96–97.

[28] H. W. A. Thirlway, *Non-appearance before the International Court of Justice* (Cambridge, 1985), p. 107.

[29] *ICJ Rep 1975*, p. 18, para. 15; and see the declaration of Judge Gros and the separate opinions of Judges Petrén and Dillard.

[30] *ICJ Rep 1994*, p. 37, paras. 72–73, and p. 102.

[31] *Sunbolf* v. *Alford* (1838) 3 M and W 218, at 252.

measure of clarification and development. I agree with the late Judge Sir Hersch Lauterpacht that it is incumbent on international tribunals to bear in mind this consideration, which places them in a different position from domestic tribunals as regards dealing with – or at least commenting on – points that lie outside the strict *ratio decidendi* of the case.[32]

Thus, it is difficult to deny the existence of a distinction in the jurisprudence of the Court between *ratio decidendi* and *obiter dictum*. Judge Anzilotti's view that 'there is no need to distinguish between essential and non-essential grounds' might well be interpreted less as a denial that no logical distinction could be drawn between the two categories, than as a denial of any practical difference in their relative precedential weight. So the question is what is the weight to be assigned to a statement of non-essential reasons. Three answers are possible: (i) *obiter dicta* have the same precedential value as *rationes decidendi*; (ii) *obiter dicta* have no precedential value; (iii) *obiter dicta* have a precedential value which, though not equal to that of *rationes decidendi*, is not markedly inferior.

Judge Anzilotti would no doubt support the first view. But it probably accords with current thinking to suppose that the fact that a pronouncement by the Court was made *obiter* can operate to lessen its authority.[33] The arguments of counsel are sometimes directed to showing that some particular proposition in a judgment of the Court was or was not part of the *ratio decidendi*.[34] In the case of international litigation generally, publicists likewise sometimes evaluate propositions on the basis of whether or not they amounted to *obiter dicta* of the relevant tribunal;[35] they appear to recognise the existence of the distinction in international law.[36] Beckett seemed disinclined to accord equal weight to each side of the distinction.[37]

---

[32] *Barcelona Traction, Light and Power Company, Limited, ICJ Rep 1970*, p. 64, para. 2, Judge Fitzmaurice, separate opinion.

[33] Lauterpacht, *Development*, pp. 339, 341, 361; and see C. F. Amerasinghe, *State Responsibility for Injury to Aliens* (Oxford, 1967), p. 33.

[34] Cf. *Application for Revision and Interpretation of the Judgment of 24 February 1982 in the Case concerning the* Continental Shelf (Tunisia/Libyan Arab Jamahiriya)*(Tunisia/ Libyan Arab Jamahiriya), ICJ Rep 1985*, p. 208, where the contention was that a certain view as to what was the Court's previous holding represented its *ratio decidendi*.

[35] See, for example, Lord McNair, *The Law of Treaties* (Oxford, 1961), p. 312; and Paul Jean-Marie Reuter, 'Une ligne unique de délimitation des espaces maritimes?', in Bernard Dutoit (ed.), *Mélanges Georges Perrin* (Lausanne, 1984), p. 255.

[36] See, for example, Condorelli, 'L'Autorité', p. 308.

[37] Beckett, 'Jurisprudence', p. 144.

Speaking of the distinction, and alluding to its utility in other fields, Judge Jennings remarked, 'It would be helpful if an analogous discipline could be applied to the citation of international cases'.[38] The distinction can be made and can carry differential precedential implications.

As to the second possibility referred to above, in *Anglo-Iranian Oil Company* Judge Read considered that the Court was not under an obligation to apply *obiter dicta*. In his view, they did not form part of the 'judicial decisions' which it was required by Article 38, paragraph 1 *(d)*, of the Statute to apply as subsidiary means for the determination of rules of law;[39] that was so because *ex hypothesi* they did not express a rule of law on the basis of which the cited case was decided.[40] The idea is implicit in a statement made in 1962 by Judge Spender. Referring to an observation made by the Permanent Court of International Justice in *Competence of the International Labour Organization*,[41] he remarked that the 'Court in point of fact had already arrived at its conclusion . . .; its observation was accordingly *obiter dicta*'.[42] It is, of course, useful to bear in mind that a decision could well be supported by more than one *ratio decidendi*; if it is, the additional or alternative ground or grounds do not fall to be regarded as *obiter dicta*.[43] Indeed, additional or alternative grounds need not be compatible with one another; in the *WHO* case Judge Mosler said:

The method of reasoning followed by the Court is, in my view, justified in the present case by the duty incumbent upon it as a judicial institution to define the legal position as precisely as possible in the operative provisions of the Opinion as well as in its essential reasoning, even if some of that reasoning contains alternatives each of which, even if incompatible with others, forms part of a logical concatenation that leads to common conclusions.[44]

---

[38] Sir Robert Jennings, 'The Judicial Function and the Rule of Law in International Relations', in *International Law at the Time of its Codification, Essays in Honour of Roberto Ago*, 4 vols. (Milan, 1987), III, p. 143.

[39] *ICJ Rep 1952*, p. 143, dissenting opinion.

[40] See, in English law, A. M. Honoré, '*Ratio decidendi*: Judges and Court', *LQR*, 71 (1955), p. 198.

[41] *1922, PCIJ, Series B, No. 2*, pp. 39–41.

[42] *Certain Expenses, ICJ Rep 1962*, p. 193, separate opinion.

[43] See *WHO* case, *ICJ Rep 1980*, p. 125, separate opinion of Judge Mosler; and Cross and Harris, *Precedent*, pp. 81 ff.

[44] *WHO* case, *ICJ Rep 1980*, p. 125.

But this does not touch the question how a proposition should be treated if it is in fact an *obiter dictum* in the sense that it does not form 'part of a logical concatenation that leads to common conclusions'.

Other judges have likewise tended to give no weight to *obiter dicta*. Commenting on the judgment of the Court in *Barcelona Traction, Light and Power Company, Limited*, Judge Gros considered that it was 'an *obiter dictum* void of judicial significance to assert at the present time the Canadian nationality of the Barcelona Traction company'.[45] But, if this means that an *obiter dictum* is void of judicial significance, it overlooks the fact that, even if Article 38, paragraph 1 *(d)*, of the Statute does not *require* the Court to apply *obiter dicta*, it does not *prevent* the Court from giving to them any weight whatsoever; as argued above, altogether apart from that provision, the very fact that the Court was established as a court of justice implied that its decisions would have some precedential effect.

One may now pass to the third possibility. If analysis of a judgment shows that a pronouncement on the law, though *obiter*, was made not in the course of a scholarly excursion (which would be unusual with the Court), but after judicial study of the law relating to the issues before it, the jurisprudential value of the pronouncement, though not equal to that of a *ratio decidendi*, is not markedly inferior; the *obiter* status of the pronouncement would operate to impair its value only to the extent that that status might have led to a reduced level of accuracy in making it. Some *obiter dicta*, even if controversial, are very influential.[46] Speaking of the Court's pronouncement on obligations *erga omnes* in the *Barcelona Traction, Light and Power Company, Limited* case,[47] Judge Lachs later observed that the statement 'was not necessary in the judgment, but it was a good opportunity to nail down certain provisions of the law and indicate where states are obliged to act vis-à-vis the international community as a whole'.[48] The pronouncement might have led to some debate, but the mere fact that it was *obiter* would not appear to be a substantial ground for treating it as of no authority. In English

---

[45] *ICJ Rep 1970*, p. 280, para. 21.
[46] See Condorelli, 'L'Autorité', p. 308.
[47] *ICJ Rep 1970*, p. 3, at p. 32, para. 33.
[48] Garry Sturgess and Philip Chubb, *Judging the World, Law and Politics in the World's Leading Courts* (Sydney, 1988), p. 464.

law, some *obiter dicta* carry as much persuasiveness as *rationes decidendi*.[49]

In sum, the distinction between *ratio decidendi* and *obiter dictum* is known in principle to the jurisprudence of the Court, but it probably carries less precedential significance than in a common law system.

The distinction at the level of individual opinions

As individual opinions do not decide cases, it may be said that there is little room to consider whether their reasoning is *ratio decidendi* or *obiter dictum*. They are, however, appended to the decision or opinion of the Court and are intended either to support or to controvert it. More particularly, they may be directed to parts of the decision or opinion which may themselves be regarded as *rationes decidendi* or as *obiter dicta*.[50] Consequently, their reasoning is susceptible of the same classification as that applicable to the reasoning of the Court. Thus, individual opinions may also include *obiter dicta*.[51]

Although they do not carry the authority of the Court, individual opinions have an institutional status in the sense that, unlike the views of a textbook writer, they have been expressed by a jurist sitting as a judge, and speaking after deliberating in that capacity over issues pleaded and argued by litigating parties. It follows that they lack that institutional status if they relate to matters which did not form part of the issues before the Court and were not considered by it. Views of that kind are indistinguishable in status from views expressed by a jurist writing in a non-judicial capacity; it may not be right to accord them the status given to *obiter dicta*. The point was recognised by Judges Forster and Singh in *Application for Review of Judgment No. 158 of the United Nations Administrative Tribunal*. Speaking of certain aspects of the procedures relating to the giving of advisory opinions on decisions of the Tribunal, they said:

---

[49] Cross and Harris, *Precedent*, p. 77.
[50] See Beckett, 'Jurisprudence', p. 144.
[51] See *Barcelona Traction, Light and Power Company, Limited, Second Phase, ICJ Rep 1970*, p. 64, para. 2, Judge Fitzmaurice, separate opinion, and p. 296, para. 6, Judge Ammoun, separate opinion; and André Gros, 'La recherche du consensus dans les décisions de la Cour internationale de Justice', in Rudolf Bernhardt and others (eds.), *Festschrift für Hermann Mosler* (Berlin, 1983), pp. 352, 354.

It may also be true that this procedural aspect is certainly not before the Court in 1973 and as such it may not be correct to make any observations directly or even by way of *obiter dictum*. Nevertheless, we would consider it not inappropriate to draw attention to it in our declaration and leave it to the authorities concerned to examine, if they so feel, whether the procedural machinery centering round the Committee could not be bettered.[52]

As in that case, other judges have also found it difficult to avoid pronouncing on issues which, though not raised, seemed relevant to them. In *Lighthouses in Crete and Samos*, Judge Hurst thought that 'it must be shown that the Ottoman law in question was also in force in Crete and Samos at' the time when the contract was entered into, and added:

In the absence of all examination of this question in the written and oral proceedings before the Court, I feel doubt whether as a member of the Court I ought to express an opinion on the point, but the material supplied by the respective Governments and annexed to the memorials and counter-memorials throws sufficient light on the problem to render it convenient that I should express the view at which I have arrived.[53]

Judge Hurst's own doubts suggest that relevance to an issue before the Court is always a minimum basis of propriety.

The interplay between *motifs* and *dispositif*

Running somewhat parallel to a distinction between arguments and conclusions in the pleadings of parties[54] is a distinction between *motifs* and *dispositif* in the judgment of the Court. A question which may be now briefly examined is the relationship between *motifs* and *dispositif* and the bearing which it has on the precedential value of a decision. It is useful to recall the way in which the Court sees the relationship.

In *Interpretation of Judgments Nos. 7 and 8 (Factory at Chorzów)*,[55] speaking of 'those points in the judgment in question which have been decided with binding force' and of 'a part of the judgment having binding force', the Court made it clear that not all parts of

---

[52] *ICJ Rep 1973*, p. 217.
[53] *PCIJ, Series A/B, No. 71*, p. 109.
[54] See generally Fitzmaurice, *Law and Procedure*, II, pp. 578 ff.
[55] *1927, PCIJ, Series A, No. 13*, p. 11.

a judgment have such force. Later in the same case Judge Anzilotti, dissenting, said that 'the binding effect attaches only to the operative part [le dispositif] of the judgment and not to the statement of reasons'.[56] But he proceeded to explain:

When I say that only the terms of a judgment are binding, I do not mean that only what is actually written in the operative part constitutes the Court's decision. On the contrary, it is certain that it is almost always necessary to refer to the statement of reasons to understand clearly the operative part and above all to ascertain the *causa petendi*. But, at all events, it is the operative part which contains the Court's binding decision and which, consequently, may form the subject of a request for an interpretation.[57]

The Court in fact construed the *dispositif* in the light of the *consideranda*.[58] A similar approach was taken by the Arbitral Court in the *United Kingdom–French Continental Shelf case (Interpretation)*.[59]

This interplay between *motifs* and *dispositif* had been noticed earlier in *Polish Postal Service in Danzig*, in which the Permanent Court said:

It is perfectly true that all the parts of a judgment concerning the points in dispute explain and complete each other and are to be taken into account in order to determine the precise meaning and scope of the operative portion. This is clearly stated in the award of the Permanent Court of Arbitration of October 14th, 1902, concerning the Pious Funds of the Californias, which has been repeatedly invoked by Danzig. The Court agrees with this statement. But it by no means follows that every reason given in a decision constitutes a decision.[60]

The last sentence no doubt visualises reasons other than those which are so necessary for an understanding of the *dispositif* as to be regarded as incorporated in it. In so far as such incorporation

---

[56] *1927, PCIJ, Series A, No. 13*, p. 24.
[57] *Ibid.*; and see *South West Africa, ICJ Rep 1966*, pp. 333–334, Judge Jessup, dissenting opinion.
[58] See *South West Africa, ICJ Rep 1966*, p. 333, Judge Jessup, dissenting opinion; and Etienne Grisel, 'Res judicata: l'autorité de la chose jugée en droit international', in Bernard Dutoit (ed.), *Mélanges Georges Perrin* (Lausanne, 1984), p. 149.
[59] 54 *ILR* 139, at p. 170; and 18 *RIAA*, 14 March 1978, p. 365, para. 28, cited in Etienne Grisel, 'Res judicata: l'autorité de la chose jugée en droit international', in Bernard Dutoit (ed.), *Mélanges Georges Perrin (Lausanne, 1984)*, p. 150.
[60] *1925, PCIJ, Series B, No. 11*, p. 30. And see *Maritime Delimitation and Territorial Questions between Qatar and Bahrain (Qatar v. Bahrain), Jurisdiction and Admissibility, ICJ Rep 1995*, p. 53, Judge Shahabuddeen, separate opinion.

is necessary, the Permanent Court impliedly accepted that reasons can have binding force when, in the same case, it said, as already noted, that 'it is certain that the reasons contained in a decision, at least in so far as they go beyond the scope of the operative part, have no binding force as between the Parties concerned'; by implication, where reasons do not go beyond the scope of the operative part, they attract its binding force. In this respect, the following statement by Judge Koretsky is interesting:

Could it possibly be considered that in a judgment only its operative part but not the reasons for it has a binding force? It could be said that the operative part of a judgment seldom contains points of law. Moreover, the reasons, motives, grounds, for a given judgment may be said to be the 'reasons part' of the judgment. The two parts of a judgment – the operative part and the reasons – do not 'stand apart' one from another. Each of them is a constituent part of the judgment in its entirety. It will be recalled that Article 56 of the Statute says: 'The judgment shall state *the reasons on which it is based*' (italics added). These words are evidence that the reasons have a binding force as an obligatory part of a judgment and, at the same time, they determine the *character* of reasons which should have a binding force. They are reasons which substantiate the operative conclusion directly ('on which it is based'). They have sometimes been called '*consideranda*'. These are reasons which play a role as the grounds of a given decision of the Court – a role such that if these grounds were changed or altered in such a way that this decision in its operative part would be left without grounds on which it was based, the decision would fall to the ground like a building which has lost its foundation.[61]

In the language of President Spender, 'The *dispositif* cannot be disembowelled from the Court's opinion as expressed in its motivations ... The content of the judgment must be obtained from reading together the decision and the reasons upon which it is based.'[62] But if the *dispositif* can seldom, if ever, be understood divorced from the *motifs*, it is possible that the reverse may also be true, at any rate in the sense that to understand the reasoning of the Court it may sometimes be necessary to see how it was applied in the decision actually made.[63] Thus, in understanding the *dispositif*, it may be necessary to bear in mind the reasons; but an

---

[61] *South West Africa, ICJ Rep 1966*, p. 241, dissenting opinion. And see *Fisheries Jurisdiction, ICJ Rep 1974*, p. 127, dissenting opinion of Judge Gros.

[62] *South West Africa, ICJ Rep 1966*, p. 56, para. 27, declaration.

[63] See Sørensen, *Les Sources*, pp. 158–159.

appreciation of the reasons may itself require consideration of the *dispositif*.[64]

It is in the light of this interplay that one should approach some of the standard statements made on the subject, such as that made at its twenty-fifth session by the Permanent Court of International Justice, when it 'recognized that it was impossible to vote upon the operative part of a decision and not upon the grounds thereof; for, under Article 56 of the St., the statement of reasons and the operative clauses are regarded as an indivisible whole'.[65] Judges of different legal formations appreciate this. Speaking on the point, Judge Gros remarked that 'a judgment of the Court comprises the reasoning part and the operative clause, and to understand the scope of the judgment it is not possible to separate either of these elements from the other, and an elliptical operative clause only reveals its meaning when read with the reasoning leading up to it'.[66]

A lawyer of the common law school does of course understand the distinction between a decision and the reasons for the decision; what may give him a little difficulty is the precise juridical value to be assigned to the formal way in which the distinction is observed when separating *motifs* from *dispositif* in a judgment of the Court. The Continental reader may in turn be puzzled at the absence from a common law judgment of anything recognisable as a *dispositif*. However, if, as it seems, the formal separation known to Continental systems does not exclude reasonable interplay between the two areas, the Court's practice may not after all be far removed from the common law model.

---

[64] Cf. Beckett, 'Jurisprudence', pp. 141–142.

[65] *PCIJ, Series E, No. 9*, p. 174.

[66] *Fisheries Jurisdiction, ICJ Rep 1974*, p. 126, para. 1, dissenting opinion; and see, *ibid.*, p. 127, para. 3. Thus, where the operative clause does not clearly define the rule applied by the Court, the reasoning has even greater weight. See Hermann Mosler, 'Supra-National Decisions and National Courts', *Hastings International and Comparative Law Review*, 4 (1981), p. 444.

12

Advisory opinions and decisions of chambers

Precedential value of advisory opinions

In the case of an advisory opinion, there are no parties to be bound within the meaning of Article 59 of the Statute of the Court. An advisory opinion may operate with binding force by virtue of some mechanism outside of the Statute proper; but, even where there is no such mechanism, the practical effect of an advisory opinion in securing conformity with a particular course of conduct is considerable. The effect of an advisory opinion is not however being considered here; it is by itself a substantial area of inquiry.[1] The aspect under review is the precedential influence of such an opinion. What is the basis of that influence?

Hersch Lauterpacht observed that Article 38, paragraph 1 (d), of the Statute 'by referring to "decisions" might seem to exclude, inadvertently, Advisory Opinions'.[2] So the view there was that, although an inadvertence might have led to it, 'decisions' (or, more fully, 'judicial decisions') did not include advisory opinions.[3] In support of that view, it may be argued that the omission fell to be explained by the circumstance that the Statute, as it finally emerged, included no express provisions relating to the subject of advisory opinions, the provisions on the matter proposed by the Advisory Committee of Jurists having been suppressed by the Sub-

---

[1] See, generally, Keith, *Advisory Jurisdiction*, pp. 195–222, 232–233; and Dharma Pratap, *The Advisory Jurisdiction of the International Court* (Oxford, 1972), pp. 234–256.

[2] Lauterpacht, *Development*, p. 22.

[3] See also Jennings, 'General Course', p. 330.

Committee of the Third Committee of the First Assembly of the League of Nations.[4] As is well known, provisions on the subject were inserted in the Statute only in 1929 (with effect from 1936), largely by way of upgrading of provisions in the Rules of Court.[5] Thus, the reference in Article 38, paragraph 1 (d), to 'judicial decisions' could not have been intended to embrace advisory opinions.[6]

This appreciation of the position may be thought to be consistent with the fact that the Council of the League of Nations introduced the words 'Subject to the provisions of Article 57bis' (now Article 59) at the beginning of paragraph 4 of Article 38. Since Article 59 concerned only decisions in contentious matters, the inference could be strong that the reference to 'judicial decisions' in Article 38, paragraph 4, was considered as not applicable to advisory opinions. On the other hand, it may be argued that the reference to Article 59 was intended to apply only in so far as appropriate and did not necessarily imply that the reference to 'judicial decisions' in Article 38, paragraph 4, was limited to decisions in contentious matters.

Two considerations may be put in favour of this latter view. First, Article 1 of the Statute spoke of the Permanent Court of International Justice having been established 'in accordance with Article 14 of the Covenant of the League of Nations'. Since the third sentence of the latter provided that the 'Court may also give an advisory opinion upon any dispute or question referred to it by the Council or by the Assembly', the Statute did, if only indirectly, refer to the giving of advisory opinions by the Court. Second, the reference in Article 38, paragraph 4 (draft Article 35, paragraph 4), to 'judicial decisions' formed part of the draft Statute proposed by the Advisory Committee of Jurists, together with the provisions relating to advisory opinions (draft Article 36) which were subsequently deleted. It seems legitimate to suppose that, in the view of the Committee, 'judicial decisions' were, at that stage, intended to include advisory opinions, no reason of principle appearing to suggest that such opinions were irrelevant to the purposes of the provision. If that was the view of the Advisory Committee, it would not appear to have been disturbed by the decision of the Assembly

---

[4] Hudson, *The Permanent Court*, pp. 210–213.

[5] *Ibid.*, p. 484.

[6] See Sørensen, *Les Sources*, pp. 168–169; Jennings, 'General Course', p. 330; and Röben, 'Le précédent', p. 395.

of the League of Nations to suppress the provisions in question as part of the Statute, for the decision to do so was coupled with a remark to the effect that the provisions 'concerned rather the rules of procedure of the Court'.[7] In effect, the Statute as it finally emerged was in fact constructed on the basis that the Court would be rendering advisory opinions. That being so, it is reasonable to hold that the term 'judicial decisions' in Article 38, paragraph 4, of the Statute was intended to include advisory opinions.[8]

Assuming, however, that the reference to 'judicial decisions' in Article 38, paragraph 1 *(d)*, of the present Statute does not include advisory opinions, the interesting question which arises is the following. No one disputes that such opinions do exert precedential influence. If this does not rest on any provision of the Statute, on what does it rest? The answer was given by Lauterpacht when he said, to cite him more fully:

> It is in their intrinsic power, and not in the fourth sub-paragraph of Article 38, paragraph 1 of the Statute – which by referring to 'decisions' might seem to exclude, inadvertently, Advisory Opinions – that lies the source of the authority of the Court's pronouncements and the explanation of their actual influence. The Statute by itself cannot give life to a source of law which circumstances do not permit to become effective.[9]

In other words, the very fact that the Court was established as a court of justice operated to invest its judicial opinions with the precedential force normally exerted by the opinions of a judicial body.

Thus, there can be little dispute that, as a matter both of principle and of fact, advisory opinions do exert precedential influence. In this respect, however, there has been some argument as to whether the Court discriminates, or should discriminate, between them and judgments rendered in contentious proceedings. In Hambro's view, the precedential weight of advisory opinions depends on their intrinsic merits.[10] Putting it differently, McNair, relying on Hudson, considered that from 'the point of view of their value as

---

[7] Report submitted to the Third Committee by Mr. Hagerup on behalf of the Sub-Committee, in *Documents concerning the Action Taken by the Council of the League of Nations*, 1921, p. 211.
[8] See Keith, *Advisory Jurisdiction*, p. 31.
[9] Lauterpacht, *Development*, p. 22.
[10] Edvard Hambro, 'The Authority of the Advisory Opinions of the International Court of Justice', *ICLQ*, 3 (1954), p. 21; and see *ICJ Pleadings, Namibia* case, I, p. 676, and II, pp. 375–376.

legal precedents, the Opinions of the Court are not on the same level as its judgments'.[11] But, as pointed out by Keith,[12] what Hudson had in mind was the fact that if 'the question upon which an opinion is given is later submitted to the Court for judgment, the matter is not *res judicata*';[13] precedential value is a different matter. Fachiri had earlier noted that 'it is the established practice of the Court not to discriminate in any way as between advisory opinions and judgments' so far as precedential value is concerned.[14] Beckett, writing in 1932, and Sørensen, writing in 1946, were of a similar view.[15] In the words of Charles De Visscher, 'Dans le plan de leur autorité doctrinale, il n'y a guère de distinction à faire entre arrêts et avis.'[16]

The fact that an advisory opinion may not be followed does not affect its precedential value[17] – no more so than in the case of an unexecuted judgment rendered in a contentious case. Even though the requesting organ need not follow the opinion, it may not disagree with it on legal grounds. Individual Member States, or jurists representing them in the requesting organ, may question the correctness of the opinion; but so far as the requesting organ is concerned, the opinion is an authoritative statement of the law.[18] It is useful to bear in mind the remark made by Judge Lauterpacht in 1956 to the effect that the 'Opinion of 1950 is not a treaty whose provisions can be discarded for the reason that South Africa has declined to comply with them'.[19]

Distinguishing between *res judicata* and jurisprudential influence, Judge Winiarski remarked:

Opinions are not formally binding on States nor on the organ which requests them, they do not have the authority of *res judicata*; but the Court must, in view of its high mission, attribute to them great legal value and

---

[11] Lord McNair, *The Law of Treaties* (Oxford, 1961), p. 168.

[12] Keith, *Advisory Jurisdiction*, p. 32, footnote 27.

[13] Hudson, *The Permanent Court*, p. 512.

[14] A. P. Fachiri, *The Permanent Court of International Justice, Its Constitution, Procedure and Work* (London, 1932), p. 81.

[15] Beckett, 'Jurisprudence', pp. 145–146, and Sørensen, *Les Sources*, p. 168.

[16] Charles De Visscher, *Aspects récents du droit procédural de la Cour internationale de Justice* (Paris, 1966), p. 195.

[17] Cf. Keith, *Advisory Jurisdiction*, p. 222.

[18] Fitzmaurice, *Law and Procedure*, I, p. 123.

[19] *Admissibility of Hearings of Petitioners by the Committee on South West Africa, ICJ Rep 1956*, p. 53.

a moral authority. This being the case and if *tantum valet auctoritas quantum valet ratio*, the Court, as a judicial organ, will surround itself with every guarantee to ensure thorough and impartial examination of the question. For the same reason, States see their rights, their political interests and sometimes their moral position affected by an opinion of the Court, and their disputes are in fact settled by the answer which is given to a question relating to them, which may be a 'key question' of the dispute. This explains the interest States have in being heard in advisory proceedings, in being represented and being permitted to designate their national judges, which would be perfectly useless if advisory opinions were mere utterances having no real importance in respect of their rights and interests. This is also why the Permanent Court did not hesitate to grant States the necessary guarantees, and, in order to exclude any possibility of introducing compulsory jurisdiction by the circuitous means of its advisory opinions, it deliberately laid down in Opinion No. 5 the principle of the consent of the parties (Article 36 of the Statute).[20]

The procedures of the Court are in fact designed to secure the objective, stated by Judge Winiarski, of surrounding the Court 'with every guarantee to ensure thorough and impartial examination of the question' to be considered in advisory proceedings; contentions of fact and law are the subject of close argument.[21]

In the *Peace Treaties* case, Judge Azevedo spoke to similar effect as Judge Winiarski.[22] Judge Zoričič stated that 'the Court's advisory opinions enjoy the same authority as its judgments, and are cited by jurists who attribute the same importance to them as judgments'.[23] In the view of Judge Tanaka:

Firstly, concerning the Advisory Opinion of 1950, it has no binding force upon those concerned, namely no *res judicata* results from an advisory opinion for the purposes of subsequent litigation, even if the issue is identical. This point constitutes a difference between advisory and contentious proceedings. The structure of the proceedings is not the same, and the concept of parties in the same sense as in the latter does not exist in the former. This legal nature of an advisory opinion does not prevent that, as an authoritative pronouncement of what the law is, its content will have an

---

[20] *Interpretation of Peace Treaties with Bulgaria, Hungary and Romania, ICJ Rep 1950*, pp. 91–92, Judge Winiarski, dissenting opinion.

[21] See Judge Jessup's remark in *South West Africa, ICJ Rep 1966*, p. 350, dissenting opinion; and *ICJ Pleadings, Namibia*, I, p. 677.

[22] *ICJ Rep 1950*, p. 80.

[23] *Ibid.*, p. 101, dissenting opinion. And see Hammarskjøld, *La Juridiction internationale* (Leiden, 1938), p. 289, cited by Judge Padilla Nervo, dissenting, in *South West Africa, Second Phase, ICJ Rep 1966*, p. 458, note 1.

influence upon the Court's decision on the same legal issue, irrespective of whether or not this issue constitutes a part of a subsequent stage of the same affairs.[24]

In his separate opinion in the *Namibia* case, Judge de Castro put it, interestingly, this way:

An organ may have functions of different kinds, both advisory and contentious; such, for example, is the case of a Council of State, a court of arbitration or a tribunal.

But in all circumstances the Court retains the elevated dignity deriving from its constitutional status and independence, and its authority may never be compared to that of a legal consultant or advisor; it must remain faithful to its judicial character.

Its advisory opinions do not carry less authority than its judgments. There is, to be sure, a difference, stemming from the *vis re judicata* of the judgments, but this is limited to the parties to the dispute (*vis relativa*: Statute, Art. 59).

On the other hand, the reasons on which judgments are based (Statute, Art. 56) are considered to constitute *dicta prudentium*, and their force as a source of law (Statute, Art. 38) derives *not* from any hierarchic power (*tantum valet auctoritas quantum valet ratio*) but from the validity of the reasoning (*non ratione imperio, sed rationis imperio*).

The essential differences between judgments and advisory opinions lies in the binding force of the former (Charter, Art. 94) and it is on that account that the Court's jurisdiction was established on a voluntary basis (Statute, Art. 36) and the effect of judgments limited to the parties and the particular case (Statute, Art. 59). However, like the reasons on which a judgment is based, the reasoning and operative part of an advisory opinion are, at least potentially, clothed with a general authority, even vis-à-vis States which have not participated in the proceedings, and may therefore contribute to the formation of new rules of international law (Statute, Art. 38, para. 1 (*d*)).[25]

And in the words of Judge Gros:

[W]hen the Court gives an advisory opinion on a question of law it states the law. The absence of binding force does not transform the judicial operation into a legal consultation, which may be made use of or not according to choice. The advisory opinion determines the law applicable to the question put; it is possible for the body which sought the opinion not to follow it in its action, but that body is aware that no position

---

[24] *South West Africa, ICJ Rep 1966*, p. 260, Judge Tanaka, dissenting opinion.
[25] *ICJ Rep 1971*, pp. 173–174.

adopted contrary to the Court's pronouncement will have any effectiveness whatsoever in the legal sphere.[26]

Thus, although an advisory opinion has no binding force under Article 59 of the Statute, it is as authoritative a statement of the law as a judgment rendered in contentious proceedings. From this point of view, it is possible to understand the argument advanced by counsel for India before the ICAO: 'if the International Court of Justice expresses an opinion, it lays down the law and I call it in that sense a judgment'.[27] Advisory opinions are treated on the same plane as judgments.[28]

Precedential value of decisions of a chamber

Article 27 of the Statute provides that a judgment of a chamber 'shall be considered as rendered by the Court'. That provision imparts to a judgment of a chamber the juridical force attaching to a judgment of the full Court. Does it also have the effect of equating the jurisprudential value of a judgment of a chamber with that of a judgment of the full Court?

The idea that equivalence of juridical authority should connote equivalence of jurisprudential authority has its supporters;[29] but it has not met with general acceptance. Speaking of judgments of a chamber, Judge Alvarez expressed the view that 'aux yeux de l'opinion publique, [les sentences] n'ont qu'une valeur moindre puisqu'elles n'expriment pas l'opinion de tous les juges et, par conséquent, elles ne peuvent pas créer un précédent juridique comme les sentences rendues par tous les membres du tribunal'.[30] Similar views have been expressed elsewhere.[31]

It is necessary to consider the institutional relationship between

[26] *Western Sahara, ICJ Rep 1975*, p. 73, Judge Gros, declaration.

[27] *ICJ Pleadings, Appeal Relating to the Jurisdiction of the ICAO Council (India v. Pakistan)*, Memorial of India, Minutes of ICAO, Mr. Palkhivala, p. 218.

[28] *South West Africa, Preliminary Objections, ICJ Rep 1962*, p. 334; *South West Africa, Second Phase, ICJ Rep 1966*, p. 261, Judge Tanaka, dissenting opinion, and pp. 327 and 338, Judge Jessup, dissenting opinion.

[29] D. M. Poulantzas, 'The Chambers of the International Court of Justice and their Role in the Settlement of Disputes arising out of Space Activities', *Revue hellénique de droit international*, 18 (1965), pp. 152–153.

[30] A. Alvarez, *Le Droit international nouveau* (Paris, 1959), p. 599.

[31] See *Land, Island and Maritime Frontier Dispute (El Salvador/Honduras), ICJ Rep 1990*, p. 9, Judge Elias, dissenting opinion; and E. Lauterpacht, *Aspects of the Administration of International Justice* (Cambridge, 1991), p. 29.

171

the Court and its chambers. Argument, which merits respect, has been made to the effect 'that the chambers envisaged in article 26 do not act in the name of the Court, but are independent organisms'.[32] If they are 'independent organisms', this must mean that Article 92 of the Charter established not only the International Court of Justice, but, at least potentially, other courts 'independent' of that Court. It is difficult to read the provision in that way. What it established was a single Court which, however, was given power to act through chambers in certain circumstances. The model is familiar to judicial organisation. In the words of Article 92 of the Charter, the Court 'shall act in accordance with the annexed Statute, which is based upon the Statute of the Permanent Court of International Justice and forms an integral part of the present Charter'. The only judicial body which the Charter contemplated as acting under the Statute was the Court. Article 25, paragraph 1, of the Statute provides that the 'full Court shall sit except when it is expressly provided otherwise in the present Statute'. The implication is that elsewhere in the Statute provision is made for the Court – the same Court – to sit otherwise than in its 'full' formation. That contemplates the Court acting through chambers. This is consistent with Hudson's view that the expression 'full Court' in Article 25 of the Statute 'serves its principal function by setting off the whole body of the judges from the chambers of the Court'.[33] Although the practice has not been consistent, it may be recalled that in the first chamber case, decided by the chamber of summary procedure of the Permanent Court of International Justice in 1924, the judgment began with the carefully chosen words, 'The Court, sitting as a Chamber of Summary Procedure . . .', and ended with a *dispositif* beginning with the words, 'For these reasons the Court decides . . .'.[34] Nothing in the revisions made in 1945 was of sufficient substance to break that mould. Admittedly, the 1924 case related to the chamber of summary procedure, and not to a chamber established under Article 26 of the present Statute; but it is not considered that this represents a material difference. Whatever may be

---

[32] Shabtai Rosenne, 'Article 27 of the Statute of the International Court of Justice', *Virg JIL*, 32 (1991), p. 230.

[33] Hudson, *The Permanent Court*, p. 335.

[34] *Treaty of Neuilly, 1924, PCIJ, Series A, No. 3*, pp. 4 and 9 respectively. And see *Interpretation of Judgment No. 3, PCIJ, Series A, No. 4*, p. 4; *Land, Island and Maritime Frontier Dispute (El Salvador/Honduras), ICJ Rep 1990*, p. 57; and Hudson, *The Permanent Court*, p. 586.

the chamber involved, the jurisdiction belongs not to it, but to the Court;[35] it is merely exercised by the chamber. A chamber is not a wholly distinct institution; it is a chamber of the Court.[36] In *East Timor (Portugal v. Australia)*, the Court stated that the principle of *Monetary Gold* was 'confirmed in several of its subsequent decisions', among which it then included two chamber decisions; it treated decisions of its chambers as decisions of the Court.[37]

Thus, a decision of a chamber is not rendered by a judicial body independent of the Court; it is given by the Court sitting in a special formation. But does it follow that it has the same precedential value as a decision rendered by the full Court? In some municipal systems the decisions of a collegiate judicial body sitting *en banc* are in practice treated as having higher authority than those of the same body sitting in divisional or other smaller formations.[38] It is difficult to see why a similar precedential relationship should not exist as between the Court and its chambers.

No particular problems have arisen so far. The Court has itself made use of the decisions of its chambers. In *Certain Phosphate Lands in Nauru*[39] it observed that its previous jurisprudence on the *Monetary Gold* principle 'was applied by a Chamber of the Court in the case concerning the *Land, Island and Maritime Frontier Dispute (El Salvador/Honduras)*'.[40] In the *Jan Mayen* case[41] it made several references to the decision of the chamber in the *Gulf of Maine* case.[42] In *Maritime Delimitation and Territorial Questions between Qatar and Bahrain*[43] it cited the recognition by a chamber[44] of the rule that the Court cannot take account of declarations, admissions or proposals which the parties may have made in the course of direct

---

[35] See Fred Morrison's remark in A. C. Arend (ed.), *The United States and the Compulsory Jurisdiction of the International Court of Justice* (Lanham, 1986), p. 158.

[36] Counsel has spoken of 'the plenary tribunal of which [a chamber] is a part'. See *Land, Island and Maritime Frontier Dispute (El Salvador/Honduras), Application by Nicaragua for Permission to Intervene*, Verbatim Record, C4/CR 90/3, p. 80, 6 June 1990, Mr. E. Lauterpacht.

[37] *ICJ Rep 1995*, p. 101, paragraph 26.

[38] See M. D. A. Freeman, 'Precedent and the House of Lords', *New Law Journal*, 121 (1971), p. 551.

[39] *ICJ Rep 1992*, p. 260, para. 52.

[40] *ICJ Rep 1990*, p. 116, para. 56.

[41] *ICJ Rep 1993*, p. 61.

[42] *ICJ Rep 1984*, p. 246.

[43] *ICJ Rep 1994*, p. 126, para. 40.

[44] *Land, Island and Maritime Frontier Dispute (El Salvador/Honduras: Nicaragua Intervening), ICJ Rep 1992*, p. 406, para. 73.

negotiations where these have not led to an agreement between them. Also, individual opinions have frequently referred to decisions rendered by chambers.

However, difficulty could arise in the event of a variance in holdings on the same point as between the full Court and a chamber. One observer considers that

> in the *Land, Island and Maritime Frontier Dispute* a Chamber of five Judges, including two Judges ad hoc, has set the parameters for intervening States as well as taking a less restrictive approach to the criteria for intervention under Article 62 than did the full Court in earlier intervention cases. It is also noticeable that the three Judges of the Chamber who are (or have been) Judges of the Court (Judges Sette-Camara, President Sir Robert Jennings and Vice-President Oda) had all stated their preferred approach to intervention through separate and dissenting opinions in those earlier cases. It remains to be seen what weight will be given to this decision by a differently constituted Chamber or a future full Court.[45]

It is right to recall that the election of those members of the chamber who were already judges of the Court was made before any question of intervention had been raised.[46] Also, it must be borne in mind that the argument in the case was as to whether what might be involved was a variance or a distinction.[47] How far there was a true variance is open to debate; the kind of intervention adopted by the chamber permitted the intervener to make observations to the Court but preserved and respected the jurisdictional link principle by taking the position that an intervener without such a link could not be a party.[48] However, if in fact a variance occurs as between holdings of the full Court and a chamber, there can be little doubt that in a later case the Court would incline to resolve the inconsistency in favour of its own holding, unless the holding of the chamber satisfies it that its own previous holding was erroneous and so should be departed from.

---

[45] Christine Chinkin, *Third Parties in International Law* (Oxford, 1993), p. viii; and see, *ibid.*, p. 177. See also Andrew F. Moore, 'Ad Hoc Chambers of the International Court of Justice and the Question of Intervention', *Case Western Reserve JIL*, 24 (1992), pp. 687, 697; and Rosa Maria Riquelme Cortado, *La Intervención de Terceros Estados en el Proceso Internacional* (Madrid, 1993), p. 125.

[46] Verbatim Record, C4/CR 90/3, p. 81, Mr. E. Lauterpacht.

[47] Verbatim Record, C4/CR 90/5, pp. 23–25, Professor Brownlie.

[48] *Land, Island and Maritime Frontier Dispute, Application to Intervene, ICJ Rep 1990*, paras. 102–105. Cf. E. Lauterpacht, *Aspects of the Administration of International Justice* (Cambridge, 1991), pp. 26 ff.

If, contrary to the foregoing, decisions of chambers exert the same degree of precedential authority as decisions of the full Court, a question may arise as to whether this will apply to *ad hoc* chambers also. There are two points. The first is how representative is such a chamber of the Court. Those members of such a chamber who are also members of the Court are elected by the Court to the chamber from among the members of the Court; but, in practice, the election is made in accordance with the previously ascertained wishes of the parties. The second point concerns the relationship between such a chamber and the international community. As laid down in Article 9 of the Statute, 'the electors shall bear in mind ... that in the body [of the Court] as a whole the representation of the main forms of civilisation and of the principal legal systems of the world should be assured'. The authority of the decisions of the Court is obviously linked to its representative character, both as regards civilizations[49] and as regards legal systems.[50] Understandably, the principle of Article 9 of the Statute is not fully reflected in the membership of all chambers; but it is indirectly at work in so far as the regular judges of the Court who are members of a chamber have been freely elected to it by their colleagues who have themselves been elected to the Court in accordance with the principle. The operation of the principle is less apparent where the election of judges as members of a chamber is done in accordance with the stated wishes of the parties to the particular case. The validity of chambers so established has been strongly defended[51]

---

[49] See Hudson, *The Permanent Court*, p. 157, para. 148.

[50] *Barcelona Traction, Light and Power Company, Limited, ICJ Rep 1970*, p. 317, separate opinion of Judge Ammoun.

[51] See E. Lauterpacht, *Aspects of the Administration of International Justice* (Cambridge, 1991), pp. 87 ff. For other arguments and observations see E. D. Brown, *The United Nations Convention on the Law of the Sea, 1982: A Guide for National Policy Making, Legislation and Administration*, (Commonwealth Secretariat, London, 1982), III, pp. 85–86; Georg Schwarzenberger, 'Present-Day Relevance of the Hague Peace System 1899–1979', *Year Book of World Affairs*, 34 (1980), pp. 349–350; also, by him, *International Law as Applied by International Courts and Tribunals*, IV: *International Judicial Law* (London, 1986), pp. 15–16, 167–168, 334, 391, 393; Paul de La Pradelle, 'Progrès ou déclin du Droit international?', in *Mélanges offerts à Charles Rousseau, La Communauté internationale* (Paris, 1974), p. 147; Edward McWhinney, *Judicial Settlement of International Disputes; Jurisdiction, Justiciability and Judicial Law-Making on the Contemporary International Court* (Dordrecht, 1991), p. 73; J. G. Starke, *The New Rules of Court of the International Court of Justice* (Institute of Advanced Studies, Australian National University, Canberra, 1973), p. 9; Thomas Franck, 'Fairness in the International Legal and Insti-

and may be assumed for present purposes. Nor, as has been remarked above, has the Court so far shown any disposition to distinguish between the precedential authority of decisions given by them and that of decisions given by the Court. However, whether it should be taken that an issue in this latter respect is foreclosed is less clear.

tutional System', *Hag R*, 240 (1993–III), pp. 315–316; *Land, Island and Maritime Frontier Dispute (El Salvador/Honduras), Application for Permission to Intervene, ICJ Rep 1990*, p. 18; and, by the present writer, 'The International Court of Justice: The Integrity of an Idea', in R. S. Pathak and R. P. Dhokalia (eds.), *International Law in Transition, Essays in Memory of Judge Nagendra Singh* (Dordrecht, 1992), p. 341.

13

The precedential impact of
individual opinions

Introductory remarks

The fact that a decision was a majority one does not render it any less a decision of the Court than a unanimous one. On the other hand, even if the judgment is unanimous, it is not infallible;[1] this possibility can scarcely be less open where the decision was a majority one. Judges who think it is erroneous in whole or in part have a statutory right to say so; so too where the decision is sought to be supported by different or additional reasons. But do dissenting and separate opinions (both referred to below as 'individual opinions') weaken the authority of the Court's judgment?

There is, indeed, an appearance of disarray in the presentation of several opinions on the same point. The argument against multiplicity not surprisingly goes back a long way.[2] It has been frequently made and as frequently resisted. Experience has not confirmed the fears expressed by Lord Phillimore in 1920, when, speaking of the work of the Advisory Committee of Jurists, he said, '[W]e came to the conclusion that a dissenting judge might insist on expanding his motifs in such a way as to make the judgment ridiculous ... Curiously enough, the Council [of the League of Nations] is about to propose to the Assembly that the dissentients shall be allowed to express their reasons.'[3] Some decades later, Judge de Castro dealt with the matter in this way:

---

[1] Lauterpacht, *Development*, p. 398.
[2] See, generally, Farrokh Jhabvala, *The Development and Scope of Individual Opinions in the International Court of Justice* (Ann Arbor, 1977), pp. 76–80.
[3] Lord Phillimore, 'Scheme for the Permanent Court of International Justice', *Transactions of the Grotius Society*, 6 (1920), pp. 95–96.

Dissenting and separate opinions are criticized, especially in countries which follow the Latin system, because they weaken the authority of judgments: it is not the Court, it is said, but only a tiny majority which takes the decision; furthermore, in separate opinions, some of the arguments on which the judgment rests are called into question by members of the majority.

On the other hand, such opinions are evidence of the life and of the evolution of legal doctrine. Some dissenting opinions are the law of the future; others are the expression of the resistance of old ideas. Personally, I think separate opinions have their uses: they give judges an opportunity to explain the reasons for their votes. The drafting of a judgment is a very delicate task, for it must, with great prudence, reflect the 'consensus' of the majority and it must do so clearly, simply and unambiguously. In these circumstances, if the arguments which a judge regards as conclusive do not find expression in the judgment, a separate opinion makes it possible for them to be stated. Separate opinions provide a means for making known the reasons for the votes of members of the majority and this may be useful for the purposes of critical studies by commentators.[4]

Judge Lachs put it thus:

It may be claimed that institutionalized dissent destroys the illusion of absolute certainty, but the workings of the Court do not depend upon illusion, and the dissent it brought into the open is particularly valuable as a reflection of reality. It preserves the ongoing counterpoint of international judicial opinion, in which a new voice is bound to emerge from time.[5]

The last phrase echoes the memorable remark of Charles Evans Hughes, a Chief Justice of the United States Supreme Court and earlier a member of the Permanent Court of International Justice, that a 'dissent in a court of last resort is an appeal to the brooding spirit of the law, to the intelligence of a future day, when a later decision may possibly correct the error into which the dissenting judge believes the court to have been betrayed'.[6]

---

[4] *Appeal Relating to the Jurisdiction of the ICAO Council, ICJ Rep 1972*, p. 116, separate opinion.
[5] Manfred Lachs, 'The Revised Procedure of the International Court of Justice', in *Essays on the Development of the International Legal Order, in Memory of Haro F. van Panhuys* (Alphen a/d Rijn, 1980), p. 42.
[6] Lauterpacht, *Development*, p. 66, note 10, citing Charles Evans Hughes, *The Supreme Court of the United States* (New York, 1928), p. 68. The passage has been cited more than once in the jurisprudence of the Court. See, *inter alia*, *South West Africa, Second Phase, ICJ Rep 1966*, p. 325, Judge Jessup, dissenting.

But the justification of the system relating to individual opinions is not being considered; the focus is on the impact of the system on the precedential authority of the Court's decisions. In this respect, a helpful distinction is that made by Hersch Lauterpacht between what he called the 'substantive' authority of a decision and what he called its 'formal authority'. The latter is not affected by the expression of a different individual view; the former can and may properly be. In his words:

Experience has shown that so long as it is clear that the decision of the Court is, within its proper limits, binding and authoritative, the individual Opinions of the Judges, far from detracting from the standing of the Judgments or Advisory Opinions, add to their vitality, comprehension and usefulness and greatly facilitate the fulfilment of the indirect purpose of the Court, which is to develop and to clarify international law. It is improbable that such disagreement, expressed in terms of moderation and restraint, impairs the authority of the Court. Undoubtedly, a dissent – whether partial or complete – may, in proportion to its intrinsic merit, impair in some measure the substantive as distinguished from the formal authority of the decision of the Court. But, then, if the dissent is in part expressive of better law or of a better judicial method, no lasting harm need ensue from the fact that the substantive authority of the Court's decision may be to that extent impaired. It would be prejudicial to the cause of international justice to assume that the weight of the Court's decisions is irrefutably entrenched behind its formal authority. From that point of view a judicial dissent is not only an appeal to enlightened and informed legal opinion. It is, indirectly, a powerful stimulus to the maximum effort of which a tribunal is capable. For no formal authority can in the long run shield a defective decision from the impact, in proportion to its merits, of a dissent. Mere dissent cannot weaken the authority of the decision. The merits of the dissent may have that effect. On the other hand, if the dissent is one-sided or extravagant, it will add emphasis to the balance and the restraint of the decision of the Court.[7]

It would, for example, have been of the substantive authority of an advisory opinion that Judge Dillard was speaking when he said that as 'a sheer practical matter . . . had a strongly reasoned dissent cast grave doubt on the validity of the resolutions, then the probative value of the Advisory Opinion would have been weakened'.[8]

---

[7] Lauterpacht, *Development*, pp. 66–67.
[8] *Namibia, ICJ Rep 1971*, p. 151.

Thus individual opinions may well affect the substantive authority of a judgment of the Court; but the formal authority remains intact.

Holdings resting on a false consensus

One area in which the substantive authority of a decision may be weakened by individual opinions relates to cases in which such opinions may show that a particular holding in a judgment rests on a false consensus.

Decision-making by the Court, as in the case of any collegiate judicial body,[9] involves a process of convergence of views in an effort to reach a consensus. Some willingness to modify a position of secondary importance in the light of different views is essential. Alluding to this aspect, Charles De Visscher remarked of Judge Hurst, 'Il lui paraissait plus essentiel d'atteindre au plus large dénominateur commun que d'exposer dans une opinion individuelle ou dissidente les points secondaires sur lesquels il réservait sa manière de voir.'[10] Simple compromise is of course impermissible;[11] on the other hand, a judge cannot abstain from voting.[12] For these reasons, the pursuit of the objective of securing the largest common denominator could result in the adoption of the easy course and a corresponding failure to confront the real issues.

Worse, as Beckett pointed out in reference to the 'Lotus', the decision could include a statement of law on a particular point which was in fact rejected by half of the bench;[13] in such a case, his view was that the relevant holding 'ne peut aucunement être considérée comme un précédent ou comme une source de droit'. Hambro later made a similar observation in respect of *Conditions of Admission of a State to Membership in the United Nations (Article 4 of*

[9] *Military and Paramilitary Activities in and against Nicaragua (Nicaragua v. United States of America), ICJ Rep 1986*, p. 155, Judge Nagendra Singh.
[10] Charles De Visscher, *ICLQ*, 13 (1964), p. 3.
[11] *Delimitation of the Maritime Boundary in the Gulf of Maine Area, ICJ Rep 1984*, p. 389, Judge Gros; and *Continental Shelf (Libya/Malta), ICJ Rep 1985*, joint separate opinion, p. 90, para. 36.
[12] *PCIJ, Series E, No. 9*, p. 174; *Western Sahara, ICJ Rep 1975*, p. 75, para. 9, declaration of Judge Gros; and Resolution concerning the Internal Judicial Practice of the Court, 1976, Article 8 (v). But the early practice of the Permanent Court of International Justice allowed abstention on voting prior to the taking of the final vote. See *PCIJ, Series E, No. 11*, p. 148.
[13] Beckett, 'Jurisprudence', p. 43, citing the *'Lotus', 1927, PCIJ, Series A, No. 10*.

Charter),[14] observing that 'the majority of 9 in reality was a minority of 7'.[15] Rosenne likewise demonstrated that the decision of the Court in the *Guardianship Convention* case rested on views which were in fact supported only by a minority.[16] Much the same thing was later pointed out by Judge Petrén in the *Nuclear Tests*, where he drew attention to the possibility that the procedures of the Court could lead to 'the adoption of judgments whose reasoning is not accepted by the majority of the judges voting in favour of them'.[17] But, even in such cases, although individual opinions may weaken the substantive authority of a judgment by showing the absence of real consensus on some particular point, the formal authority of the judgment is unaffected.

Criticism of judgment

Criticisms of a judgment are not confined to dissenting opinions; they may occur in separate opinions also. For a number of reasons, judges are often in the position of agreeing with the conclusion but not fully with the reasoning.[18] In a 1985 case Judge Ruda, having voted for the operative clauses of the judgment, stated in a separate opinion that he subscribed 'to most of its reasoning' but felt 'bound to dissent from the conclusion reached in paragraphs 41, 42 and 43'.[19] The extent of the difference may raise questions as to whether an opinion should be entitled a separate opinion or a dissenting opinion.[20] Some separate opinions are critical of the judgment to such an extent as to raise doubt as to whether the vote should not

---

[14] *ICJ Rep 1947–1948*, p. 57.

[15] Edvard Hambro, 'Dissenting and Individual Opinions in the International Court of Justice', *ZöV*, 17 (1956–1957), p. 345.

[16] S. Rosenne, 'Sir Hersch Lauterpacht's Concept of the Task of the International Judge', *AJIL*, 55 (1961), p. 861, and footnote 134.

[17] See his separate opinion in the *Nuclear Tests (Australia v. France)*, *ICJ Rep 1974*, p. 306, and, also by him, 'Forms of Expression of Judicial Activity', in Leo Gross (ed.), *The Future of the International Court of Justice*, 2 vols. (Dobbs Ferry, 1976), II, p. 452.

[18] *Certain Norwegian Loans*, *ICJ Rep 1957*, p. 34, Judge Lauterpacht, separate opinion.

[19] *Application for Revision and Interpretation of the Judgment of 24 February 1982 in the Case concerning the* Continental Shelf (Tunisia/Libyan Arab Jamahiriya) *(Tunisia/Libyan Arab Jamahiriya)*, *ICJ Rep 1985*, p. 232, para. 1.

[20] See *Certain Norwegian Loans*, *ICJ Rep 1957*, p. 66, Judge Lauterpacht, separate opinion.

have been a dissenting one.[21] The judge's position can be complicated where his disagreement extends to part of the conclusion as well, as can happen in a case in which the *dispositif* contains several holdings, the judge voting for some and against the rest. According to the publications of the Court:

In May 1948, the Court decided that the opinion of a Judge who disagreed with a judgment or advisory opinion should be called a 'dissenting' opinion; and that a separate opinion given by a Judge who supported the view of the majority should be called an 'individual' opinion.[22]

It is apparent that this does not provide adequate guidance; in practice, a judge exercises a right to choose the title of his statement.[23] Thus, criticisms may be presented in individual opinions generally; but to what extent?

Sometimes a distinction is made between the right of a judge to express his own point of view and the offering of any criticism by him of the judgment of the Court; it is said that individual opinions, whether separate or dissenting, should not be critical of the judgment. On 1 December 1927 the Permanent Court of International Justice agreed that the object of dissenting opinions 'was to show the reasons for which a judge could not agree with the majority and that they were not intended to be a reasoned criticism of the judgment or opinion'.[24] This view was reflected in Judge Anzilotti's statement in 1930 that a 'dissenting opinion should not be a criticism of that which the Court has seen fit to say, but rather an exposition of the views of the writer'.[25] A similar standpoint was taken in 1953 by Judge Basdevant, speaking thus:

While concurring in the operative part of the Judgment, I am bound to say that the reasons for which I do so are to a great extent different from those stated by the Court. I therefore think that I should indicate in outline, but without exhaustive consideration of each separate point, the

---

[21] See Jennings, 'The Collegiate Responsibility and the Authority of the International Court of Justice', in Yoram Dinstein (ed.), *International Law at a Time of Perplexity, Essays in Honour of Shabtai Rosenne* (Dordrecht, 1989), p. 348.

[22] *ICJYB*, 1948–1949, p. 80. And see *ICJYB*, 1950–1951, p. 118.

[23] Farrokh Jhabvala, 'Declarations by Judges of the International Court of Justice', *AJIL*, 72 (1978), p. 854. And see Rosenne, *Law and Practice* (1965), II, p. 596.

[24] *PCIJ, Series E, No. 4*, p. 291.

[25] *Free City of Danzig and ILO, 1930, PCIJ, Series B, No. 18*, p. 18. See, likewise, Baron Schenk von Stauffenberg, *Statut et Règlement de la Cour permanente de Justice internationale* (Berlin, 1934), p. 414; and Manley O. Hudson, 'The Twenty-Eighth Year of the World Court', *AJIL*, 44 (1950), p. 20.

means by which I arrive at agreement with the operative part. I do not propose, in doing this, to embark upon a criticism of the reasoning adopted by the Court, nor to express my views on all the points dealt with in the at times over-complete arguments of the Parties; to do either would be to go beyond the bounds within which an individual opinion ought, in my view, to be kept.[26]

In 1955 he remarked:

While fully accepting the operative clause of the Opinion, I have, to my regret, reached the same view by a different path from that followed by the Court. I in no way intend any criticism of the latter which, I consider, would be out of place in a separate opinion written by a Judge, but I believe that I should indicate briefly the means by which I am enabled to subscribe to the Opinion given by the Court.[27]

The problem presented by these views is to see how it is possible for an individual opinion which suggests an approach different from that taken by the judgment of the Court to avoid being in some sense critical of the latter. Although he considered that a 'dissenting opinion should not be a criticism of that which the Court has seen fit to say', it is not possible to read the opinions, concurring or dissenting, of Judge Anzilotti without appreciating that in several instances the differences which emerged between them and the Court's judgment constituted substantial criticisms of the latter. This is apparent from his dissenting opinion in *Diversion of Water from the Meuse*.[28] The fact that he tended to avoid making direct comparisons between his position and that of the Court was a sign of courtesy, not an indication of absence of criticism; even so, it is to be observed that he made such a comparison in the *Interpretation of the Convention of 1919 concerning Employment of Women during the Night*.[29]

Obviously, individual opinions should not assume the form of hostile criticism. That, unfortunately, has sometimes been the case; as remarked by Rosenne, 'some of them give the appearance of having been written *cum ira et sine studio*'.[30] But to suggest simply, as is

---

[26] *Minquiers and Ecrehos, ICJ Rep 1953*, p. 74.
[27] *Voting Procedure on Questions relating to Reports and Petitions concerning the Territory of South West Africa, ICJ Rep 1955*, p. 80.
[28] *1937, PCIJ, Series A/B, No. 70*, p. 45.
[29] *1932, PCIJ, Series A/B, No. 50*, p. 387, para. 3.
[30] Shabtai Rosenne, *The Practice and Methods of International Law* (London, 1984), p. 98.

sometimes done, that such an opinion may not be critical is an exaggeration. Anand put the position correctly when he said: 'A dissent should indeed afford a critique of the Court's judgment. It should express disagreement without being disagreeable.'[31] It should strike a balance between institutional loyalty to the Court of which the judge is a member, and devotion to the law whose servant he remains. On this view of the matter, it may be accepted that it should not be the enterprise of an individual opinion simply to undermine the authority of the Court's judgment; its purpose should, indeed, be to set out the judge's views. But, if the latter cannot be stated without presenting a criticism of the Court's reasoning, to say that the judge cannot criticise the judgment is to deny him a right to express his opinion and to offer to the judgment a shield which a robust jurisprudence should not need. Gratuitously polemical remarks are another matter; yet, in the words of Edvard Hambro, 'These utterances are regrettable, but are not in themselves very dangerous for the Court.'[32] They may be quietly put down with the words of Chief Justice Hughes, 'Independence does not mean cantankerousness and a judge may be a strong judge without being an impossible person. Nothing is more distressing on any bench than the exhibition of a captious, impatient, querulous spirit.'[33] The present bench, let it be said, does not suffer from this infirmity.

An allied view is that a dissenting opinion should not offer an alternative decision to that determined by the Court. In *Continental Shelf (Libyan Arab Jamahiriya/Malta)*, Judge Mosler prefaced his dissenting opinion with the statement, 'Since it cannot be the legitimate purpose of a separate opinion of a judge being in the minority to offer an alternative decision, but rather to explain why he is not able to follow the reasoning and result of the Judgment, my remarks will concentrate only on the principal points of divergence of views.'[34] This is attractive; the difficulty for a dissenting judge is that it is not always practicable to 'explain why he is not able to

---

[31] R. P. Anand, *Studies in International Adjudication* (Delhi, 1969), p. 215.

[32] Edvard Hambro, 'Dissenting and Individual Opinions in the International Court of Justice', *ZöV*, 17 (1956–1957), p. 243.

[33] Charles Evans Hughes, *The Supreme Court of the United States* (New York, 1936), pp. 67–68, cited in C. W. Jenks, *The Common Law of Mankind* (London, 1958), pp. 440–441.

[34] *ICJ Rep 1985*, p. 114. And see his separate opinion in *Aegean Sea Continental Shelf, ICJ Rep 1978*, p. 25, second paragraph.

follow the reasoning and result of the Judgment' without in effect having 'to offer an alternative decision'. Judge Anzilotti, dissenting, was offering an 'alternative decision' in the *Diversion of Water from the Meuse* when he indicated how he considered 'that the Court should have proceeded',[35] adding:

For these reasons, I consider that the Court should have accepted submission I° of the Counter-claim, should have rejected submission III (1) of the Reply, and should have adjudged and declared that the fact of making it impossible, by the construction of the Borgharen barrage, for the quantity of Meuse water discharged through the treaty feeder to vary according to the level of the Meuse, as provided in Article IV of the Treaty, and of constantly maintaining that quantity at its maximum amount, is an infraction of the Treaty.[36]

In the *Nuclear Tests (Australia* v. *France)*, the joint dissenting opinion of Judges Onyeama, Dillard, Jiménez de Aréchaga and Waldock expressly said, 'Dissenting, as we do, from the Court's decision that the claim of Australia no longer has any object, we consider that *the Court should have now decided* to proceed to pleadings on the merits.'[37] This also seemed equivalent to offering an 'alternative decision' on the particular phase of the proceedings then before the Court. In any event, it is important not to complicate the problem by the adoption of misleading terminology. The minority cannot and do not really present an 'alternative decision': they can at most indicate an alternative solution. Their opinion does not result in two decisions being delivered by the Court.[38]

One last observation. While accepting the propriety of individual dissenting opinions, Fachiri considered that joint dissenting opinions were 'highly undesirable'. Speaking of the *Customs Régime between Germany and Austria*,[39] he said:

This is the second occasion upon which dissenting judges of the Court have taken the course of delivering a joint opinion, and in my respectful submission this is highly undesirable. Every one will agree that any wide measure of disagreement within the Court is, in itself, regrettable, but its unfortunate effect is magnified if an impression is created of the Bench

---

[35] *1937, PCIJ, Series A/B, No. 70*, p. 50.
[36] *Ibid.*, p. 52.
[37] *ICJ Rep 1974*, p. 371, para. 119, emphasis added.
[38] See, generally, Farrokh Jhabvala, *The Development and Scope of Individual Opinions in the International Court of Justice* (Ann Arbor, 1977), p. 208.
[39] *1931, PCIJ, Series A/B, No. 41*, p. 37.

being divided into two camps, one against the other, as tends to be done by two opinions representing an almost equal numerical strength. The Rules of Court do not indeed appear to contemplate this procedure, but, quite apart from any technical objection, it seems to be objectionable in principle. The judgment or opinion of the Court should represent the combined labours of the whole Bench working in collaboration, and any irreconcilable dissent should be that of the individual judge concerned – as it were an addendum expressing his personal views. This is the spirit in which the Court has worked in the past and continues to work at the present time, but in order that this may be apparent to all, it is earnestly to be hoped that a practice of joint dissenting opinions will not be allowed to grow up'.[40]

One can see the point, sometimes still heard, about magnification of differences. That, however, would not seem to be a sufficient objection; joint dissenting opinions do not appear frequently, but the right to append them is not in doubt.

A dissent on a point may not necessarily oppose the majority view on the point

The counterpart of the proposition that the judgment of the Court may not in fact represent majority opinion on a particular point is the proposition that a dissenting opinion may not necessarily be opposed to the position taken by the majority on a particular point. Judge Jennings gave the reason as follows:

In a case like the present where an important question of jurisdiction had to be left to be dealt with at the merits stage, it is incumbent upon those Judges who have felt it necessary to vote 'No' to some of the items of the *dispositif*, to explain their views, if only briefly. The reason is that the scheme of the *dispositif* is necessarily designed to enable the majority to express their decision. Even amongst them, reasons for the decision may differ; but the actual decision, expressed by the vote 'Yes', will be essentially the same decision for all of them. Not so for those voting 'No'. An example is the very important subparagraph (3) of paragraph 292 in the present case, by which those voting 'Yes' express their common view that the respondent State has acted in breach of its obligation not to intervene in the affairs of another State: – a vote, 'No', however, might mean that in the opinion of that

---

[40] A. P. Fachiri, 'The Austro-German Customs Union Case', *BYBIL*, 13 (1932), p. 75.

Judge, the Respondent's acts did not amount to intervention; or that there was a legal justification by way of collective self-defence; or that the action was justified as a counter measure; or that, as in the case of the present Judge, the Court had no jurisdiction to decide any of these things, and therefore the vote 'No', of itself, expressed no opinion whatsoever on those other substantive questions.[41]

Judge Ignacio-Pinto likewise had occasion to explain that his dissent did not necessarily signify opposition. In his words:

To my regret, I have been obliged to vote against the Court's Judgment. However, to my mind the negative vote does not, strictly speaking, signify opposition, since in a different context I would certainly have voted in favour of the process which the Court considered it should follow to arrive at its decision. In my view that decision is devoted to fixing the conditions for exercise of preferential rights, for conservation of fish species, and historic rights, rather than to responding to the primary claim of the Applicant, which is for a statement of the law on a specific point.[42]

That would seem to mean that the judge was not opposed to what the Court in fact determined, but that, in his view, the point which the Court determined was not the point presented for determination.

A somewhat similar situation occurred in *Certain Phosphate Lands in Nauru (Nauru v. Australia), Preliminary Objections.* In part 1 (f) of the *dispositif* the Court rejected Australia's preliminary objection based on the fact that New Zealand and the United Kingdom were not parties to the proceedings. Vice-President Oda was one of a minority of four who voted against that holding. In his dissenting opinion he however said 'that my negative vote on operative part 1 (f) is motivated by my belief that it is premature to close the door on the objection concerned, which I find too closely connected with the merits for present decision; this particular vote on my part does not therefore signify that I necessarily accept this objection without further examination'.[43] Thus, the vote cast against the Court's holding on the point did not necessarily signify disagreement with the substance of the holding.

[41] *Military and Paramilitary Activities in and against Nicaragua, ICJ Rep 1986*, pp. 528–529.
[42] *Fisheries Jurisdiction (United Kingdom v. Iceland), ICJ Rep 1974*, p. 35.
[43] *ICJ Rep 1992*, p. 303.

When a judge is bound by the decision of the Court

There are certain limits to the right to dissent. A judge is bound at the merits stage by the decision of the Court on a preliminary point from which he earlier dissented in the same case; though entitled to maintain that his original opinion was right, he must now proceed on the basis that it stands decided as it has been by the Court.[44] So too where, more than one preliminary objection having been raised, the Court upholds jurisdiction on a point on which a judge would have held that there was no instrument before it by reference to which it could assume jurisdiction in relation to any aspect of the dispute; he must proceed to consider any remaining objections on the basis of the Court's ruling on that particular point.[45] This is also the situation where a point in the nature of a preliminary point is considered at the merits; a judge who upholds the point when it is expressly or implicitly rejected by the Court has to proceed with the remainder of the case on the basis of the Court's decision.[46]

A judge cannot at the preliminary stage anticipate the merits. This was what President Khan sought to point out in his declaration in the *Fisheries Jurisdiction* cases,[47] what he had in mind being presumably Judge Padilla Nervo's dissenting opinion in which the substance of the case was entered into.[48] A similar situation may arise where preliminary issues have been joined to the merits; a judge

---

[44] See the *Free Zones of Upper Savoy and the District of Gex (Second Phase), 1930, PCIJ, Series A, No. 24*, joint dissenting opinion, p. 20, the point made about intervening changes in the composition of the bench not being, it is submitted, material to the point made in the text above; *Namibia, ICJ Rep 1971*, p. 130, Judge Petrén, separate opinion; *Application for Review of Judgment No. 158 of the United Nations Administrative Tribunal, ICJ Rep 1973*, p. 223, Judge Onyeama, separate opinion; *Military and Paramilitary Activities in and against Nicaragua, (Nicaragua v. United States of America), Merits, ICJ Rep 1986*, pp. 176–177, para. 16, Judge Ruda, separate opinion, and p. 182, para. 2, Judge Ago, separate opinion; and Nagendra Singh, *The Role and Record of the International Court of Justice* (Dordrecht, 1989), pp. 187–189. As to the position as between different cases, see *ICJ Pleadings, South West Africa* cases, VII, p. 187, argument of Mr de Villiers.

[45] *Interhandel, ICJ Rep 1959*, pp. 119–120, Judge Lauterpacht; and see Shabtai Rosenne 'Sir Hersch Lauterpacht's concept of the task of the International Judge', *AJIL*, 55 (1961), at pp. 843–844.

[46] *Maritime Delimitation of the Area between Greenland and Jan Mayen (Denmark v. Norway), ICJ Rep 1993*, p. 91, para. 2, Vice-President Oda, separate opinion.

[47] *ICJ Rep 1973*, pp. 22–23.

[48] *Ibid.*, p. 36. And see *South West Africa, ICJ Rep 1966*, p. 263, dissenting opinion of Judge Tanaka, and Judge Petrén's remarks in *Nuclear Tests (Australia v. France), ICJ Rep 1974*, p. 307, penultimate paragraph.

who dissents from the later judgment of the Court upholding an objection which has been so joined cannot go on to pronounce on the merits. So too, it is submitted, where, by agreement of the parties, objections are heard together with the merits.[49] The reason, of general principle, is that the upholding of the objection means that the Court itself cannot consider the merits, even if they were in fact presented to it.[50] Nor can a judge pronounce at the preliminary stage on an objection which has been joined to the merits.[51] A more complicated situation arises where, in preliminary proceedings in which the adjudication has been split into two separate stages, a judge opines on jurisdiction at a stage when the Court itself has not fully dealt with the issue.[52]

There could also be a question as to whether a judge is bound in a later case to follow a previous holding in a different case with which he disagreed at the time. In *International Status of South West Africa*[53] Judge Read dissented from the Court's holding on the question of accountability to, and supervision by, the United Nations. However, joining the majority in *Admissibility of Hearings of Petitioners by the Committee on South West Africa*,[54] he proceeded on the basis (to quote counsel in a later case) 'that his function now was not to reconsider the question [but] purely to interpret the majority opinion on a particular point raised in the request of the Assembly'.[55] But, where there is no similar function, there is no reason to suppose that a judge who dissented on a point in a previous case may not reopen the point in a later one; he may certainly reopen a point supported by the dissenting opinion of other judges in a previous case.[56]

---

[49] Cf. *East Timor (Portugal* v. *Australia), ICJ Rep 1995,* p. 90, separate opinion of Judge Oda, at p. 107, dissenting opinion of Judge Weeramantry, at p. 142, and dissenting opinion of Judge *ad hoc* Skubiszewski, at p. 226.

[50] *Barcelona Traction, Light and Power Company, Limited, ICJ Rep 1970,* p. 164, para. 9, Judge Jessup, separate opinion.

[51] *Barcelona Traction, Light and Power Company, Limited, ICJ Rep 1964,* pp. 49–50, Judge Jessup's remarks, probably directed to Vice-President Koo's separate opinion at p. 51.

[52] See the somewhat unusual procedure employed in *Qatar* v. *Bahrain, ICJ Rep 1994,* p. 112, and the dissenting opinion of Judge Oda, at p. 133.

[53] *ICJ Rep 1950,* p. 164, separate opinion.

[54] *ICJ Rep 1956,* p. 23.

[55] *ICJ Pleadings, South West Africa,* VII, p. 187, Mr. de Villiers.

[56] See the approach taken by Judge Tanaka in *Barcelona Traction, Light and Power Company, Limited, ICJ Rep 1964,* pp. 72 ff, in which he preferred to follow a previous joint dissenting opinion of other judges. See also *Land, Island and Maritime Frontier Dispute (El Salvador/Honduras), Application by Nicaragua for Permission*

President Spender's much discussed position in *South West Africa, Second Phase*,[57] on the right to append opinions, seems to be an extension of the generally understood position. The Court had already dealt with preliminary issues;[58] the merits were now before it. What it now effectively did was to dismiss the claims on the merits; that truth was not diminished by the circumstance that it did so on a particular aspect of the merits. The claims having been dismissed on the merits, minority judges were entitled to give their reasons for disagreeing with what the Court in fact did, and accordingly to say why the claims should have been upheld on the merits and not dismissed. They could not do this if they were limited to the particular ground on which the claims were dismissed.

It is submitted that similar reasoning would apply where, in a phase of a case dealing with admissibility and jurisdiction, the Court holds that the applicant's claim 'no longer has any object and that the Court is therefore not called upon to give a decision thereon'. In the *Nuclear Tests*, in which that was the position, it was questioned whether minority judges could properly deal with jurisdiction.[59] The matter should, however, be considered from the point of view of what was really before the Court. What was really before it was a question whether the applicant was entitled to a hearing on the merits. The Court, on the basis of a holding that the claim no longer had any object, held that the applicant was not entitled to a hearing on the merits. Minority judges, who considered that the case should be heard on the merits, could not give their reasons if they were limited to the particular ground which sufficed to found the Court's decision; they had to deal with jurisdiction also. In *East Timor (Portugal v. Australia)* minority judges dealt with all the preliminary issues even though the Court dealt with some only.[60]

A word may be said on the position of members of the drafting committee. As they come from amongst judges who appear to form

to Intervene, Verbatim Record, C4/CR 90/3, pp. 82–83, afternoon, Mr E. Lauterpacht.

[57] *ICJ Rep 1966*, p. 51.

[58] *South West Africa, Preliminary Objections, ICJ Rep 1962*, p. 319.

[59] *Nuclear Tests (Australia v. France), ICJ Rep 1974*, p. 307, Judge Petrén, separate opinion.

[60] *ICJ Rep 1995*, p. 90, dissenting opinion of Judge Weeramantry at p. 142, and dissenting opinion of Judge *ad hoc* Skubiszewski at p. 226.

part of the emerging majority,[61] they would only exceptionally dissent; a chamber exception exists. However, there is little to support the view that it is not proper for a member of the committee to append a separate opinion to the judgment. The factors which may lead a non-member of the committee to append a separate opinion could apply equally in the case of a member. As early as 1931 there was recognition that members of the drafting committee might have opposing views on some aspects.[62] Because of confidentiality, it is difficult to find material in the public domain indicative of every case in which a separate opinion was appended by a member of the drafting committee. The difficulty is not, however, insurmountable in the case of a President who appends such an opinion, he being in the normal way the chairman of the committee in respect of a judgment with which he agrees. Concurring declarations or opinions were issued by Presidents in some cases.[63] Apart from cases involving the President, it is certain that there have been instances in which other members of a drafting committee have appended concurring declarations or separate opinions.

The utility of separate opinions and dissenting opinions

In the case of a common law collegiate court, the explanation has been given that the 'fundamental reason why the opinions of

---

[61] Resolution concerning the Internal Judicial Practice of the Court, 12 April 1976, Article 6, para. (i). Exceptionally, different arrangements could be made, as for the drafting to be done by a single judge. See *PCIJ, Series E, No. 16*, p. 197. The Court is 'entirely free to suspend the application of the Resolution in a given case'. See, *ibid.*, and *PCIJ, Series E, No. 12*, p. 197. This is recognised in the fact that the *chapeau* of the Resolution provides for departure from its requirements.

[62] *PCIJ, Series D, Addendum to No. 2*, 1931, p. 221, Judge Anzilotti.

[63] See *Anglo-Iranian Oil Company, ICJ Rep 1952*, p. 116, separate opinion of President McNair; *Barcelona Traction, Light and Power Company, Limited, Preliminary Objections, ICJ Rep 1964*, p. 47, declaration of President Spender; *ibid., Second Phase, ICJ Rep 1970*, p. 54, separate opinion of President Bustamante y Rivero; *Namibia, ICJ Rep 1971*, p. 59, declaration of President Khan; *Appeal Relating to the Jurisdiction of the ICAO Council, ICJ Rep 1972*, p. 71, declaration of President Khan; *Fisheries Jurisdiction, ICJ Rep 1973*, p. 66, declaration of President Khan; *Application for Review of Judgment No. 158 of the United Nations Administrative Tribunal, ICJ Rep 1973*, p. 214, declaration of President Lachs; *Fisheries Jurisdiction (United Kingdom v. Iceland), ICJ Rep 1974*, p. 35, declaration of President Lachs; *Aegean Sea Continental Shelf, Interim Protection, ICJ Rep 1976*, p. 15, separate opinion of President Jiménez de Aréchaga; *Military and Paramilitary Activities in and against Nicaragua, ICJ Rep 1986*, p. 151, separate opinion of President Singh; and the *Lockerbie* case, *ICJ Rep 1992*, p. 17, declaration of acting President Oda.

minority judges cannot form part of the *ratio decidendi* of a case is that they are not reasons for the order made by the court; a *ratio decidendi* is entitled to authority not as the opinion of one or more judges but as the reason for a judicial order'.[64] In the case of the International Court of Justice, that would apply to any variant views, whether set out in separate opinions or in dissenting opinions. Such opinions do not form part of the Court's decision; whatever their intrinsic merits, it is the decision of the Court which has legal effect. So the question may be asked what value such opinions have within the framework of the Court's functions.

One may begin by first considering the views of the Court itself. Speaking of opinions appended to judgments of the United Nations Administrative Tribunal, it observed:

> In order to interpret or elucidate a judgement it is both permissible and advisable to take into account any dissenting or other opinions appended to the judgement. Declarations or opinions drafted by members of a tribunal at the time of a decision, and appended thereto, may contribute to the clarification of the decision. Accordingly the wise practice of the Tribunal, following the example of the Court itself, has been not only to permit such expressions of opinion but to publish them appended to the judgement. It is therefore proper in the present case, in order better to grasp the position of the Tribunal on the point now under examination, to refer not only to the Judgement itself, but also to the 'Statement' of Mr. Endre Ustor and the dissenting opinion of Mr. Arnold Kean.[65]

Thus, in the view of the Court, the expression of individual opinions by its own members represents a 'wise practice'. For the purpose of understanding the *Aerial Incident of 27 July 1955 (Israel v. Bulgaria)*,[66] it consulted 'some of the separate but concurring opinions' in that case, even though it added that the point in question was 'evident in other ways'.[67] In the *Continental Shelf (Tunisia/Libyan Arab Jamahiriya), Application for Permission to Intervene*,[68] it likewise referred to the declarations of a number of judges appended to its

---

[64] A. M. Honoré, '*Ratio decidendi*: Judges and Court', *LQR*, 71 (1955), p. 198. Cf. J. L. Montrose, '*Ratio decidendi* and the House of Lords', *MLR*, 20 (1957), p. 127.

[65] *Application for Review of Judgment No. 333 of the United Nations Administrative Tribunal, ICJ Rep 1987*, p. 45, para. 49. And see S. Rosenne, *The World Court, What It is and How It Works*, 4th ed. (Dordrecht, 1989), p. 137.

[66] *ICJ Rep 1959*, p. 127.

[67] *Barcelona Traction, Light and Power Company, Limited, Preliminary Objections, ICJ Rep 1964*, p. 29.

[68] *ICJ Rep 1981*, p. 16, para. 27.

order in the *Nuclear Tests (Australia v. France), Application for Permission to Intervene*,[69] in which they emphasised the importance of Fiji's application.

Individual opinions may also show that, although an issue is not referred to in the decision, the Court was in fact aware of it,[70] with the consequence that the decision may fall, depending on the circumstances, to be construed as either treating the issue as not necessary to be decided, or as tacitly resolving it in a manner that is consistent with the decision. The first explanation probably accounts for the silence in the order made in *Land, Island and Maritime Frontier Dispute (El Salvador/Honduras)*,[71] on the question adverted to in some of the dissenting opinions as to the propriety of the method of selecting members of an *ad hoc* chamber. The second explanation probably applies to the *Aerial Incident of 3 July 1988 (Islamic Republic of Iran v. United States of America)*[72] in which two of the separate opinions considered the question whether the order made was at variance with a precedent of the Court, one holding that it was not, the other that it was;[73] the order implicitly proceeded on the basis that there was no inconsistency. The second explanation probably also applies to *Maritime Delimitation in the Area between Greenland and Jan Mayen (Denmark v. Norway)*,[74] in which the Court implicitly proceeded on the basis that it had jurisdiction on a certain point; the question, though not raised by the parties, was considered in two of the separate opinions appended to the judgment, one holding that there was no jurisdiction, the other that there was.[75]

'An over-speaking Judge', says Bacon, 'is no well tuned cymball'.[76] Silence is always an option, and, although size is by itself not a logical ground of criticism, a lengthy opinion given just for the sake of speaking is indefensible. However, an individual opinion may,

---

[69] *ICJ Rep 1974*, pp. 531–533.
[70] *Report of the Informal Inter-Allied Committee on the Future of the Permanent Court of International Justice*, HMSO, Cmnd. 6531 (1944–II), p. 23.
[71] *ICJ Rep 1990*, p. 3.
[72] *ICJ Rep 1989*, p. 132.
[73] See the separate opinions of Judges Schwebel and Shahabuddeen, *ICJ Rep 1989*, at pp. 136 and 145 respectively.
[74] *ICJ Rep 1993*, p. 38.
[75] See the separate opinions of Vice-President Oda and Judge Shahabuddeen, *ICJ Rep 1993*, at pp. 91 and 202 respectively, as well as the declaration of the former at p. 83.
[76] *Bacon's Essays* (London, 1896), pp. 224–225.

without prolixity, clarify or restate the law in a way which proves to be helpful to its development. It is possible to discuss legal issues more fully in an individual opinion than in the Court's decisions. There are reasons for this. First, as was said by Judge Gros, 'the Court normally determines the law without elaborating the theory'.[77] Discussion tends to take place in individual opinions, which will in consequence be fuller than the Court's judgment on the particular points. This will be especially the case if it is accepted that, as suggested by Jenks, it is the expository style which is appropriate to the particular developing phase through which international law is currently passing.[78] Judge Gros, who may be considered as belonging to a school which favoured an economical use of the right to express an individual opinion, appended a dissenting opinion of thirty printed pages to the judgment of the chamber in the *Gulf of Maine*.[79]

Then, as to the range of issues which may be treated of in an individual opinion, it must be recalled that the Court 'retains its freedom to select the ground upon which it will base its judgment'.[80] In many cases the Court will select the simplest ground. It is not necessary to go the entire way with Judge Lauterpacht's ideas as to the extent to which the Court should deal with legal issues in order to appreciate his observation to the effect that there 'may be force and attraction in the view that among a number of possible solutions a court of law ought to select that which is most simple, most concise and most expeditious. However, in my opinion such considerations are not, for this Court, the only legitimate factor in the situation.'[81] A point which is both relevant and important should not be avoided merely because of the difficulty which it presents.[82]

Counsel in argument have been known to contend that a dissenting opinion was authoritative on a particular point. Speaking

---

[77] *Delimitation of the Maritime Boundary in the Gulf of Maine Area, ICJ Rep 1984*, p. 384, Judge Gros.

[78] C. W. Jenks, *The Common Law of Mankind* (London, 1958), p. 437.

[79] *ICJ Rep 1984*, pp. 360–389.

[80] *Application of the Convention of 1902 Governing the Guardianship of Infants, ICJ Rep 1958*, p. 62. And see *Certain Norwegian Loans, ICJ Rep 1957*, p. 25; *South West Africa, ICJ Rep 1966*, p. 19, para. 8, referring to Art. 53, para. 2, of the Statute; and the *Aegean Sea Continental Shelf, ICJ Rep 1978*, p. 17, para. 40.

[81] *Certain Norwegian Loans, ICJ Rep 1957*, p. 36. See also his remarks in *Voting Procedure on Questions relating to Reports and Petitions Concerning the Territory of South West Africa, ICJ Rep 1955*, pp. 92–93.

[82] See *Expenses* case, *ICJ Rep 1962*, p. 198, separate opinion of Judge Fitzmaurice.

in 1963 of the maxim 'No interest, no action', Attorney General Sir John Hobson submitted that the 'dictum is authoritatively dealt with in a dissenting opinion in the recent *South West Africa* cases (*ICJ Rep 1962*, p. 455)'.[83] In the *Nuclear Tests (Australia v. France)* case, Solicitor General Ellicott, referring to a dissenting opinion of Judge Lachs in the *North Sea Continental Shelf cases*,[84] said:

The development of the law relating to the protection of the environment from atmospheric nuclear testing is, I would respectfully suggest, one of those developments analogous to the emergence of the law of outer space of which you, Mr. President, spoke in your dissenting opinion in the *North Sea Continental Shelf* case. And in relation to such developments you expressed the view (at p. 232) that 'the Court would ... take cognizance of the birth of a new rule, once the general practice States have pursued has crossed the threshold from haphazard and discretionary action into the sphere of law'.

The fact that these observations were made in a dissenting opinion does not, I venture to submit, mean that they do not have the support of the Court as a whole. They are not to be read as inconsistent with what the Court itself then said.[85]

Individual opinions are part of the collective work of the Court

Referring to Judge Lauterpacht's liberal use of his right to append separate and dissenting opinions, Rosenne observed:

It has for some time been commonly felt among competent observers of the Court that individual opinions which, so to speak, underpin the anonymous decisions of the Court, thanks to their greater freedom of expression and emphasis on underlying principles which the anonymous author of the majority view cannot always articulate fully, or which, in another direction, by indicating other legal principles which can govern the particular circumstances, may correct any misleading impression which the majority opinion might convey, or which, by flatly contradicting it, are seen by enlightened legal opinion to be expressive of better law, have a value of their own not so much for the development of the law as for the proper functioning of the Court.[86]

[83] *ICJ Pleadings, Northern Cameroons*, p. 393.
[84] *ICJ Rep 1969*, p. 232.
[85] *ICJ Pleadings, Nuclear Tests (Australia v. France)*, I, pp. 185–186.
[86] S. Rosenne, 'Sir Hersch Lauterpacht's Concept of the Task of the International Judge', *AJIL*, 55 (1961), p. 861.

Rosenne's view that individual opinions 'have a value of their own not so much for the development of the law as for the proper functioning of the Court' is important. Although not forming part of the Court's decision, individual opinions are appended to it. The term 'appended' may conjure up the image of something dangling as a useless appendix to the matter of real importance. That would not be correct; individual opinions are an integral part of the collegiate work of the Court. In the view of Fitzmaurice, 'It would . . . be to give a wrong impression of the worth of the Court's work, collegiately considered, if due place was not given to the individual opinions that are essentially a part of its collective product.'[87] Judge Jennings has spoken to similar effect.[88]

President Anzilotti saw the matter correctly when he said, 'The opinion of the Court is not, to my mind, a collection of individual opinions coinciding as regards their conclusion; rather is it the result of the opposition and interpretation of different opinions.'[89] The judgment is framed by all judges, including dissenting judges. It is prepared by a drafting committee of judges, the draft being subsequently discussed and amended by the Court as a whole, inclusive of judges who might later append concurring or dissenting opinions. The system is such as to enable the judgment to take into account or to meet objections raised in such opinions; the latter may result in substantial changes being made to the former. On the other hand, as was remarked by Judge Hughes, each judge labours 'in his own sanctum on his own opinion, knowing that it will be analyzed and eviscerated by equally if not more able men who have studied the case with the same attention'.[90] Thus, a judge, if indeed he does not altogether abandon the idea, may well end up by making important modifications in the opinion which he originally intended to give;[91] and, though the speed of the procedures

---

[87] Fitzmaurice, *Law and Procedure*, I, preface, p. xxxii. See also, *ibid.*, pp. 1–2.

[88] Jennings, 'Collegiate Responsibility', pp. 346, 348, 351.

[89] *PCIJ, Series E, No. 4*, p. 23.

[90] D. F. Fleming, *The United States and the World Court 1920–1966* (New York, 1968), p. 102.

[91] See, for example, the evolution in the thinking of Judge Finlay in *Certain German Interests in Polish Upper Silesia, Merits, 1926, PCIJ, Series A, No. 7*, p. 84; his reconsideration of the evidence no doubt proceeded in the light of the thinking of the Court. Also in practice, the Court, or more usually the drafting committee, may request the deletion or modification of a passage in an opinion. See R. Y. Jennings, 'The Internal Judicial Practice of the International Court of Justice',

at this stage may be an impediment, he may need to do so if only to ensure that he is not responding to a passage in the draft which does not in fact form part of the text of the judgment as it finally emerges.[92] An individual opinion may, in practice, also take account of another, provided that there is no degeneration into a debate at this stage.

Looking at these procedures, Judge Jennings makes the point that the fact that changes may be made in the draft judgment in response to individual opinions and *vice versa* shows not only that the authors of such opinions are involved in the preparation of the judgment, but equally that the Court itself exerts an influence on the preparation of such opinions. In his words, 'the whole Court is much involved in the separate, even dissenting, opinions, just as the judges making separate opinions are all the time involved in the Court's own decision'. Hence, the 'judgment of the Court and the separate opinions belong to each other, and, ideally, illuminate each other ... Where arguments alternative to those of the judgment are offered – even dissenting arguments – this can show the range from which the Court has chosen its stance.'[93] This consideration is of particular importance in the case of an opinion appended by a judge *ad hoc*. In the words of Judge *ad hoc* Elihu Lauterpacht, such a judge has

the special obligation to endeavour to ensure that, so far as is reasonable, every relevant argument in favour of the party that has appointed him has been fully appreciated in the course of collegial consideration and,

---

BYBIL, 59 (1988), p. 43. The final decision is however left with the judge concerned.

[92] See para. 45 at p. 89, and compare it with the reference to that paragraph at p. 138 of *Border and Transborder Armed Actions (Nicaragua v. Honduras), ICJ Rep 1988*, p. 69; and see para. 76, at pp. 38–39, and compare it with the reference to that paragraph at p. 102 of *Territorial Dispute (Libyan Arab Jamahiriya/Chad), ICJ Rep 1994*, p. 6. See also Sir Robert Jennings, 'Collegiate Responsibility', pp. 349–350.

[93] Sir Robert Jennings, 'The Internal Judicial Practice of the International Court of Justice', *BYBIL*, 59 (1988), p. 43. Putting it perhaps a little more strongly, counsel submitted that 'to the extent that the majority judgment differs from dissentient opinions, it differs knowingly and deliberately. One may therefore conclude that if the judgment of the Court contains the highest expression of what is thought by the Court to be the law, the dissenting opinions contain – as regards the points on which they dissent – the highest expression of what is thought by the Court *not* to be the law.' See *Land, Island and Maritime Frontier Dispute (El Salvador/Honduras), Application by Nicaragua for Permission to Intervene*, Verbatim Record, C4/CR 90/3, pp. 82–83, afternoon, Mr E. Lauterpacht.

ultimately, is reflected – though not necessarily accepted – in any separate or dissenting opinion that he may write.[94]

These remarks about individual opinions being part of the collective product of the work of the Court do not exaggerate; they come to life when regard is had to the fact that the original practice was that opinions were read out in open Court.[95] In the *S.S. 'Wimbledon'*,[96] on the instructions of the President, the Registrar read the dissenting opinions of Judges Anzilotti and Huber and also that of Judge *ad hoc* Schücking.[97] On 25 August 1924 'it was decided that dissenting opinions might be read by dissenting judges themselves in French or English, but that no translation would be read at the sitting'.[98] It was from the bench that Judge Finlay delivered his 'Observations' in *Certain German Interests in Polish Upper Silesia*;[99] Judge Rostworowski delivered his dissenting opinion in like manner.[100] The *Fourth Annual Report* of the Permanent Court of International Justice stated:

Prior to the reading of the judgment in the *Lotus* case, the question was raised whether dissenting judges must read their separate opinions in open Court. It was decided that that was a matter resting entirely with the judges themselves. In practice, some judges have, for reasons of expediency, either confined themselves to summarizing orally their separate opinions or have renounced their right to read them (in the case concerning the jurisdiction of the European Commission of the Danube, in which the Court's opinion was very lengthy, of the three judges who had appended separate observations or dissenting opinions, one summarized his observations, another waived his right to read them and the third simply read the conclusions of his dissenting opinion). On the other hand, in the case concerning the interpretation of Judgments Nos. 7 and 8, the only judge submitting a dissenting opinion read it in full, whilst in the case concerning Minority Schools in Upper Silesia all the dissenting judges waived their right to read their opinions.[101]

---

[94] *Application of the Convention on the Prevention and Punishment of the Crime of Genocide, Provisional Measures, ICJ Rep 1993*, p. 409, para. 6.

[95] Hudson, *The Permanent Court*, p. 589.

[96] *1923, PCIJ, Series A, No. 1*.

[97] *PCIJ, Series C, No. 3*, I, p. 37.

[98] *PCIJ, Series E, No. 1*, p. 259.

[99] *PCIJ, Series A, No. 7*, p. 84.

[100] *Ibid.*, p. 86; and see *PCIJ, Series C, No. 11*, I, p. 39, and *PCIJ, Series C, No. 15*, II, p. 187.

[101] *PCIJ, Series E, No. 4*, p. 292.

As late as 1948 Vice-President Basdevant read a joint separate opinion in *Corfu Channel, Preliminary Objection*;[102] in the same case, the dissenting opinion of Judge *ad hoc* Daxner was also read. In *Asylum*, individual opinions were not read, but merely appended to the judgment.[103] In the first *Admission* case, the President asked whether two of the judges wished to read their individual opinions, and received an answer in the negative.[104] In *Certain Norwegian Loans*, judges declined to read their opinions, having informed the President that they did not wish to do so.[105] So too in *Right of Passage over Indian Territory*.[106] In the *Guardianship Convention* case, it appears that the President extended no invitation for opinions to be read;[107] the existing practice was in the course of settling down to the effect that opinions were only appended and not read.[108] But this development, or degeneration, could not efface the significance of the earlier history of opinions being read out from the bench: that significance was, and continues to be, that, as stated by Fitzmaurice, they are essentially part of the collective product of the Court.

The character of individual opinions as part of the functioning of the Court was also recognised by Judge Ammoun when stating:

I must emphasize in the first place that the authority of the precedents of the two international courts derives, *inter alia*, from the very fact that their judgments include the dissenting or separate opinions of their members. This is no paradox; for, in order to assess the value of a judicial decision, it is necessary to be able to ascertain the extent to which it expresses the opinion of the Court, and what objections judges no less qualified than those who supported it were able to bring against it ...

This authority [of individual opinions] is nothing other than that of particularly well-qualified jurists and takes its place in the general context of legal teaching. Thus, Mr. St. Korowicz, in a study of the opinion of the seven dissenting judges in the *Customs Régime between Germany and Austria* case, places it under the head of 'the teachings of publicists', which are

---

[102] *ICJ Pleadings, Corfu Channel*, III, p. 161.
[103] *ICJ Pleadings, Haya de la Torre*, II, p. 14.
[104] *ICJ Pleadings, Conditions of Admission of a State to Membership in the United Nations (Article 4 of the Charter)*, p. 41.
[105] *ICJ Pleadings, Certain Norwegian Loans*, II, p. 18.
[106] *ICJ Pleadings, Right of Passage over Indian Territory*, IV, p. 12.
[107] *ICJ Pleadings, Application of the Convention of 1902 Governing the Guardianship of Infants*, p. 136.
[108] See *ICJYB, 1953–1954*, p. 120; and, *ibid., 1954–1955*, p. 99.

regarded in Article 38, paragraph 1 *(d)*, of the Statute of the Court as 'subsidiary means for the determination of the rules of law'.[109]

Judge Ammoun's view that the authority of separate and dissenting opinions is 'nothing other than that of particularly well-qualified jurists and takes its place in the general context of legal teaching' might admit of qualification. It is true that, as it has been remarked, the influence of individual opinions will depend on their legal craftsmanship, the cogency of their reasoning, and their proximity to the decision of the Court and its own reasoning.[110] But it is influence which carries special weight in view of the fact that, though not forming part of the judgment of the Court, such opinions are appended thereto pursuant to Article 57 of the Statute by judges functioning in that capacity; they are delivered not by jurists *simpliciter*, but by jurists sitting as judges in a particular case, expressing views on issues duly presented and carefully argued.[111] The authority which they possess exceeds in principle that of an opinion given by a jurist writing only as such.[112]

The Court's view

The connection suggested by Judges Ammoun and Fitzmaurice between the decision of the Court and individual opinions was later emphasised by the Court itself. It did so in a document sent by it on 6 November 1986 to the Secretary-General of the United Nations under the title 'Observations of the International Court of Justice on the Report of the Joint Inspection Unit'. An issue had arisen as to whether, for reasons of economy, the Court's decisions might be published without such opinions. The 'Observations'

---

[109] *Barcelona Traction, Light and Power Company, Limited, Second Phase, ICJ Rep 1970*, pp. 316–317.

[110] Leo Gross, *AJIL*, 68 (1974), p. 552.

[111] For the distinction between academic and judicial or forensic work, see Sir Arnold McNair, *The Development of International Justice* (New York, 1954), pp. 16–17; Sir Gerald Fitzmaurice, 'Some Problems Regarding the Formal Sources of International Law', in *Symbolae Verzijl* (The Hague, 1958), pp. 171–172; Sir Humphrey Waldock, 'The ICJ as seen from Bar and Bench', *BYBIL*, 54 (1983), p. 34; Fitzmaurice, *Law and Procedure*, II, pp. 638–639; and *ICJ Pleadings, The Temple of Preah Vihear*, II, p. 69 (M. Pinto: 'quelquefois les avocats et les auteurs ne sont pas toujours d'accord ensemble', said of the same jurist).

[112] S. Rosenne, *The Practice and Methods of International Law* (London, 1984), p. 97.

included the following statements which, because of their importance, are set out *in extenso*:

8. In this regard, it may be helpful to indicate certain characteristics
essential to the texts of its judicial decisions, whether judgments, advisory
opinions, or orders disposing of substantive issues. In so doing, the Court
must stress that an indissoluble relationship exists between such decisions
and any separate opinions, whether concurring or dissenting, appended to
them by individual judges. The statutory institution of the separate opinion has been found essential as affording an opportunity for judges to
explain their votes. In cases as complex as those generally dealt with by
the Court, with operative paragraphs sometimes divided into several inter-
linked issues upon each of which a vote is taken, the bare affirmative or
negative vote of a judge may prompt erroneous conjectures which his
statutory right of appending an opinion can enable him to forestall or
dispel. To disseminate the Court's decisions without the appended opinions would therefore give rise to misconceptions affecting individual
judges. It should in any case be apparent that the reasoning of a decision
simply represents a highest common denominator. Therefore, given the
multiplicity of judges dealing with a case, it is likely that some individual
judges will feel that one or more of the considerations that determined
their votes require more specific treatment; or there may remain points
of great legal interest that a judge feels impelled to raise or explain, and
such is the interplay of views during the Court's deliberations that these
points will shed light on, or themselves be illuminated by, corresponding
passages in the Court's decision. Thus not only do the appended opinions
elaborate or challenge the decision, but the reasoning of the decision
itself, reviewed as it finally is with knowledge of the opinions, cannot be
fully appreciated in isolation from them. In short, the individual opinions
are or may be essential to the full understanding of the Court's decision.

9. The foregoing explanations are founded upon Articles 56 and 57 of
the Statute of the Court. These are worded as follows:

'Article 56

1. The judgment shall state the reasons on which it is based.
2. It shall contain the names of the judges who have taken part in the
decision.

Article 57

If the judgment does not represent in whole or in part the unanimous
opinion of the judges, any judge shall be entitled to deliver a separate
opinion.'

It must be added that the sense of the English text of Article 57 is illuminated by the French text, which provides:

'Si l'arrêt n'exprime pas en tout ou en partie l'opinion unanime des juges, tout juge aura le droit d'y joindre l'exposé de son opinion individuelle.'

It is clear that the use of the word '*joindre*' confirms that the opinions are integrated with the judgment. Any official publication of the judgment without the opinions must represent an abridgement of the judgment – a truncation – to which the judges constituting the membership of the Court at any given time cannot lend authority without compromising the Court in its future decision-making processes.

10. In sum, no text omitting any statement delivered for final inclusion by one or more of the participant judges listed at the head of the decision is the complete and authentic decision of the Court.

11. Even independently of the foregoing conclusions flowing from the Statute and the judicial character and tradition of the institution, the Court feels bound to stress the importance of the element of balance to the impact of its collegiate work. By this element is meant the full and fair presentation in a decision of all the legal options on which the Court has exercised its powers of distinction. This presentation will be thrown out of balance if separate and dissenting opinions are removed, especially where decisions taken by a narrow majority are concerned. To take an extreme case, it would not be proper to present a judicial decision adopted by a casting vote of the President without the opinions that could be expected to accompany it. What would the international community have thought if the United Nations had translated and disseminated the Judgment of the Court rejecting the claims of Ethiopia and Liberia in the *South West Africa* cases while omitting the separate and dissenting opinions which had been joined to it? And, in the Court's view, no line can reasonably and regularly be drawn between cases where little harm supposedly would be done by excluding the opinions, and cases where, on the contrary, the harm would be great.[113]

The roots of these observations go back in time. Without seeking to retrace them, one may notice a statement which Vice-President Huber was recorded as making in 1929 as follows:

He was not revealing any secret in stating that M. Anzilotti and he himself had, during the discussions of this question in the Court, when it had drafted and revised its Rules, supported the publication of dissentient opinions. The Court had considered that the publication of such opinions not only had all the advantages to which M. Politis had referred, but that the possibility of the publication of those opinions made it necessary for the Court to examine very carefully the different points of view brought

---

[113] *Observations of the International Court of Justice on the Report of the Joint Inspection Unit (A/41/591)*, paras. 8–11; footnotes omitted.

forward by the judges, and to state clearly the reasons for its awards. The Court had also felt that the possibility of publication was a guarantee against any subconscious intrusion of political considerations, and that judgments were more likely to be given in accordance with the real force of the arguments submitted. He felt that it was essential to retain the right of individual judges to publish their views, and he would urge that this right was an essential condition for the exercise of their liberty of conscience and their impartiality.[114]

The thought of individual opinions not being published would have been unintelligible to Vice-President Huber; it is known that he would not have accepted a position on the bench of the Court if dissenting opinions were not allowed.[115] It is not surprising that, in his own time, Fitzmaurice should speak as follows of the value of separate and dissenting opinions:

These play a valuable part in the functioning of the Court, and to ignore them would be to give but an incomplete portrayal of its work as a whole, as well as to disregard material of primary importance from the stand-point of the present study; for although dissenting Judges differ from the Court as to the actual conclusion, they may well, in the course of so doing, make general statements or explanations of principle which are in them-selves not in any way inconsistent with the views of the Court, but merely differently applied to the facts. Again, a Judge who delivers a separate but not dissenting opinion, agrees with the conclusion of the Court, but for different reasons, or prefers to give his own reasoning. His views clearly form a valuable supplement to those of the Court. Finally, even where the views of an individual Judge are definitely contrary to those of the Court, on matters of principle, it may be desirable to quote them, because it is often the case, particularly with difficult or controversial questions, that a decision can only properly be appreciated in the light of a contrary view.[116]

The influence of the legal cultures represented in the Court

One last comment. The judges of the Court forgather from different parts of the world; but for practical purposes, the differences in outlook reduce themselves broadly, if not entirely, to

---

[114] League of Nations, Committee of Jurists on the Statute of the Permanent Court of International Justice, *Minutes of the Session held at Geneva, March 11th–19th, 1929* (Geneva, 1929), p. 52.

[115] S. Rosenne, *The World Court, What it is and How it Works*, 4th edn, (Dordrecht, 1989), p. 137.

[116] Fitzmaurice, *Law and Procedure*, I, pp. 1–2.

those between the civilian system and the common law system.[117] There is no appreciable difference between judges of either group so far as concerns the substantive law to be applied. In whichever of Cardozo's six judicial styles they write,[118] in a fundamental sense all members of the Court speak a common language.[119] Differences in outlook can, however, influence approach and style, particularly in respect of opinions.[120] As it has been observed, 'there is a close connection between the legal civilization of a country and the way in which its judges justify their decisions'.[121]

Now, as John Dewey observed, 'Courts not only reach decisions; they expound them, and the exposition must state justifying reasons.'[122] That, it is believed, applies to all legal systems; but there can be differences in application. French courts, which typify the Continental outlook, are required by law to state reasons, but these are given succinctly, generally following a single-sentence syllogistic form;[123] the 'doctrine' is developed by commentaries on decisions and on the Code produced by legal scholars. 'Leading academics do in France what judges do in England, and the patterns of reasoning and length are not without resemblance; the French "notes" [by academics] are much more akin to English judgments than French judgments

---

[117] In this respect, it has been remarked that Third World judges speak and write like Western judges. See Lyndel V. Prott, 'The Style of Judgment in the International Court of Justice', *Aust YBIL* (1970–1973), p. 82. This is not strange; most, if not all of them, have been exposed directly or indirectly to some Western system.

[118] See generally J. A. R. Nafziger, 'Some Remarks on the Writing Style of the International Court of Justice', in Thomas Buergenthal (ed.), *Contemporary Issues in International Law, Essays in Honour of L. B. Sohn* (Kehl, 1984), p. 325, at p. 331.

[119] Kotaro Tanaka, 'The Character of World Law in the International Court of Justice', *Japanese Annual of International Law*, 15 (1971), p. 15; and *Military and Paramilitary Activities in and against Nicaragua (Nicaragua v. United States of America), ICJ Rep 1986*, pp. 158–159, Judge Lachs, separate opinion.

[120] See T. M. Cooper, 'The Common and the Civil Law – A Scot's View', *Harvard Law Review*, 63 (1950), p. 470.

[121] Jean Louis Goutal, 'Characteristics of Judicial Style in France, Britain and the USA', *American Journal of Comparative Law*, 24 (1976), p. 43.

[122] John Dewey, 'Logical Method and Law', in R. D. Henson (ed.), *Landmarks of Law, Highlights of Legal Opinion* (London, 1963), p. 123.

[123] See L. Neville Brown and Francis Jacobs, *The Court of Justice of the European Communities*, 3rd edn (London, 1989), p. 43; and Lauterpacht, *Collected Papers*, II, p. 474.

are.'[124] If French judges have views in addition to those set out in the judgment of the court, 'they will express them in articles – something English judges will almost never do'.[125] That does not happen frequently and, when it happens, it is limited to questions of principle raised by the case. On the other hand, English judges are now more 'media-friendly';[126] but, even so, the fundamental inhibition in expressing extra-judicial opinions on issues judicially decided by them has not much diminished. Sometimes traces of that attitude could follow them into the International Court of Justice: speaking of Judge Lauterpacht, Jessup and Baxter remarked, 'Quite properly, he refrained from comment upon cases which had come before the Court after his election.'[127]

Thus, the French 'system leaves most of the task of commenting, construing and constructing to law professors. Hence, their influential position. In contrast, the somewhat remote position of English academics is tied to the fact that judges leave them so little room in the task of critique and elaboration so typical of legal science.'[128] Judicial opinions in 'revision'-type procedures in Germany, as in France, 'have the appearance of being addressed to other judges, much like notes and instructions by a teacher or a superior are formally communicated to students and

---

[124] Jean Louis Goutal, 'Characteristics of Judicial Style in France, Britain and the USA', *American Journal of Comparative Law*, 24 (1976), p. 64. For the substantial role played by doctrine in civil law systems, see A. P. Sereni, 'Les Opinions individuelles et dissidentes des juges des tribunaux internationaux', *RGDIP*, 68 (1964), p. 819, at p. 825.

[125] Jean Louis Goutal, 'Characteristics of Judicial Style in France, Britain and the USA', *American Journal of Comparative Law*, 24 (1976), p. 64.

[126] See Frances Gibb, 'Justice on the Screen', *The Times*, 23–29 October 1993; letter from Lord Woolf, *The Times*, 23 October 1993, written from 'Lords of Appeal Corridor, House of Lords'; and 'Law Chief Blames Lack of Press Restraint for Disquiet over Sentences' (press interview by Lord Chief Justice Taylor), *The Times*, 27 June 1994, p. 7.

[127] Philip C. Jessup and R. R. Baxter, 'The Contribution of Sir Hersch Lauterpacht to the Development of International Law', *AJIL*, 55 (1961), p. 100. And see Lauterpacht, *Development*, preface, p. xiv.

[128] Jean Louis Goutal, 'Characteristics of Judicial Style in France, Britain and the USA', *American Journal of Comparative Law*, 24 (1976), p. 65. For the interesting fusion of the code style and the common law style of judicial writing in Quebec, see W. Friedmann, '*Stare decisis* at common law and under the Civil Code of Quebec', *Canadian Bar Review*, 31 (1953), p. 723. 'Professor' seems to be a more honourable title in Europe. See P. C. Jessup, *The Price of International Justice* (New York, 1971), p. 75.

subordinates'.[129] By contrast, the text of a common law judgment is designed to carry persuasion with the wider public and to elicit professional appreciation by lawyers in general without the need for mediating academic exposition;[130] its function is to make the 'conclusion plausible, to justify it to the legal world and to society's conscience'.[131] Interestingly, speaking of contemporary legal developments in Germany, Karl Doehring remarks that 'German law ... offers the judges of the Constitutional Court the possibility to give separate and dissenting votes, whereas before the Court spoke with one voice only. This new system was inspired by looking at the Anglo-American practice and that of the International Court of Justice.'[132]

One only needs to reflect on the special position occupied by the International Court of Justice as a World Court to appreciate that the syllogistic style does not provide a suitable vehicle for conveying its determinations. It is employed by the Court in the framing of orders, but with much flexibility; the only judgments in which it was used were two judgments of the Chamber of Summary Procedure, given in the *Treaty of Neuilly, Article 179, Annex, Paragraph 4 (Interpretation)*[133] and *Interpretation of Judgment No. 3.*[134] With those exceptions, it is the discursive style which is used.

Arguments against separate opinions are often inspired by the judicial arrangements in force in code systems. The arrangements in those systems command admiration; but perhaps they do not provide a model for the World Court. First, judgments of the Court are not rendered within a judicial hierarchy; even in the case of advisory opinions concerning administrative tribunals, they are not

---

[129] See J. G. Wetter, *The Styles of Appellate Judicial Opinions, A Case Study in Comparative Law* (London, 1960), p. 71.

[130] *Ibid.*, pp. 70–71, and Lyndel V. Prott, 'Judicial Reasoning in the Common Law and Code Law Systems', *Archiv für Rechts und Sozialphilosophie*, 64 (1978), pp. 417–420.

[131] B. H. Levy, *Cardozo and Frontiers of Legal Thinking, with Selected Opinions* (New York, 1938), p. 84.

[132] Karl Doehring, 'The Auxiliary Function of Comparative Law for the Interpretation of Legal Rules of National and International Law', in *International Law at the Time of its Codification, Essays in Honour of Roberto Ago*, 4 vols. (Milan, 1987), IV, p. 61.

[133] *PCIJ, Series A, No. 3.*

[134] *PCIJ, Series A, No. 4.* And see S. Rosenne, *The Practice and Methods of International Law* (London, 1984), pp. 94 ff.

directives addressed by a superior body to a lower body operating within a common court system. Second, they are not produced within the homogeneous arrangements of a single domestic system and are not intended to be doctrinally elaborated in a systematic way by a group of legal scholars having any kind of accredited responsibility to do so; it is not the recognised task of any body of academics to produce a 'doctrine' based on the case law of the Court in the sense in which that is authoritatively done in certain code systems.[135] Moreover, as Edward Gordon remarked:

> For the most part, the international legal community does not provide an ongoing process equivalent to the association of judges, practising lawyers, law professors and students characteristic of domestic professional life. The 'invisible college of international lawyers', to borrow Professor Schachter's familiar and apt phrase, is too diffuse outside domestic professional circles to exert a significant international cultural influence.[136]

Third, the judgments of the Court are by contrast intended to carry persuasion, on a self-sufficient basis and throughout a heterogeneous world community, that the Court's judicial authority has been correctly exercised. And, fourth, while the judges of the Court are all committed to deciding cases in accordance with international law, they are chosen in a way designed to ensure that 'in the body as a whole the representation of the main forms of civilization and of the principal legal systems of the world should be assured' (Article 9 of the Statute of the Court). It was the understanding of Baron Descamps, President of the 1920 Advisory Committee of Jurists, that this provision would serve 'to make the Court a really representative world-tribunal'.[137]

In connection with the last point, it is also useful to bear in mind that the style employed by the Permanent Court of International Justice, upon which the restrictive view of the scope of opinions is largely based, was due to the fact that the Court's judgments were directed to a European audience. Writing of the period, it has been said:

---

[135] For the role of the 'accredited jurisconsult' in writing up *doctrine*, see C. K. Allen, *Law in the Making*, 7th edn (Oxford, 1964), p. 181.

[136] Edward Gordon, 'Observations on the Independence and Impartiality of the Members of the International Court of Justice', *Connecticut JIL*, 2 (1987), p. 411.

[137] *Procès-Verbaux*, 1920, p. 754.

[T]he arguments of the Court in general were specially directed to a European audience. African, Asian and most Islamic peoples were not of interest to the Court during this period. They were with a few exceptions (eg Ethiopia, Liberia, Turkey, Japan) not even members of the League. They were therefore not regarded as important to the work of the International Court and were not counted as part of its audience.[138]

The constituency of the present Court has progressively broadened out from the narrower province of that of its predecessor, and its composition is correspondingly more diversified. Within a judicial scheme intended to serve a constituency of that kind, there should be room for reasonable freedom in the exercise of a judge's statutory right to speak separately.[139] In 1970 Judge Ammoun asked: '[D]o not the opinions of the judges of the two International Courts derive increased authority from the fact that those judges were elected, according to Article 9 of the Statute of both Courts. . .?'[140] It is because of the representative principle referred to by Judge Ammoun that weight has in turn to be given to the observation of Judge Jennings that 'it is right and proper that a Judge should be able to comment on the Court's decision in terms of the form of civilization and of the legal system that he represents. He can, so to speak, both interpret it for that part of the world, and even lend an additional and peculiar authority to it.'[141]

The Court was designed to be a World Court; it is now more truly so than ever. The disciplined play within it of the different legal cultures which compose it is essential to its capacity to speak with the authority of the principal judicial organ of the United Nations.

[138] Lyndel V. Prott, 'The Style of Judgment in the International Court of Justice', *Aust YBIL (1970–1973)*, p. 80.
[139] See Edvard Hambro, 'Dissenting and Individual Opinions in the International Court of Justice', *ZöV*, 17 (1956–1957), p. 247; and Manfred Lachs, 'Le juge international à visage découvert (les opinions et le vote)', in *Estudios de Derecho Internacional, Homenaje al Profesor Miaja de la Muela* (Madrid, 1979), II, p. 949.
[140] *Barcelona Traction, Light and Power Company, Limited, ICJ Rep 1970*, p. 317.
[141] Jennings, 'Collegiate Responsibility', p. 350.

14

Effect and scope of the
Court's case law

Some practical effects

The jurisprudential importance which the Court attaches to its previous decisions was discussed in chapter 2. The practical consequences have to be borne in mind in considering the proper scope of its case law. New cases sometimes influence the development of State practice. As illustrations, D. J. Harris[1] cites the *Fisheries* case,[2] the *Reservations* case[3] and the *Reparation* case.[4] The speed with which the jurisprudence of the *Fisheries* case was translated into the provisions of the 1958 Geneva Convention on the Territorial Sea and the Contiguous Zone[5] may be recalled. The development had been anticipated in a general sense; in his speech before the Court, Attorney General Sir Frank Soskice had observed:

It is common ground that this case is not only a very important one to the United Kingdom and to Norway, but that the decision of the Court on it will be of the very greatest importance to the world generally as a precedent, since the Court's decision in this case must contain important pronouncements concerning the rules of international law relating to

[1] D. J. Harris, *Cases and Materials on International Law*, 3rd edn (London, 1983), p. 48. And see Condorelli, 'L'Autorité', pp. 307–308.
[2] *ICJ Rep 1951*, p. 116.
[3] *Ibid.*, p. 15. And see Section 2 (Reservations) of the Vienna Convention on the Law of Treaties, 1969. Correspondingly, a holding of the Court may be reversed conventionally. See the '*Lotus*' and Article 1 of the Brussels Convention on Penal Jurisdiction in Matters of Collision, 1952.
[4] *ICJ Rep 1949*, p. 174.
[5] Herbert Thierry, 'L'Evolution du droit international', *Hag R*, 222 (1990–III), p. 42.

coastal waters. The fact that so many governments have asked for copies of our Pleadings in this case is evidence that this is the general view.[6]

A common lawyer might be more easily disposed to see it that way. But judges of different legal traditions have spoken likewise. In his individual opinion, Judge Alvarez cited the Attorney General's statement with evident approval, adding, 'The present litigation is of great importance, not only to the Parties to the case, but also to all other States.'[7] In the *Asylum* case, Judge Azevedo, dissenting, said:

It should be remembered, on the other hand, that the decision in a particular case has deep repercussions, particularly in international law, because views which have been confirmed by that decision acquire quasi-legislative value, in spite of the legal principle to the effect that the decision has no binding force except between the parties and in respect of that particular case (Statute, Art. 59).[8]

Referring to the *Aerial Incident of 27 July 1955*,[9] Judge Tanaka observed:

Although this Judgment was given in consideration of the particular circumstances of the case and its binding force was limited to the parties and to this particular case (Article 59 of the Statute), it has exercised tremendous influence upon the subsequent course of the Court's jurisprudence and the attitude of parties vis-à-vis the jurisdictional issues relative to this Court.[10]

Another judge from a non-common law tradition was equally clear about the effect of the Court's decisions. Speaking on the question of the right of intervention in pending proceedings, Judge Morozov remarked:

This is the first time in the administration of international justice and, more particularly, in the experience of the International Court of Justice, that the Court has been obliged to take a decision on a request invoking Article 62. Therefore the impact of this decision unavoidably goes far beyond the specific request of Malta and may in future be considered as a precedent which, from my point of view, could be used for justification

---

[6] *ICJ Rep 1951*, p. 145.
[7] *Ibid.*
[8] *Asylum, ICJ Rep 1950*, p. 332, Judge Azevedo.
[9] *ICJ Rep 1959*, p. 127.
[10] *Barcelona Traction, Light and Power Company, Limited, ICJ Rep 1964*, p. 67, Judge Tanaka, separate opinion.

of a practice which is not consistent with the Statute and might, moreover, undermine the guiding principle of the consent of States.[11]

Thus, the fear was that such a decision might be considered as a precedent justifying a practice even though this was thought not to be consistent with the Statute.[12]

One consequence of the influence exerted by decisions of the Court is interesting. Continuity of language does not always betoken continuity of meaning or practice.[13] However, as was recognised by Judge Read, 'draftsmen, in deciding upon the language to be used in a treaty provision, e.g., The Disputes Article, have constantly in mind the principles of interpretation as formulated and applied by the Permanent Court and by this Court'.[14] The tendency to follow language tested by settled principles is a general one in the practice of the law, even though sometimes subject to important qualifications.[15]

In view of the possible repercussions of a decision, in maintaining consistency the Court not only looks backwards to its previous decisions; it may look forward with a view to forecasting the more general implications of the decision which it is called upon to make in the case before it, even if not controlled by those implications.[16] This is apart from the 'forward reach' which a judgment, particularly of a declaratory character, may have on future developments relating to the particular matter decided.[17] Adverting to the wider possibilities, in *Barcelona Traction, Light and Power Company, Limited*, the Court observed:

---

[11] *Continental Shelf (Tunisia/Libyan Arab Jamahiriya), Application for Permission to Intervene, ICJ Rep 1981*, p. 22, para. 3. On the question of the right to intervene, see the later case of *Land, Island and Maritime Frontier Dispute (El Salvador/Honduras), Application for Permission to Intervene, ICJ Rep 1990*, pp. 3 and 92.

[12] See also his separate opinion in *Continental Shelf (Libyan Arab Jamahiriya/Malta), Application for Permission to Intervene, ICJ Rep 1984*, p. 30.

[13] For a significant example, see Rosenne, *Law and Practice* (1985), p. 56, relating to the election of judges of the Court.

[14] *Peace Treaties, ICJ Rep 1950*, p. 233.

[15] See, generally, *Maxwell on the Interpretation of Statutes*, 12th edn (London, 1969), p. 24; *Craies on Statute Law*, 7th edn (London, 1971), pp. 136, 167–168; Cross and Harris, *Precedent*, pp. 177 ff; and *Halsbury's Laws of England*, 4th edn, XXVI, p. 293, para. 573.

[16] Common law judges also consider the future relevance of their decisions and their implications. See J. G. Deutsch, 'Precedent and Adjudication', *Yale Law Journal*, 83 (1974), p. 1584.

[17] *Northern Cameroons, ICJ Rep 1963*, p. 37.

[A]ny decision of the Court, relative to Article 37, must affect a considerable number of surviving treaties and conventions providing for recourse to the Permanent Court, including instruments of a political or technical character, and certain general multilateral conventions of great importance that seem likely to continue in force. It is thus clear that the decision of the Court in the present case, whatever it might be, would be liable to have far-reaching effects. This is in no way a factor which should be allowed to influence the legal character of that decision: but it does constitute a reason why the decision should not be regarded as already predetermined by that which was given in the different circumstances of the *Israel v. Bulgaria* case.[18]

A decision of the Court may also influence international organisational arrangements. In *Effect of Awards of Compensation made by the United Nations Administrative Tribunal*[19] the Court considered that the General Assembly was not entitled to refuse to give effect to awards of compensation made by the United Nations Administrative Tribunal properly constituted and acting within the limits of its statutory competence. It went on to speak of possible arrangements under which a challenge might be brought to the validity of an award on grounds of excess of competence or other defect capable of vitiating it. Having also held that the Tribunal was a judicial body, it said:

In order that the judgments pronounced by such a judicial tribunal could be subjected to review by any body other than the tribunal itself, it would be necessary, in the opinion of the Court, that the statute of that tribunal or some other legal instrument governing it should contain an express provision to that effect. The General Assembly has the power to amend the Statute of the Administrative Tribunal by virtue of Article 11 of that Statute and to provide for means of redress by another organ. But as no such provisions are inserted in the present Statute, there is no legal ground upon which the General Assembly could proceed to review judgments already pronounced by that Tribunal. Should the General Assembly contemplate, for dealing with future disputes, the making of some provision for the review of the awards of the Tribunal, the Court is of opinion that the General Assembly itself, in view of its composition and functions, could hardly act as a judicial organ – considering the arguments of the parties, appraising the evidence produced by them, establishing the facts and declaring the law applicable to them – all the more so as one party to the disputes is the United Nations Organization itself.[20]

[18] *ICJ Rep 1964*, pp. 29–30.
[19] *ICJ Rep 1954*, p. 47.
[20] *Ibid.*, p. 56.

Here then was a suggestion by the Court, guardedly made, that what was desired was a system of judicial review in which appeals would not lie to the General Assembly. Provision for this purpose was made in 1955. Judge Jiménez de Aréchaga later remarked:

The basic purpose of the 1955 amendments to the Statute of the Administrative Tribunal thus appears to have been to deal with the question raised in the general observations of the Court which have been cited above in the way suggested therein. This explains why the system of judicial review established in 1955 is confined to certain specific grounds upon which the validity of a judgment may be challenged: excess of or failure to exercise jurisdiction or a fundamental error in substantive law or in procedure. This also explains why the amendments adopted exclude the possibility that the General Assembly may itself pronounce on the validity of an award which has been challenged.[21]

Mention may also be made of certain observations made by Judge Lachs in his separate opinion in *Application for Review of Judgment No. 158 of the United Nations Administrative Tribunal*[22] on the desirability of uniformity of procedure as between the ILO Administrative Tribunal and the United Nations Administrative Tribunal. Although uniformity has not been achieved, some initiatives in that direction were taken. Referring to these, he later remarked:

I welcome these developments, not only in themselves but because observations made by a Member of the International Court of Justice have been taken up by the United Nations General Assembly with a view to enacting some legislative measures in their respect. This indicates that, in its functioning, the principal judicial organ of the United Nations may not only decide contentious issues or give advisory opinions, but also contribute in practical terms to the improvement or operation of the law within the United Nations system.[23]

The influence of case law on the litigation strategy of parties

As a matter of course, arguments at the bar of the Court habitually draw on decided cases, the effort being to show that the legal

---

[21] *Application for Review of Judgment No. 158 of the United Nations Administrative Tribunal, ICJ Rep 1973*, p. 243.

[22] *ICJ Rep 1973*, p. 214.

[23] *Application for Review of Judgment No. 333 of the United Nations Administrative Tribunal, ICJ Rep 1987*, p. 75.

structure of the case fits, or does not fit, into some relevant pattern established by the Court's case law. But there have also been instances in which substantive elements of the litigation strategy of a party were directly inspired by a decided case. In the view of Vice-President Badawi, the *Norwegian Loans* case had 'been presented by the French Government as a reproduction of the two cases on the *Serbian and Brazilian Loans*'.[24] In *Barcelona Traction* Judge Tanaka observed, 'There is not the slightest doubt that this objection denying the Court's jurisdiction in the present case has been motivated and inspired by the existence of two precedents, namely the Judgments in the *Aerial Incident* case of 26 May 1959 *(ICJ Reports 1959*, p. 127), and the *Temple of Preah Vihear* case of 26 May 1961 *(ICJ Reports 1961*, p. 17).'[25] A little later he added:

The first repercussion of the Judgment in the *Aerial Incident* case may be seen in the Judgment in the *Temple of Preah Vihear* case delivered on 26 May 1961, precisely two years after the delivery of the Judgment in the *Aerial Incident* case.

It is to be noted that the repercussion is found not in the conclusion of the Judgment itself, but in the argument of the party raising a preliminary objection to the Court's jurisdiction, and in the reasoning of the Court in disposing of this objection.[26]

And, referring specifically to Thailand's objection in the *Temple of Preah Vihear*, he said, 'It is not unreasonable to suppose that this objection of Thailand was encouraged by the Judgment in the *Aerial Incident* case'.[27]

In the *Continental Shelf (Libyan Arab Jamahiriya/Malta), Application for Permission to Intervene*,[28] referring to the *Nuclear Tests*[29] and the *Continental Shelf (Tunisia/Libyan Arab Jamahiriya)*,[30] Judge Mbaye observed that

in neither case did the Court have to consider the problem of whether or not a jurisdictional link must exist between the intervening State and the original States parties.

The position is quite different in the present case, where the instigator (Italy) was inspired by past experience, especially by the Judgment of the Court in 1981 in which it stated:

---

[24] *Norwegian Loans, ICJ Rep 1957*, p. 31, separate opinion.
[25] *ICJ Rep 1964*, p. 66.
[26] *Ibid.*, p. 67.
[27] *Ibid.*, p. 68.
[28] *ICJ Rep 1984*, p. 3.
[29] *ICJ Rep 1974*, pp. 253 and 457.
[30] *ICJ Rep 1981*, p. 20, para. 35, and p. 10, para. 34.

214

'If in the present Application Malta were seeking permission to submit its own legal interest in the subject-matter of the case for decision by the Court, and to become a party to the case, another question would clearly call for the Court's immediate consideration. That is the question mentioned in the Nuclear Tests cases, whether a link of jurisdiction with the Parties to the case is a necessary condition of a grant of permission to intervene under Article 62 of the Statute.'[31]

Italy seemed to be in the very situation envisaged by the Court in its Judgment.[32]

Thus, in the view of Judge Mbaye, Italy's Application had been 'inspired' by a previous judgment by the Court.

It is possible too that the position taken by a party may be based on views expressed in a separate opinion or dissenting opinion. In the *Nuclear Tests (Australia v. France)*,[33] France, though not appearing, let it be known that it was of the view that the terms of its 1966 optional clause declaration prevailed over the jurisdictional provisions of Article 17 of the General Act for the Pacific Settlement of International Disputes of 1928 on the ground that the optional clause declarations of itself and Australia were equivalent to a later treaty relating to the same subject-matter as the 1928 Act, to which both States were parties. As remarked in the joint dissenting opinion, this proposition seemed 'probably to take its inspiration from the dissenting opinions of four judges in the *Electricity Company of Sofia and Bulgaria* case,[34] although the case itself is not mentioned in the French Government's letter of 16 May 1973'.[35] The joint dissenting opinion proceeded, however, to observe that quite 'apart . . . from any criticisms that may be made of the actual reasoning of the opinions, they provide very doubtful support for the proposition advanced by the French Government'.[36]

Judicial self-restraint

'Careful as it is to keep its pronouncements "in accordance with international law", as required by its Statute, the Court does not

---

[31] *Ibid.*, pp. 18–19, para. 32.
[32] *ICJ Rep 1984*, pp. 36–37.
[33] *ICJ Rep 1974*, p. 253.
[34] *PCIJ, Series A/B, No.* 77.
[35] *ICJ Rep 1974*, p. 352, para. 87.
[36] *Ibid.*

shrink, when confronted with situations that are clearly new, from a certain boldness in striking out a path towards new developments in the law.'[37] However, the fact that the Court appreciates the use to which its decisions may be put in other cases as well as their wider repercussions within the international community tends to impose some restraint on its holdings. Sometimes it is possible to argue that this restraint has led it to miss an opportunity to develop the law in a desirable direction. Speaking on the question of the right to intervene in pending proceedings in the *Continental Shelf (Libyan Arab Jamahiriya/Malta), Application for Permission to Intervene,* Judge Mbaye considered that the Court should 'take advantage of the excellent opportunity provided by the case before it to breathe life into Article 62 of its Statute, and make a clear pronouncement on the very important question of the "jurisdictional link" which may or may not be required between the intervening State and the main parties, and in respect of which there are so many queries'.[38] There, in effect, the thought was that the Court should deliberately create a precedent on the point in question.

A similar approach was taken by Judge Tanaka in the *Barcelona Traction* case, in which he was not persuaded by the distinction sought to be drawn by the Court between the position under Article 36, paragraph 5, and Article 37 of the Statute. Even though the *Aerial Incident* case might have lost all practical value by reason of the possible disappearance of relevant optional clause declarations, he considered

that the Court should have dealt primarily with the Judgment in the *Aerial Incident* case as this involved the same legal question as the present issue rather than evade it because it was an inconvenient obstacle. General international law might have benefited by such an attitude of the Court by finding a common solution to the jurisdictional question which has arisen or might arise concerning Articles 36, paragraph 5, and 37.[39]

But the Court may have sound reason for caution. In *Interpretation of Judgments Nos. 7 and 8 (the Chorzów Factory)*, the Permanent Court of International Justice said that the 'obligation incumbent upon

---

[37] De Visscher, *Theory and Reality*, p. 397; and see Lauterpacht, *Development*, pp. 77 and 83.

[38] *ICJ Rep 1984*, pp. 35–36, separate opinion.

[39] *ICJ Rep 1964*, pp. 71–72.

the Court under Article 60 of the Statute to construe its judgments at the request of any Party, cannot be set aside merely because the interpretation to be given by the Court might possibly be of importance in another case which is pending'.[40] The particular situation which gave rise to that statement does not remove an implication that, in principle, the reasoning out of a case should not fail to consider a point merely because of possible repercussions on another pending or possible case. At the same time, the expression of the Court's reasoning may properly take account of its more general future consequences; it may make an express reservation on a point which, though seemingly related, does not have to be decided. In *Certain German Interests in Polish Upper Silesia, Merits*, the Permanent Court of International Justice, in referring to the guarded position which it had taken in a previous advisory case, wrote:

The Court has already been confronted with the problem of the scope of the Armistice Convention and of the Protocol of Spa in relation to the Polish law of July 14th, 1920, in connection with the question which formed the subject of Advisory Opinion No. 6. In that affair, however, the Court had only to consider certain less important aspects of the problem: in particular, it had not to decide the question whether Poland is entitled to rely on the two instruments in question. For the purposes of that affair, it sufficed to observe that the Armistice Convention did not possess the importance which Poland attempted to attribute to it; but the Court was careful to make an express reservation in regard to the point above mentioned.[41]

Likewise, the Court may tailor its decision in such a way as expressly to exclude its application to other cases presenting significantly different features, even though there may be no necessity to do this. Thus, the advisory proceedings in *Application for Review of Judgment No. 158 of the United Nations Administrative Tribunal* were set in train by a staff member's application to the Committee on Applications for Review of Administrative Tribunal Judgments. Distinguishing proceedings of this kind from similar proceedings instituted on the application of a Member State, the Court stated that it was not to be understood as 'expressing any opinion in regard to

---

[40] *1927, PCIJ, Series A, No. 13*, p. 21.
[41] *1926, PCIJ, Series A, No. 7*, p. 27. And see Sørensen, *Les Sources*, p. 167.

any future proceedings instituted under Article 11 by a member State'.[42] The point of that caution became evident in 1982, when the Court observed:

Hence the Advisory Opinion given by the Court on the *Application for Review of Judgement No. 158 of the United Nations Administrative Tribunal* is relevant to its approach to the present request on two main counts: because that Opinion recognized that it would be incumbent upon the Court to examine the features characteristic of any request for advisory opinion the Committee decides to submit at the prompting of a member State, and because it indicated that the Court should bear in mind during that examination not only the considerations applying to the review procedure in general but also the 'additional considerations' proper to the specific situation created by the interposition of a member State in the review process.[43]

An allied situation arose in the case of *Judgments of the Administrative Tribunal of the International Labour Organisation upon Complaints made against the United Nations Educational, Scientific and Cultural Organisation*. There, reviewing the particular circumstances of the case relating to the hearing procedure, the Court said that it was 'not bound for the future by any consent which it gave or decisions which it made with regard to the procedure thus adopted'.[44] That could only mean that the special characteristics of the case would have to be borne in mind in considering whether, on the points in question, it would exert precedential influence in later cases; it could not mean that the Court was assuming a power to divest a particular opinion of any precedential influence which it would normally be capable of exerting. It is, however, consistent with the view that possible implications for other cases should be taken into account, as far as reasonable, in the formulation of a decision on the point in question.

In the *Aegean Sea Continental Shelf* case the Court took the position that, even if the General Act for the Pacific Settlement of International Disputes of 1928 was in force as between Greece and Turkey, a Greek reservation operated to exclude jurisdiction thereunder. The Court did not therefore find it necessary to determine whether the Act was still in force as between the parties. Giving the reasons for its abstention, it observed:

[42] *ICJ Rep 1973*, p. 178, para. 31.
[43] *Application for Review of Judgment No. 273 of the United Nations Administrative Tribunal, ICJ Rep 1982*, p. 332, para. 17.
[44] *ICJ Rep 1956*, p. 86.

Although under Article 59 of the Statute 'the decision of the Court has no binding force except between the parties and in respect of that particular case', it is evident that any pronouncement of the Court as to the status of the 1928 Act, whether it were found to be a convention in force or to be no longer in force, may have implications in the relations between States other than Greece and Turkey.[45]

Judge *ad hoc* Stassinopoulos disagreed. It was precisely because of the possible implications for other States that he considered that in 'an organized international society ... the settlement of this question, after the three cases already submitted to the Court (*Nuclear Tests* and *Trial of Pakistani Prisoners of War*), would present a more general interest'.[46] Arguing in favour of the continuance in force of the 1928 Act as between the parties, he made an interesting use of the cases referred to, contending that, in the light of the publicity given in them to the existence of the Act, it was 'inconceivable that Turkey could have forgotten to take any action needed to manifest its desire to be bound by that instrument no longer'.[47] This view did not prevail over the understandable prudence of the Court.

A careful policy of not deciding a point until the necessity arises is consequently observable. An example is furnished by the *Status of Eastern Carelia*, in which the Permanent Court of International Justice said that there 'has been some discussion as to whether questions for an advisory opinion, if they relate to matters which form the subject of a pending dispute between nations, should be put to the Court without the consent of the parties. It is unnecessary in the present case to deal with this topic.'[48] Thus, the Court explicitly refrained from deciding the point. Curiously, the opposite assumption was to be made for some time to come.[49]

The Court's policy of self-restraint is well known. It will not decide a point which 'can have only an academic interest'.[50] Judge Ammoun remarked on the policy in *Barcelona Traction, Light and Power Company, Limited*. He was dealing with the question 'whether diplomatic protection derives from a general principle of law

---

[45] *ICJ Rep 1978*, pp. 16–17, para. 39.
[46] *Ibid.*, p. 72, para. 1.
[47] *Ibid.*, p. 73, para. 3.
[48] 1923, *PCIJ, Series B, No. 5*, p. 27.
[49] See p. 112 above.
[50] *Northern Cameroons, ICJ Rep 1963*, p. 35.

recognized by the nations (Article 38, para. 1(c), of the Court's Statute) or from an international custom (para. 1(b) of that Article)'.[51] His comment ran:

The Judgment of the Permanent Court of International Justice of 1924 in the *Mavrommatis Palestine Concessions* case does not seem to have taken any stand on this point, when it stated, with some emphasis, in an axiomatic form that diplomatic protection 'is an elementary principle of international law'. One cannot hazard a guess as to the sense in which the expression 'elementary principle' was taken, given as it is without any other qualification. And when other judgments have referred to this precedent, they do not seem to have been any more explicit. The terminology of the two international Courts does not permit of there being attributed to them, on this point, an opinion which they seem designedly to have kept *in petto*, following a prudent practice which has already been remarked on.[52]

Another illustration is furnished by the *Fisheries Jurisdiction* case. The Court was directing its mind to 'a possible objection based on views expressed by certain authorities to the effect that treaties of judicial settlement or declarations of acceptance of the compulsory jurisdiction of the Court are among those treaty provisions which, by their very nature, may be subject to unilateral denunciation in the absence of express provisions regarding their duration or termination'. However, finding that 'those views cannot apply to a case such as the present one', it considered that it did 'not need to examine or pronounce upon the point of principle involved'.[53]

This policy of judicial self-restraint runs in parallel with the general view that it is inappropriate for the Court to over-crystallise the law. In *Panevezys-Saldutiskis Railway* Judge van Eysinga cited a statement by Borchard reading: 'An extensive jurisprudence has established and crystallized the rule to the effect that a claimant must have possessed the nationality of the claimant State where the claim originated.' The judge then observed:

It may be that this jurisprudence has *crystallized* the rule which Borchard has in mind. But it may be observed that 'crystallize' implies the idea of rigidity. When the Court has to apply unwritten law, of course it often encounters difficulties. But there are also advantages, in particular the

---

[51] *ICJ Rep 1970*, p. 300, para. 10.
[52] *Ibid.*, pp. 300–301, para. 10.
[53] *ICJ Rep 1973*, pp. 16–17, para. 29.

advantage that such rules of law, not being written, are precisely not rigid. It will suffice to read, *inter alia*, the observations of M. Politis (*Year Book, 1931*, II, pp. 206–209) to see that it is a happy thing that the rule adduced by Lithuania, which may be binding in a certain number of cases, is by no means crystallized as a general rule. And in this connection the question also arises whether it is reasonable to describe as an unwritten rule of international law a rule which would entail that, when a change of sovereignty takes place, the new State or the State which has increased its territory would not be able to espouse any claim of any of its new nationals in regard to injury suffered before the change of nationality. It may also be questioned whether indeed it is any part of the Court's task to contribute towards the crystallization of unwritten rules of law which would lead to such inequitable results.[54]

The jurisprudence of the present Court also contains warnings against 'over-systematisation'.[55] These warnings are particularly important in situations in which the law is in a state of motion. Referring in 1974 to the evolution of the law relating to fisheries jurisdiction, the Court remarked that to 'declare the law between the Parties as it might be at the date of expiration of the interim agreement (was) a task beyond the powers of any tribunal'.[56]

The caution observed by the Court is not, of course, a limitation on the value of case law; it is an indication of the Court's concern to preserve that value and not to dissipate it through extravagance. Of importance too is the need to safeguard the judicial character of the Court; the ultimate danger is that, as Judge Singh observed, 'a tribunal indulging in unnecessary pronouncements, by making them when not legally required to do so, could easily undermine its judicial character. This would particularly apply in the context of administering inter-State law.'[57]

The scope of the Court's developmental function

The question of the authority and value of the Court's pronouncements may also be considered on the basis of the view

---

[54] *1932, PCIJ, Series A/B, No. 76*, at pp. 34–35.

[55] *North Sea Continental Shelf Cases, ICJ Rep 1969*, p. 53, para. 100; *Fisheries Jurisdiction, ICJ Rep 1974*, p. 143, para. 27, Judge Gros, dissenting opinion; *Continental Shelf (Tunisia/Libyan Arab Jamahiriya), ICJ Rep 1982*, p. 92, para. 132; C. H. M. Waldock, review article, *BYBIL*, 32 (1955–1956), p. 348; and De Visscher, *Theory and Reality*, preface, pp. vii–viii.

[56] *Fisheries Jurisdiction, ICJ Rep 1974*, p. 19, para. 40.

[57] *Aegean Sea Continental Shelf, ICJ Rep 1978*, pp. 47–48. And see the reference to 'judicial restraint' in *ICJ Rep 1982*, p. 347, para. 45.

taken of the extent of its developmental responsibilities. The Court has a power, and, arguably, a corresponding duty, to develop the law.[58] As is well known, Judge Alvarez devoted some thought to this responsibility: the Court should not only state, or restate, the law but should also develop it to meet the new requirements of a dynamic international society, that dynamism appearing to him to be particularly urgent as a result of the upheavals connected with the Second World War and its aftermath.[59] Arguing for a new international law, in 1952 he said:

[T]he present Court is, according to its Statute, a Court of *justice* and, as such, and by virtue of the dynamism of international life, it has a double task: to *declare* the law and *develop* the law. Its first task includes the *settlement of disputes* between States as well as the *protection of the rights* of those States as recognized by the law of nations. As regards the Court's second task, namely, the development of law, it consists of deciding the existing law, modifying it and even creating new precepts, should this be necessary. This second mission is justified by the great dynamism of international life. The Third Session of the General Assembly of the United Nations has recognized the Court's rights to develop international law in its Resolution No. 171. The Institute of International Law has on its side in the recently held Session at Siena expressly recognized this right of the Court. In creating a commission, the Institute unanimously adopted the following Resolution: *[Translation]* 'The Institute of International Law, keenly aware of the growing importance of the International Court of Justice and of its rôle in the development of international law . . .' In discharging this task the Court must not proceed in an arbitrary manner, but must seek inspiration in the great principles of the new international law.[60]

Judge Alvarez's views on the need for a new international law have occasioned discussion; there could be little dispute, however, as to his central point concerning the Court's developmental func-

---

[58] As to the distinction between development and codification, see Sir Ian Sinclair, *The Vienna Convention on the Law of Treaties*, 2nd edn (Manchester, 1984), p. 11. The distinction is not always clear. See J. Monnier, 'Observations sur la codification et le développement progressif du droit international', in Bernard Dutoit (ed.), *Mélanges Georges Perrin* (Lausanne, 1984), pp. 239–241.

[59] *Competence of the General Assembly for the Admission of a State to the United Nations*, *ICJ Rep 1950*, pp. 12–13, dissenting opinion; *Status of South West Africa*, *ICJ Rep 1950*, p. 177, dissenting opinion; and the *Fisheries* case, *ICJ Rep 1951*, p. 146, separate opinion.

[60] *Anglo-Iranian Oil Company*, *ICJ Rep 1952*, p. 132, dissenting opinion.

tions.[61] The 1947 General Assembly resolution, to which he referred, was also cited by Judge Elias.[62] The General Assembly is coordinate in legal status with the Court, both being principal organs of the United Nations; it could not competently confer on the Court powers not confided, at any rate *in globo*, to the latter by the Charter or the Statute.[63] The Resolution of the Assembly could, however, recognise, and even stress, the existence of the Court's power to develop the law. It is possible that the Court had that power in mind when it said in the *Reparation* case, 'Throughout its history, the development of international law has been influenced by the requirements of international life.'[64] The requirements of contemporary international life would seem to be moving, on the one hand, in the direction of a limitation of earlier notions of relatively unbridled sovereignty,[65] and, on the other, in the direction of growing recognition of the responsibility of individual States as members of an increasingly cohesive international community. These ideas lay at the centre of Judge Alvarez's views. He might have been somewhat forceful and insistent in his statements;[66] but the substance of his thesis would not appear to have been markedly at variance with the actual course of developments.[67]

The Court, though a place of learning, is not a learned scientific institute.[68] Addressing the Permanent Court of International Justice in *Nationality Decrees Issued in Tunis and Morocco*, Professor de Lapradelle observed:

---

[61] See *Guardianship Convention* case, *ICJ Rep 1958*, p. 102, Judge Moreno Quintana; and *Military and Paramilitary Activities in and against Nicaragua, ICJ Rep 1986*, p. 332, para. 155, Judge Schwebel, dissenting.

[62] *Aegean Sea Continental Shelf, ICJ Rep 1976*, p. 29.

[63] Georg Schwarzenberger, 'Trends in the Practice of the World Court', *Current Legal Problems*, 4 (1951), pp. 5–8; Rosenne, *Law and Practice* (1985), p. 48; and Dharma Pratap, *The Advisory Jurisdiction of the International Court* (Oxford, 1972), pp. 261–262.

[64] *ICJ Rep 1949*, p. 178; and see *Barcelona Traction, Light and Power Company, Limited, ICJ Rep 1964*, p. 56, Judge Koo, separate opinion.

[65] There was always some limitation on sovereignty. See James Crawford, 'The Criteria for Statehood in International Law', *BYBIL*, 48 (1976–1977), p. 146.

[66] See, too, Alejandro Alvarez, *Le Droit international nouveau – son acceptation, son étude* (Paris, 1960).

[67] See Keith Highet, 'Reflections on Jurisprudence for the "Third World": The World Court, the "Big Case", and the Future', *VirgJIL*, 27 (1987–II), p. 296; and Charles Rousseau, 'Alejandro Alvarez (1868–1960)', *RGDIP*, 64 (1960), pp. 690–691.

[68] See also *Western Sahara, ICJ Rep 1975*, p. 108, Judge Petrén, separate opinion, stating that 'it is not an historical research institute'.

[I]f at certain moments, exchanging as we hope courtesy for courtesy and English citation for French citation, our arguments take the character of a technical controversy which we may perhaps be allowed to call an academic controversy, we must never allow ourselves to fall into a misconception. This is not an abstract controversy; this is not science for the sake of science; it is not law for law's sake. It is law applied to political issues, law upon which life itself depends.[69]

In the *Northern Cameroons* case, Judge Fitzmaurice put it this way:

[C]ourts of law are not there to make legal pronouncements in *abstracto*, however great their scientific value as such. They are there to protect existing and current legal rights, to secure compliance with existing and current legal obligations, to afford concrete reparation if a wrong has been committed, or to give rulings in relation to existing and continuing legal situations. Any legal pronouncements that emerge are necessarily in the course, and for the purpose, of doing one or more of these things. Otherwise they serve no purpose falling within or engaging the proper function of courts of law as a judicial institution.[70]

Thus, uncalled for intellectual excursions are misguided. The duty of the Court is to decide the case; to do that, it is not necessary for it to respond to every argument.[71]

But a superior abstention can be pedantic too. To what extent, if any, should the Court go beyond the strict duty to decide the case so as to take account of the possibility that the parties may have an interest in learning its reaction to their main legal positions? The idea that the Court could properly move some way in that direction is not without support. In 1937 Judge Anzilotti said:

The operative clause of the judgment merely rejects the submissions of the principal claim and of the Counter-claim. In my opinion, in a suit the main object of which was to obtain the interpretation of a treaty with reference to certain concrete facts, and in which both the Applicant and the Respondent presented submissions indicating, in regard to each point, the interpretation which they respectively wished to see adopted by the Court, the latter should not have confined itself to a mere rejection of the submissions of the Applicant: it should also have expressed its opinion on the submissions of the Respondent; and, in any case, it should have declared what it considered to be the correct interpretation of the Treaty.

---

[69] *PCIJ, Series C, No. 2*, p. 58.
[70] *ICJ Rep 1963*, pp. 98–99, separate opinion.
[71] *Application for Review of Judgment No. 158 of the United Nations Administrative Tribunal, ICJ Rep 1973*, p. 210, para. 95.

It is from the standpoint of this conception of the functions of the Court in the present suit that the following observations have been drawn up.[72]

Speaking on the same theme, Judge Lauterpacht later stated:

In my opinion, a Party to proceedings before the Court is entitled to expect that its Judgment shall give as accurate a picture as possible of the basic aspects of the legal position adopted by that Party. Moreover, I believe that it is in accordance with the true function of the Court to give an answer to the two principal jurisdictional questions which have divided the Parties over a long period of years and which are of considerable interest for international law. There may be force and attraction in the view that among a number of possible solutions a court of law ought to select that which is most simple, most concise and most expeditious. However, in my opinion such considerations are not, for this Court, the only legitimate factor in the situation.[73]

In 1957 he wrote:

The administration of justice within the State can afford to rely on purely formal and procedural grounds. It can also afford to disregard the susceptibilities of either of the parties by ignoring such of its arguments as are not indispensable to the decision. This cannot properly be done in international relations, where the parties are sovereign States, upon whose will the jurisdiction of the Court depends in the long run, and where it is of importance that justice should not only be done but that it should also appear to have been done.[74]

Similar views may be found in separate opinions given by him in 1955 and 1956.[75] Not to be overlooked too is the fact that a case may involve aspects of the law of special interest to the relevant region; the question is a delicate one, but it raises considerations which may be difficult to ignore in the case of a judicial body with a global mandate.[76]

In 1964 Judge Tanaka had occasion to observe that the 'more important function of the Court as the principal judicial organ of

---

[72] *Diversion of Water from the Meuse, 1937, PCIJ*, Series A/B, No. 70, p. 45, Judge Anzilotti, dissenting opinion.

[73] *Certain Norwegian Loans, Judgment, ICJ Rep 1957*, p. 36.

[74] Lauterpacht, *Development*, p. 39; and see, *ibid.*, pp. 37, 61 and 75.

[75] *Voting Procedure on Questions relating to Reports and Petitions concerning the Territory of South West Africa, ICJ Rep 1955*, pp. 90 ff; and *Admissibility of Hearings of Petitioners by the Committee on South West Africa, ICJ Rep 1956*, p. 57.

[76] See *Arbitral Award Made by the King of Spain on 23 December 1906, ICJ Rep 1960*, pp. 217–218, declaration of Judge Moreno Quintana; and see *Asylum, ICJ Rep 1950*, p. 290, Judge Alvarez, dissenting opinion.

the United Nations is to be found not only in the settlement of concrete disputes, but also in its reasoning, through which it may contribute to the development of international law'.[77] Judge Jessup spoke to the like effect. Citing Lauterpacht's views and a number of cases favouring a liberal approach, he said:

The specific situations in each of the cases cited can be distinguished from the situation in the instant case, but all of the quoted extracts are pervaded by a certain 'conception of the functions of the Court' which I share but which the Court does not accept. Article 59 of the Statute indeed provides: 'The decision of the Court has no binding force except between the parties and in respect of that particular case'. But the influence of the Court's decisions is wider than their binding force.[78]

As a matter of general practice, the 'conception of the functions of the Court' favoured by Judge Jessup, and also by Judge Lauterpacht, is not followed by the Court; but to the extent that the Court occasionally expresses *obiter dicta* it is permissible to suppose that the essence of the conception is not rigidly excluded. What might be the proper balance between the opposed positions?

Referring to the liberal view favoured by Lauterpacht and comparing it with a narrower if more cautious one preferred by others, Fitzmaurice says:

If it be asked which of these two attitudes is the better, the answer may well be 'both', or at any rate that each is defensible; but clearly much depends on the circumstances. The sort of bare order or finding that may suit many of the purposes of the magistrate or county court judge will by no means do for the Court of Appeal, the House of Lords or the Judicial Committee of the Privy Council, and their equivalents in other countries. International tribunals at any rate have usually regarded it as an important part of their function, not only to decide, but, in deciding, to expound generally the law having a bearing on the matters decided.[79]

Some judges are remarkable for the lapidary quality of their compositions; some are less terse. As observed by Fitzmaurice, 'many if not most judges achieve a position of balance between the two pos-

---

[77] *Barcelona Traction, Light and Power Company, Limited, Preliminary Objections, ICJ Rep 1964*, p. 65, separate opinion.

[78] *Barcelona Traction, Light and Power Company, Limited, ICJ Rep 1970*, p. 163, para. 9, Judge Jessup, separate opinion.

[79] Fitzmaurice, *Law and Procedure*, II, p. 648. And see his separate opinion in *Barcelona Traction, Light and Power Company, Limited, ICJ Rep 1970*, p. 64, para. 2.

sibilities'.[80] And for good reason. Brevity has its virtues; but it has limitations also. Speaking of the Court, Schwarzenberger said, 'The persuasive character of its judgments and advisory opinions depends on the fullness and cogency of the reasoning offered. It is probably not accidental that the least convincing statements on international law made by the International Court of Justice excel by a remarkable economy of argument.'[81]

The difficulty, therefore, is one of harmonising the need for full reasoning with the Court's established position that it is only concerned with the decision of the particular issues before it and eschews any further pronouncement. On the one hand, as Judge Carneiro remarked, 'the Court should not reduce its decision to a doctrinal, abstract or theoretical assertion; it must necessarily relate its decision to the specific case'.[82] Or, as it was put by Judge Gros, 'A court only decides the case before it without being able to deliver judgments of principle with a general scope.'[83] On the other hand, however limited may be the particular issue, the decision has to be justified by reference to more general norms. The Court recognised this when, speaking of the application of equitable principles in the field of maritime delimitation, it said:

Thus the justice of which equity is an emanation, is not abstract justice but justice according to the rule of law; which is to say that its application should display consistency and a degree of predictability; even though it looks with particularity to the peculiar circumstances of an instant case, it also looks beyond it to principles of more general application.[84]

So the task of formulating general norms cannot always be escaped. But care needs to be used. The 'complex jurisprudential problem', as observed by Judge Dillard, is one of 'knowing how best to reconcile the need for general norms in the interest of some degree of predictability versus the need to avoid them in the interest of the particularistic and individualistic nature of the subject-matter to which the norms are applicable'.[85] The problem may

---

[80] Fitzmaurice, *Law and Procedure*, II, p. 648.
[81] Georg Schwarzenberger, *International Law as Applied by International Courts and Tribunals*, 3rd edn (London, 1957), I, p. 32.
[82] *Ambatielos* case, *ICJ Rep 1952*, p. 52, para. 6, separate opinion.
[83] *Continental Shelf (Tunisia/Libyan Arab Jamahiriya)*, *ICJ Rep 1982*, p. 152.
[84] *Continental Shelf (Libyan Arab Jamahiriya/Malta)*, *ICJ Rep 1985*, p. 39, para. 45.
[85] *Fisheries Jurisdiction*, *ICJ Rep 1974*, p. 61, separate opinion.

present itself in terms of a distinction between principles and rules. Lauterpacht put it this way:

It is in relation to the problem of judicial caution that the Court has been constantly confronted with the question whether in deciding the issue before it the Court must not only act on legal principle but also state that principle; whether it ought to state not only the legal rule which it applies but also the wider legal principle underlying the rule; and whether in stating that principle it must limit itself to the exigencies of the case before it or state the principle in all its generality, and by reference to all qualifying exceptions, against the background of relevant international doctrine and practice. It is possible to hold that in its capacity as an organ which may be expected to develop international law, in addition to deciding cases before it, and to secure the requisite degree of certainty in the administration of justice, the Court ought to give a wider interpretation of the scope of its task. On the other hand, there is room for the view, frequently acted upon by the Court, that the systematic generalisation of the rules applied by it or of its decisions not accompanied by a statement of the underlying rules is the function of writers – a function which has occasionally been fulfilled with signal success and authority.[86]

In 1929 M. Fromageot was reported to have stated the position thus:

The Court of Justice was a judicial body, and its task was not to attempt the scientific solution of legal questions, but to judge disputes between States and decide upon their cases and claims. It would be for the experts in doctrine, by a study and analysis of the judicial decisions, to extract from them general principles, and subsequently, by a synthetic study, to elaborate universal rules of international law.[87]

No doubt, it was for all of these reasons that both Judge Dillard and Charles De Visscher referred with approval to Brierly's view that the 'nature of international society does not merely make it

---

[86] Lauterpacht, *Development*, pp. 82–83, footnote omitted. And see Oscar Schachter, 'Creativity and Objectivity in International Law', in Rudolf Bernhardt and others (eds.), *Festschrift für Hermann Mosler* (Berlin, 1983), pp. 820–821. Possibly because of these reasons, it has been 'frequently argued that on matters of great importance law is less precise while on other, minor matters it contains much more detail'. See *Military and Paramilitary Activities in and against Nicaragua, ICJ Rep 1986*, p. 168, Judge Lachs, separate opinion. For 'problems of grand theorizing,' see also Friedrich Kratochwil, 'The Limits of Contract', *EJIL*, 5 (1994), p. 486.

[87] League of Nations, Committee of Jurists on the Statute of the Permanent Court of International Justice, *Minutes of the Session held at Geneva, March 11th–19th, 1929*, (Geneva, 1929), p. 24.

difficult to develop rules of international law of general application, it sometimes makes them undesirable'.[88]

It has also to be remembered that, unlike a legislature, the Court has no general legislative mandate; it is not creating a new rule out of whole cloth. This is no less true in the case of a common law judge; he may make law, but he may not do so as if he were a 'law-giver'.[89] Far from being able to act as if it were initiating legislation,[90] the Court at The Hague is narrowly restricted by the framework of the particular case before it.[91] The process of development was put by Fitzmaurice thus:

It is axiomatic that courts of law must not legislate: nor do they overtly purport to do so. Yet it is equally a truism that a constant process of development of the law goes on through the courts, a process which includes a considerable element of innovation. Without it, the common law of England would never have come into being, as the record clearly shows. Nor, for that matter, would the civil law of ancient Rome; for the great codifications came only after a long legal evolution, much of which resulted from the action of the magistrature. Modern experience shows that even in fully developed legal systems this process is necessary, and goes on all the time; for it is beyond the normal capacity of any legislature to provide in advance for all the subtleties, the twists, the turns and the by-ways resulting from novel and constantly changing conditions. Only through the day-to-day action of the courts can these be handled. Nor can the legislature anticipate great issues of principle which may arise suddenly, and indeed for the first time, through the medium of a litigation. In practice, courts hardly ever admit a *non liquet*. As is well known, they adapt existing principles to meet new facts or situations. If none serves, they in effect propound new ones by appealing to some antecedent or more fundamental concept, or by invoking doctrines in the light of which an essentially innovatory process can be carried out against a background of received legal precept.[92]

In response to the proposition that the Court has no legislative mandate, it may be argued that the absence on the international

---

[88] Brierly, 'Règles générales du droit de la paix', pp. 17–18; and *ICJ Rep 1974*, p. 61.

[89] See Jennings, 'General Course', p. 341.

[90] See, as to common law courts, J. A. Hiller, 'The Law Creative Roles of Appellate Courts in the Commonwealth', *ICLQ*, 27 (1978), p. 92.

[91] See, generally, Sørensen, *Les Sources*, p. 156; and Cross and Harris, *Precedent*, pp. 34 ff, and 216 ff, in relation to a common law court.

[92] See Gerald Fitzmaurice, 'Judicial Innovation – Its Uses and its Perils – As exemplified in some of the Work of the International Court of Justice during Lord

plane of anything corresponding to a national legislature competent to keep the law adjusted to changing social requirements is a reason for the Court to take a liberal view of the scope of its pronouncements.[93] But, the argument can cut both ways; for the presence of a legislature at the national level also means that an agency is constantly available to amend the law as formulated by the municipal court, if necessary.[94] Again, depending on the circumstances, legislative inactivity at the national level may or may not be interpreted as indicative of a warrant for compensating judicial lawmaking.[95] Even though municipal courts can at times introduce important legal changes, they are not equipped to undertake law reform of the kind which needs to be supported by appropriate institutional and administrative procedures;[96] legislative inactivity would not justify that. As it was put by Lord Devlin, a judge should not 'be the complete lawmaker'.[97] The remark is no less applicable to the International Court of Justice. The Court is not a legislature and should not be astute to creep into the habits of one.

No doubt, as it is said in the jurisprudence, 'the judicial settlement of international disputes . . . is simply an alternative to the direct and friendly settlement of such disputes between the Parties'.[98] There are indeed times when recourse to the Court has the advantage of enabling a State to accept a solution which, unaided by independent adjudication, it may find politically difficult to countenance though otherwise willing to contemplate. But governments do not in fact always consider it as an expression of friendly regard to be arraigned before the Court,[99] even on the basis of consensual

McNair's Period of Office', in *Cambridge Essays in Honour of Lord McNair* (London, 1965), pp. 24–25, footnote omitted.

[93] *South West Africa, Preliminary Objections, ICJ Rep 1962*, p. 363, Judge Bustamante, separate opinion; and *Barcelona Traction, Light and Power Company, Limited, ICJ Rep 1970*, p. 64, para. 2, Judge Fitzmaurice, separate opinion. And see W. Friedmann, 'The International Court of Justice and the Evolution of International Law', *Archiv des Völkerrechts*, 14 (1969–1970), pp. 317–318.

[94] Röben, 'Le précédent', p. 400.

[95] See W. Friedmann, 'Limits of Judicial Law-Making and Prospective Overruling', *MLR*, 29 (1966), p. 593.

[96] *Ibid.*, p. 602.

[97] Lord Devlin, 'Judges and Lawmakers', *MLR*, 39 (1976), p. 5.

[98] *Free Zones of Upper Savoy and the District of Gex, 1929, PCIJ, Series A, No. 22*, p. 13. The principle is reflected in the Manila Declaration on the Peaceful Settlement of International Disputes, adopted on 15 November 1982 by General Assembly Resolution A/37/590.

[99] P. C. Jessup, 'International Litigation as a Friendly Act', *Col LR*, 60 (1960), pp. 24 ff; and Guy de Lacharrière, in Garry Sturgess and Philip Chubb, *Judging the*

jurisdiction, and more particularly where there is a risk of losing the case through newly-made case law.

However, as observed by Judge Lauterpacht, 'Reluctance to encroach upon the province of the legislature is a proper manifestation of judicial caution. If exaggerated, it may amount to unwillingness to fulfil a task which is within the orbit of the functions of the Court as defined by its Statute.'[100] And, to recall the words of Fitzmaurice, the Court does not fulfil its responsibilities by limiting itself to the 'sort of bare order or finding that may suit many of the purposes of the magistrate or county court judge'; that, as he says, 'will by no means do for the Court of Appeal, the House of Lords or the Judicial Committee of the Privy Council, and their equivalents in other countries'.[101] It will not do for the International Court of Justice. Further, while, as mentioned above, it is possible that sovereign States litigating before the Court may conceive a sense of dissatisfaction about losing a case because of new law made by the Court for the purpose of deciding it,[102] it is possible that the character of its case may be such as to discourage a State from agreeing to litigate before a Court which is incapable of a reasonable degree of flexibility to accommodate the changing expectations of the international community.[103]

The case for steering a middle course between caution and boldness is obvious.[104] The task is not easy. It could get bogged down in 'Polonius-like homilies' about balancing the need for development against the importance of stability and certainty.[105] Inactivity invites charges of judicial timidity; activism invites charges of judicial legislation. This has led to restrained statements on the functions of the Court, as by President Winiarski and Judge

---

World: Law and Politics in the World's Leading Courts (Sydney, 1988), p. 455. Cf. the *Aegean Sea Continental Shelf, ICJ Rep 1978*, p. 52, Judge Lachs, separate opinion.

[100] *Admissibility of Hearings of Petitioners by the Committee on South West Africa, ICJ Rep 1956*, p. 57.

[101] Fitzmaurice, *Law and Procedure*, II, p. 648.

[102] See Sir Robert Jennings, in *Judicial Settlement of International Disputes* (Max Planck Institute, Berlin, 1974), pp. 37–38.

[103] See Sir Gerald Fitzmaurice, 'Judicial Innovation – Its Uses and Its Perils – As exemplified in some of the Work of the International Court of Justice during Lord McNair's Period of Office', in *Cambridge Essays in International Law* (London, 1965), p. 26.

[104] For the differential pull of these two factors, see Lauterpacht, *Development*, Pt II.

[105] Oscar Schachter, 'The Nature and Process of Legal Development in International Society', in R. St J. Macdonald and D. M. Johnston (eds.), *The Structure and Process of International Law* (Dordrecht, 1986), p. 768.

Tanaka.[106] More recently, the matter was put this way by Judge Jennings:

[T]he primary task of any court of justice is not to 'develop' the law much less to 'make' it, but to dispose in accordance with the law of the particular dispute between the particular parties before it. This is not to say that it is no part of the Judge's task to develop the law. It clearly is, not least in international law. But it *is* to say that any 'development' must be necessary for, and incidental to, the disposal of the actual issues before the court. For the strength of 'case law' is supposed to be precisely that it arises from actual situations rather than conceived *a priori*.[107]

He added:

[T]he Court must – and this is perhaps the most important requirement of the judicial function – be seen to be applying existing, recognized rules, or principles of law. Even where a court creates law in the sense of developing, adapting, modifying, filling gaps, interpreting, or even branching out in a new direction, the decision must be seen to emanate reasonably and logically from existing and previously ascertainable law. A court has no purely legislative competence. Naturally the court in probably most difficult cases – and for the most part it is only difficult cases that are brought before international tribunals – may have to make a choice between probably widely differing solutions. It may even choose a course which has elements of novelty. But whatever juridical design it decides to construct in its decision, it must do so, and be seen to do so, from the building materials available in already existing law. The design may be an imaginative artifact, but the bricks used in its construction must be recognisable and familiar.[108]

These wise caveats do not deny, but impliedly recognise, that the Court has a faculty of limited creativity. There is little doubt that in the course of its acknowledged function of developing the law, it has created law. It is prudent to speak in terms of the Court having 'enriched the law by developing it and making it progress'; but the real meaning of the observation is clear when it is followed by the question 'whether by so doing the Court has acted *ultra*

---

[106] *ICJ Pleadings, Temple of Preah Vihear*, II, p. 122, President Winiarski; and *South West Africa, ICJ Rep 1966*, p. 277, Judge Tanaka.

[107] Judge Jennings, 'The Judicial Function and the Rule of Law in International Relations', in *International Law at the Time of its Codification, Essays in Honour of Roberto Ago*, 4 vols. (Milan, 1987), III, pp. 141–142.

[108] *Ibid.*, pp. 144–145.

vires'.[109] If, as it seems, its mission has not been exceeded, this is due to the fact that its law-making activity, in cases going beyond the marginal, has been confined to developments almost certain to enjoy consensus support within the international community.[110]

The experience of the Court tempts comparison with the municipal process. 'In a changing society', said Lord Devlin, 'the law acts as a valve. New policies must gather strength before they can force an entry: when they are admitted and absorbed into the consensus, the legal system should expand to hold them, as also it should contract to squeeze out old policies which have lost the consensus they once obtained.'[111] However, the nature of international society, based as it is on relations between sovereign States, imposes limits on the extent to which this elegant portrait can be transported to the functioning of the International Court of Justice. In practice, the position of the Court would appear to lie closer to Lord Wright's cautious view of judges navigating 'from case to case, like the ancient Mediterranean mariners, hugging the coast from point to point and avoiding the dangers of the open sea of system and science'.[112]

[109] Manfred Lachs, 'Some Reflections on the Contribution of the International Court of Justice to the Development of International Law', *Syracuse Journal of International Law and Commerce*, 10 (1983), p. 277, and, also by him, 'Thoughts on the Recent Jurisprudence of the International Court of Justice', *Emory International Law Review*, 4 (1990), p. 92.

[110] See Oscar Schachter, 'The Nature and Process of Legal Development in International Society', in R. St J. Macdonald and D. M. Johnston (eds.), *The Structure and Process of International Law.* (Dordrecht, 1986), p. 772; and, also by him, 'Creativity and Objectivity in International Law', in Rudolf Bernhardt and others (eds.), *Festschrift für Hermann Mosler* (Berlin, 1983), p. 820. Possibly for these reasons, it has been remarked that the Court has had a disappointingly modest role in the evolution of contemporary international law. See W. Friedmann, 'The International Court of Justice and the Evolution of International Law', *Archiv des Völkerrechts*, 14 (1969–1970), p. 305.

[111] Lord Devlin, 'Judges and Lawmakers', *MLR*, 39 (1976), p. 1.

[112] Lord Wright, 'The Study of the Law', *LQR*, 54 (1938), p. 186, cited in Lord Devlin, 'Judges and Lawmakers', *MLR*, 39 (1976), p. 5.

15

Conclusion

In his speech of welcome to the present Court at its inaugural meeting, The Netherlands Foreign Minister remarked as follows on the inevitability of judge-made law:

Montesquieu, in a well-known passage of his *Esprit des lois*, has described the function of a judge as follows: 'Judges are but the mouthpiece which recites the law – inanimate beings who cannot moderate either its force or its vigour.' This judgment of the great French philosopher is very far from having met with universal acceptance; it represents too rigid an interpretation of the *trias politica* and a conception of the administration of justice which was typical of a period in which the importance of written law was exaggerated, but was later subjected to severe criticism. This conception of the judge's function is still less applicable in international law, in which a written, established rule seldom exists. Here the judge finds himself only too often, and whether he wills it or not, obliged to assume the rôle of the law-maker. The increasing difficulties which, in recent times, have hampered the codification of international law have shown the importance of this aspect of a judge's work. The part played by case law in the formation of law becomes ever more vital; the world seems disposed to accept and to generalize a ruling given by a Court of high repute; whereas international conferences, after endless discussion, succeed neither in reconciling divergent standpoints nor in framing uniform rules of law.[1]

It is not necessary to underrate the value of conference 'legislated' law to appreciate the point made about case law.

---

[1] H.E. M. J. van Roijen, Minister for Foreign Affairs of The Netherlands, *ICJYB, 1946–1947*, p. 33.

Conclusion

As was observed by President Huber in 1925, the output of decisions by a national supreme court exceeds that of the World Court.[2] This affects the speed and extent to which the decisions of the Court influence the general development of international law.[3] Understandably, Charles De Visscher considered that '[d]oubtless long years must still pass and many more judgments be rendered before the Court's decisions can be synthesized in a systematic body of principles or rules'.[4] Synthesisation will take its time; meanwhile, however, the work of the Court is continually passing into the bloodstream of the law, as reference to the literature will attest. Indeed, as President Huber pointed out in 1925, it may well be that the comparative infrequency of international judicial decisions serves to enhance their value.[5]

Nor should the extent of the ground already covered be under-estimated. In his 1949 presidential address to the Holdsworth Club of the Faculty of Law in the University of Birmingham, McNair noted that 'the past fifty years have transformed the essential character of International Law and consolidated it into a body of 'hard law' consisting of arbitral and judicial case-law on the one hand and treaties on the other, much in the same way as English law consists of case-law and statute'.[6] In the nearly fifty years which have passed since that statement was made, much additional ground has been covered.

The transformation referred to by McNair is not surprising. As observed by Judge Armand-Ugon, 'The very idea of a *decision for a particular case* . . . is inadmissible.'[7] It cannot be otherwise: regard being

---

[2] See p. 14 *supra*.
[3] In this respect, consider the relationship between the *Fisheries* case, *ICJ Rep 1951*, p. 116, and the Geneva Conventions of 1958 on the law of the sea.
[4] De Visscher, *Theory and Reality*, p. 403.
[5] See p. 14 *supra*; PCIJ, *Series C, No. 7–I*, pp. 16–17; Lauterpacht, 'Schools of Thought in International Law', *BYBIL*, 12 (1931), p. 57; and Condorelli, 'L'Autorité', p. 311.
[6] Sir Arnold Duncan McNair, 'The International Court of Justice', in *Lord McNair: Selected Papers and Bibliography* (Leiden/Dobbs Ferry, 1974), p. 213.
[7] *Barcelona Traction, Light and Power Company, Limited, ICJ Rep 1964*, p. 165. Cf., at the municipal level, Lord Wright's remark: 'Nor is it right to say in general terms that a judgment is only an authority for what it decides. A judgment in itself as such is not an authority at all save in so far as it constitutes an estoppel between the actual parties. The authority, if any, is the *ratio decidendi*, the general rule which it embodies.' See Wright, 'Precedents', p. 124.

had to the fact that cases are decided by the application of principles of international law, it would be wrong to over-extend the stress on particularism.[8] So there is room for the operation of a system of precedents connecting one holding to another. But on what basis?

In the *Guardianship Convention* case, Professor Kisch, for The Netherlands, submitted that the Court should 'rule out all would-be precedents where the case is not covered by the same law, that is, by the Convention' of 1902 between The Netherlands and Sweden governing the Guardianship of Infants.[9] His reference to 'precedents' drew fire. Henri Rolin, the formidable Belgian advocate who spoke for Sweden, responded:

J'ai à peine besoin de dire à la Cour que, avec tout le respect que je dois à M. le professeur Kisch, cette invocation est totalement étrangère à la question qui nous occupe. Les règles relatives aux *'precedents'* sont des règles anglaises. Elles énumèrent les conditions auxquelles doivent satisfaire des décisions judiciaires en Angleterre pour avoir force obligatoire auprès des tribunaux anglais. En Angleterre, une décision judiciaire s'impose à l'observation de la Chambre des Lords elle-même dans les instances ultérieures, à moins qu'on ne puisse relever dans le cas nouveau des différences justifiant qu'on s'écarte de la solution précédemment adoptée.

Mais nous sommes ici devant la Cour internationale de Justice, qui elle n'est même pas liée par ses propres arrêts ni par ceux de la Cour permanente. Il n'y a donc pas de *'precedents'* possibles. J'ai à peine besoin de vous dire que votre article 59 du Statut l'a formellement écarté: 'La décision de la Cour n'est pas obligatoire que pour les Parties en litige et dans le cas qui a été décidé.' ...

Mais s'il n'y a pas de *'precedents'*, il y a la jurisprudence, ce qui est tout à fait différent. Et je suis en droit d'invoquer tout à fait librement l'autorité de décisions judiciaires de divers pays en attirant l'attention sur les principes qui y sont énoncés, sauf bien entendu à mon estimé contradicteur à s'insurger contre leur autorité ou à s'efforcer de vous démontrer qu'en réalité, en l'espèce, les principes que j'invoque ne s'appliquent pas.[10]

Faced with the severity of this criticism, Kisch restated his position as follows:

My learned friend has chided me somewhat for speaking of precedents, assuming, or pretending to assume, that I was trying to seduce the

---

[8] See De Visscher, *Theory and Reality*, p. 143.
[9] *ICJ Pleadings, Application of the Convention of 1902 Governing the Guardianship of Infants*, p. 169.
[10] *Ibid.*, pp. 224–225.

Court into adopting the English or American rule of *stare decisis*. He has dealt with this question at some length, but I may put his mind at rest. Of course I am well aware that the Court is not bound by the *stare decisis* principle, British or American style. Of course I use the word 'precedents' in the general and not in the strictly technical sense, and what I wanted to convey was this: that any lawyer in any country, any judge and any advocate, when confronted with a difficult case, tries to find, if not some support, at least some enlightenment and some inspiration, from what judges, and particularly the best judges, have found in similar cases. I refer to precedents in that wide sense, including even such situations – as we have had in this very country – where a judge has explicitly declared himself inspired by French or English or German decisions. Certainly that is not a phenomenon of precedents in the Anglo-American sense.[11]

The position as thus clarified by Professor Kisch understandably moved away from the common law model, but only perhaps to tilt a little in the direction of the idea of precedents being only part of the general legal material to be considered by a judge in ascertaining what is the law on a given point. The fact that previous decisions of the Court are not precedentially binding means that they are not binding precedents; it does not mean that they are not 'precedents'. So far as terminology is concerned, the word occurs with sufficient frequency in the case law of the Court, in the individual opinions of judges, in the pleadings of advocates and in the writings of jurists to justify its use.

It is not right to suggest that the Court's system of precedents is more fully formed than it is. In particular, the Court has not sought to lay down rules regulating the use of its decisions as precedents. But that does not represent as great a hardship as may be thought; much of the need to establish rules in a common law jurisdiction is attributable to the existence of a hierarchical legal order. In such an order, precise rules are required to define the way in which decisions of courts at one level are to be treated by courts at a different level. Elaborate rules are unnecessary in the case of a system which consists of a single court having no hierarchical relationship with other tribunals; it is perhaps this which has, to some extent, led to the impression that the Court has nothing in the nature of a system of precedents. In the absence of necessity for formal rules, all that is required is a working understanding of

[11] *Ibid.*, p. 259.

237

how the Court treats its own decisions. Such an understanding exists; its main elements are as follows.

A decision of the Court (including its predecessor), which is relevant, cannot be ignored; the Court has to take account of it.[12]

The distinction between *ratio decidendi* and *obiter dictum* is known to the Court in so far as it recognises that some of its reasoning may surpass its operative holding;[13] but the distinction probably carries less significance than in a common law system. The Court has not indicated whether it would treat the two categories as possessing the same precedential value; but the likelihood is that it will draw little practical distinction except, possibly, where the fact that *dicta* were made *obiter* can be shown to have contributed to a lower degree of accuracy in making them.

Stare decisis does not apply. This fact is generally taken as a feature which radically separates the Court's practice from that in common law systems. But there have been interesting developments on both sides. On the side of the Court, its jurisprudence has developed in the direction of a strong tendency to adhere closely to previous holdings. On the common law side, courts of last resort have come to accept that they are not obliged to follow their previous decisions; within careful bounds, they may depart. The World Court may do likewise. Naturally, it will not do so except with caution.

The Court has not had occasion to consider whether its decisions create law. It may incline towards avoiding the question; if it has to give an answer, it would probably do so in the negative. But, on balance, it is possible to hold that the arguments, which run both ways, support the view that the Court has a power of limited creativity.

However, even if its decisions do not create law, the Court regards them as authoritative expositions of the law. Fitzmaurice's view, which commands respect, is that such a decision may be cited as ' "authority", but not necessarily as authoritative'.[14] If it is asked why 'not necessarily as authoritative', the probable answer will be that the Court is free to depart from its previous decisions. The

---

[12] Michel Dubisson, *La Cour internationale de Justice* (Paris, 1964), p. 29; and Fitzmaurice, 'Some Problems Regarding the Formal Sources of International Law', in *Symbolae Verzijl* (The Hague, 1958), pp. 172–173.

[13] *Polish Postal Service in Danzig*, PCIJ, Series B, No. 11, pp. 29–30.

[14] Fitzmaurice, *Law and Procedure*, I, p. xxxii, footnote 22.

present writer has also spoken in terms of decisions of the Court being 'only influential, not controlling'.[15] In view of the power to depart, they are not strictly controlling; but the first part of the statement is open to upward appreciation. The Court has not rested any decision on its power to depart, even though the power unquestionably exists. Cases of apparent departure are explained in terms of distinguishing. A decision which is distinguished on valid grounds does not raise any question of the decision not being followed. The fact that the Court avoids accepting that it is departing even when it may in fact be doing so is itself an affirmation of the tenacity with which it wishes to be seen to be adhering to its previous holdings.

Thus, the position taken by the Court itself may be interpreted to mean that it considers that it is always following its previous decisions. In that sense, it seems permissible to say that it regards its decisions as authoritative. They are no less authoritative than are decisions of the House of Lords. The House also has a power to depart; in contrast with the Court, it has openly and repeatedly exercised the power;[16] nevertheless, until and unless the power is exercised, a previous decision is regarded as authoritative. A similar position suggests itself in the case of the Court. When Fitzmaurice went on to accept that 'even controversial [decisions] tend in the course of years to be generally regarded as law',[17] he would seem to be accepting that, at least in such cases, decisions of the Court may be cited not only as 'authority', but also as 'authoritative'. With submission, the view is offered that there is an acceptable sense in which, subject to a power to depart, decisions of the Court may be regarded as authoritative.[18]

In the result, a decision which cannot be distinguished on valid grounds will be followed in a later case unless it is shown to have been clearly wrong, in which case the power to depart will be exercised. It is possible that there is a second exception where the earlier holding, though right when made, is in need of modification by way of further judicial development to fit any new requirements of

---

[15] *Certain Phosphate Lands in Nauru, ICJ Rep 1992*, p. 298.

[16] See *Halsbury's Laws of England*, 4th edn, XXVI, p. 296, para. 577.

[17] Fitzmaurice, *Law and Procedure*, Vol. I, p. xxxii.

[18] See Lauterpacht, *Development*, p. 9, stating that the Court's practice 'ranges from mere illustration and 'distinguishing' to a form of speech apparently indicating the *authoritative* character of the pronouncement referred to'. Emphasis supplied.

evolving international life, in which case the Court may, within limits, amend the earlier holding in exercise of the same power through which it was first made. Outside of these cases, it is difficult to imagine the Court refusing to follow its previous holding; such a refusal would seem arbitrary and out of keeping with its fundamental judicial responsibility to adjudicate on a verifiably normative basis.

This position is not materially different from that relating to the European Court of Justice. In an opinion delivered to that Court in 1963, Advocate General Lagrange said, 'Clearly no one will expect that, having given a leading judgment, the Court will depart from it in another action without strong reasons, but it should retain the legal right to do so.'[19] Referring to this in 1981, Lord Mackenzie Stuart and J.-P. Warner remarked, 'It is interesting to observe that that statement accurately describes the stance now adopted by the House of Lords.'[20] The stance referred to, as stated in a work of authority, is this: 'Where too rigid an adherence to precedent may lead to injustice in a particular case and an undue restriction of the proper development of the law, the House of Lords may depart from its previous decisions when it appears right to do so.'[21] On the one hand, the grounds on which the House may exercise its power of departure are scarcely more or less than those on which the World Court may be expected to exercise its own power to depart from its previous decisions. On the other hand, where those grounds do not exist, the Court would in practice regard its previous decisions, even if they do not create law, as authoritative as the House would regard its own.

There is, of course, no question of the Court having consciously decided to model its practice on that of any legal system. It should have found that difficult to do; each system has its merits. The Court's practice is not identical with that existing anywhere. And there has probably been movement everywhere. As remarked above, the treatment of precedent in common law courts of last resort has

---

[19] *Da Costa v. Nederlandse Belastingadministratie (Cases 28, 29 and 30/62)*, [1963] *ECR* 31, at 42. For Advocate General Lagrange's understanding of the subject of precedent in the European Court of Justice, see Bernard Rudden, *Basic Community Cases* (Oxford, 1987), p. 39.

[20] Lord Mackenzie Stuart and J.-P. Warner, 'Judicial Decision as a Source of Community Law', in W. G. Grewe and others (eds.), *Europäische Gerichtsbarkeit und nationale Verfassungsgerichtsbarkeit, Festschrift Kutscher* (Baden-Baden, 1981), p. 277.

[21] *Halsbury's Laws of England*, 4th edn, XXVI, p. 293, para. 573.

been becoming more flexible; on the other hand, the case law of the Court has been moving in the direction of a marked attachment to precedential authority. Thus, if in its developed form the Court's practice shows some similarity with that now prevailing at a certain level of a particular system, this is the coincidental consequence of forces independently at work on both sides. What is relevant is the nature of the position reached. A reasonable conclusion is that the position reached at this stage of the evolution of the Court's practice represents a balance between the maintenance of stability and capacity for change which is suited to the orderly development of the jurisprudence of a global judicial institution.

Index

Index

243

Index